WOMEN SOCIETY AND CHRISTIANITY

ENCYCLOPAEDIA OF WOMEN SOCIETY AND CULTURE SERIES-7

Women Society and Christianity

RAJ PRUTHI
&
BELA RANI SHARMA

ANMOL PUBLICATIONS PVT LTD
New Delhi-110 002

ANMOL PUBLICATIONS PVT LTD
4374/4B, Ansari Road, Daryaganj
New Delhi-110 002

Women Society and Christianity

First Edition 1995
Reprint : 1997
ISBN 81-7488-088-7

PRINTED IN INDIA

Published by J.L. Kumar for Anmol Publications Pvt. Ltd., New Delhi and Printed at Tarun Offset Printers, Maujpur, Delhi-53, Phone : 2260794

Acknowledgement

Some good work has been published on the otherwise neglected area of gender studies in the recent past. While compiling the present series we have collated relevant information to answer some of the present day queries pertaining to women studies. In doing so many distinguished contributors have earned our gratitude and we are deeply indebted to them.

Prof. Sheik Ali, Prof. G.C. Pande, Prof. M.N. Das, Prof. Romila Thapar, Prof. Aparna Basu, Prof. Vina Majumdar, Prof. Suvra Jaiswal, Prof. Leela Dubey, Prof. Devaki Jain, Prof. Sardamani have constantly inspired us. We are obliged to them.

Dr. (Mrs.) S. Pruthi, Dr. M. Lakshman and Dr. Neelam Khurana have facilitated the preparation of this series and we are sincerely grateful to them too.

Last but not the least, we are thankful to Shri J.L. Kumar without whose help and cooperation this series would not have seen the light of the day.

Editors

Preface

It has been observed that Indian studies on women, by and large, suffer from a crucial lacuna such as lack of an integrated approach, which takes into consideration both the micro and the macro level region. Women and their problems have acquired growing importance in our social milieu. After realising the significant role of women, it is desirable that a greater emphasis should be given for her all round development by imparting education and providing employment.

The present volume, *Women Society and Christianity* comprising of nine chapters is an attempt to provide an overall views on issues and problems related to women society and the influence of christianity upon economic conditions of women.

We hope that present volume will be of immense value not only to the masses but also to the students, researchers and teachers who are interested in Women Studies.

Editors

Contents

1

Historians on Christianity

Introduction

Long-standing traditions reinforced by strong religious commitments limited the vulnerability of most Catholic and Protestant scholars to passing whims and even more significant shifts in European scholarly opinion in the centuries following the Reformation. Yet cultural influences which developed in Europe in the seventeenth and eighteenth centuries inevitably left a mark or the work of church historians and theologians. Only a superficial observer would fail to discern beneath the polemical thrust of much Catholic and Protestant writing clear signs of change extending beyond style and language to basic approaches and even fundamental scholarly aims.

Among the influences to which Catholic scholarship in Germany clearly responded, three deserve special note: the impact of Enlightenment thought, the influences of Hegelian philosophy, and the heritage of Rankean historiographic principles. The Enlightenment had been more positively appropriated by Catholic scholars in Germany than in France, particularly in university circles, where the abolition of the Jesuit order in 1773 had opened wide possibilities for new academic directions. Catholic intellectuals' tendency during this period to stress the inward voice of reason over external dogmatic revelation loosened rigid confessional structures, and the clearly irenic implications of this stance were mirrored concretely in common participation by Catholics and Protestants in the nation's cultural life. Hegelian dialectical philosophy, inherently inimical to notions of truth as monolithic and unchangeable, profoundly influenced leading Catholic intellectuals, such as Franz Xaver von Baader (1765-1841), a social philosopher, lay theologian, and leader of the Munich circle of "Romantic" Catholics working for renewal of the Church. A pioneer of ecumenism, Baader argued that confessional differences were a stage on the road by which Papist and Protestant would ultimately find a renewal of unity greater than both. Finally, and most significantly for the future, leading Catholic historians enthusiastically embraced the methodology of Ranke.

Johann Adam Mother (1796-1838)

The first two factors go a long way to explain the significance of Catholic scholar Johann Adam Mohler, theologian and church historian at Tubingen and later Munich. Mohler was strongly influenced by Hegelian idealism, and his remarkably irenic disposition led him to seek out and maintain contacts with leading protestant scholars and pursue a lifelong preoccupation with the question of unity and division in the Church. His first work on that subject, *Die Einbeit in der Kirche,* written in 1825, demonstrates a deep sympathy with Reformation ideas about the Church's mystical and invisible character. Mohler never entirely lost these ideas, although in response to accusations of modernism and heterodoxy he later stressed the divine institution of the Catholic Church and the objective truth of its faith.

Mohler's investigations of early and medieval Christianity led him to a study of the Reformation and, in particular, the doctrinal differences between protestantism and Catholicism: he publicly acknowledged the need for a Reformation in the sixteenth century, although he argued that it had been unnecessarily revolutionary and destructive. He became increasingly preoccupied with close study of doctrinal differences, as evidenced in creeds or "symbols", and was the first Catholic scholar to develop the hitherto exclusively Protestant science of "symbolics": the comparative study of creeds and confessions.

In his major work *Symbolics* (1832), Mohler used a detailed study of the sources, especially Lutheran confessional writings, and presented the differences between Catholic and Protestant theology in an essentially calm and dispassionate manner, even when he sharply criticized the protestant position. Even more significant is the fact that Protestant doctrine appears as a reasonably coherent and self-consistent whole rather than a series of isolated propositions. Mohler genuinely attempted to understand not only its individual features but also its fundamental structure and the relationship among its parts. In this respect his work could scarcely be further from that of his sixteenth-century forebears.

As a theologian studying confessional documents, Mohler was not particularly interested in biographical comment on Luther's personal life and theological development. Yet his analysis of Reformation doctrine clearly implies a view of Luther as a man whose motivation was genuinely religious, despite the one-sidedness of his ideas and the perverse way be applied them. (The view is remarkably similar to Joseph Lortz's a century later). Although Mohler's writings are by no means free of religious bias they form a significant landmark in Catholic historiography, and not merely because of their pervasive conciliatory spirit Committed to work from genuine historical sources, Mohler was also sensitive in his use of them. Earlier scholars had treated the doctrinal confessions as an arsenal of polemical ammunition; Mohler sought to understand their inner logic and the relationship of each part to the whole.

The historical seriousness in Mohler's work was symptomatic of an increasingly evident development in both Protestant and Catholic scholarship. For the Catholic Church the Romantic era became a time of profound renewal and some notable conversions to the cause. Intellectually, it was marked by the revival of a sense of history, which at times manifested itself in a naive and idealized recovery of the Middle Ages but among more profound thinkers emerged in a more highly developed historical sensitivity. Although the Protestant scholar Leopold von Ranke provided the most obvious stimulus to channel these intentions into a more "scientific" form of historical writing, some Catholics eagerly embraced his principles, not least because they disputed Ranke's success in following those principles and saw his work as an implicit apologia for the Protestant Reformation. Accordingly, the nineteenth century witnessed a new flowering of Catholic historical writing which was intended at least in part, as a corrective to Ranke. This was, for instance, the explicit purpose behind the massive three-volume study of the Reformation by Ignaz von Dollinger, and even if Dollinger seems in the end more obviously biased than Ranke, there is no need to doubt his sincere commitment to historical accuracy.

Ignaz von Dollinger (1799-1890)

Catholic historiography of the Reformation from Dollinger in the middle of the nineteenth century to Grisar in the early twentieth is often interpreted as a grand finale to a tradition of confessional polemic extending back to the sixteenth century. But such a view, although plausible, can only be admitted if one recognizes a concurrent development of serious and painstaking historical scholarship, sometimes mitigating the power of polemics, sometimes reinforcing it. Dollinger's long and stormy academic career had its center in Munich, where he served as professor of church history from 1826 to 1873, but his influence extended through correspondence and personal contacts across Europe. His writings reveal a fascinating interplay between polemical and historical interests. In his history of the Reformation and his 1851 "sketch" of Luther, we can see the beginnings of the intense psychobiographic preoccupation with Luther which became such a prominent part of modern Roman Catholic research on the Reformation.

Dollinger differed radically from the early polemicists in his concern with Luther's inward dispositions and motives rather than with merely external factors and in his use of biographical investigation as the key to Luther's thought. He highlighted Luther's pride as the source of his problems and noted a propensity to distort and pervert true ideas, an innate tendency to violence, and a morbid preoccupation with evil, all of which influenced not only Luther's doctrine but his conduct as a theologian. Notwithstanding his scathing criticism of the Reformer and his ponderous moral judgments, Dollinger's writings are a far cry from the superficial abuse and demonological fantasies of the early polemicists. His analysis at least derives from the Reformer's self-analysis and is plausibly related to the major tenets of his thought, such as the omnipotence of God, the doctrine of imputed righteousness, and man's inability to cooperate with God's grace.

Dollinger remained intensely fascinated by Luther, and his understanding of the Reformation underwent significant change, not only because of the great length of his academic career—he died at age ninety-one—but because of his changing relationship with the papacy. A stern Ultramontane in his early period, he became increasingly opposed to the notion of papal infallibility in the years leading up to the Vatican Council and was finally excommunicated when he refused to subscribe to the newly proclaimed dogma.

In his later writings, Dollinger increasingly stressed Luther's Germanic qualities and portrayed him as the leader who personified the yearnings of the German people and was able to manipulate them to his purposes. Concurrently, Dollinger moved away from his intense preoccupation with psychobiography and no longer saw the Reformation as the product of Luther's tortured spirit. Instead, he delineated with some care the historical situation into which Luther came: the long German tradition of devotion to the Catholic faith and the prevalence of clerical abuses and justifiable hostility to Rome.

Dollinger's Luther, it should be stressed, does not shrink in stature through this broadening and deepening of historical perspective. He remains a towering individual. But if he moves history, it is because he is the spokesman of his people and the man of the moment. In his 1871 lectures on church reunion, Dollinger offered the most mature statement of his new perspective, stressing the fundamental crisis among the German Church and people, which would have drawn them away from Rome even without the "Titan of the world of mind." In elaborating on the Curia's heavy responsibility for the Reformation schism, Dollinger emphasized the decades of papal silence in the face of manifest abuses and doctrinal confusion, and a refusal to confront the question of reform because of the threat to papal power and profits. No longer is the Reformation understood as the product of Luther's diseased and violent mind. Rather Luther is seen as the catalyst of reform in a Church which had been unable to bring about the changes it desperately needed.

This alteration of outlook is symptomatic of a more fundamental process in Dollinger's maturing as a historian. His early writings, although intended as history based on sources, remain basically polemical, whereas his later work, despite the continued rejection of Luther as the "great heresiarch and seducer of the German notion", is historical writing with a high degree of objectivity. His discussion of the relative significance of Luther's personal influence and the deeper forces in German society is an admirable piece of sensitive, balanced judgment, and his identification of the Church's doctrinal confusion anticipates the position developed more substantially by Lortz. Dollinger's ability to realize so impressively in his later writings his early commitment to historical accuracy was undoubtedly assisted by his personal alienation from the ideological assumptions of the papacy, which gave him the freedom to be more open-minded about Luther and more critical of Rome. Nevertheless, his estrangement from the papacy made it highly unlikely that Dollinger's mature views would exercise any normative influence in Catholic scholarship.

Johannes Janssen (1829-1891)

More influential in the long run was the Frankfurt church historian Johannes Janssen, whose life and career were marked by intellectual consistency and a uniformly harmonious relationship with ecclesiastical authority. Perhaps for this very reason, advances in historical objectivity are harder to discern in his massive *History of the German People since the Close of the Middle Ages* (1876-1894), which was to provide a dominant historical framework for Catholic interpretation of the Reformation during subsequent generations.

Despite his deep dependence on the early writings of Dollinger

Janssen did not lack originality. His use of archival sources was more extensive, and he was less intensely preoccupied with the person of Luther. As his title indicates, Janssen's subject was the German people, not just towering individuals. He was, therefore, less interested in political history than in what he called *Kulturgeschichte*. His purpose, he declared later, was "not to give marked preference to so-called leading state events, campaigns and battles, but to depict the German national life in all its varying conditions and stages and phases of destiny". When Janssen did attend to Luther's person, echoes of the early Dollinger are unmistakable. But he was more preoccupied with Luther's impact on the Church, and the image of the Reformer which dominates his history and unifies all his statements above Luther is that of the destroyer.

Such a judgment depends very much on a prior verdict about the condition of the Church into which Luther came. It is one of Janssen's most distinctive features that he attempted to refute the notion, derived especially from Protestant writings, that the fifteenth and early sixteenth centuries were a period of degeneration in the Church. He argued that evidence depicted the less medieval Church as fundamentally healthy and flourishing, and that the mid-fifteenth century in Germany witnessed the beginnings of a great period of reform in all levels of society—expressed in a prodigious output or sermons, scriptural translations, and devotional writings and a great blossoming of religious art.

Julius Kostlin (1826-1901)

Janssen's charges were ably rebutted from the Protestant side by Julius Kostlin, professor of church history at the University of Halle/Wittenberg, whose writings on Luther were widely influential not only in Germany but especially in Britain and the United States. Kostlin had followed up a major study of Luther's theology with a substantial two-volume work on Luther's life and writings, which he subsequently rewrote as a popular one-volume biography. In the course of an essentially fair and balanced narrative account of the Reformation, Kostlin paid tribute to Luther as the one who "has united in his own person the true German nature with the deepest Christian piety", yet also recognized his personal failings and the divisive results of his work, noting that "even the highest aims and noblest principles are liable to suffer from human weakness and the human conditions by which they are sunounded". Apart from his substantial personal contribution to studies of the Reformation, Kostlin was instrumental in forming the *Verein fur Reformationsgeschichte* and publishing the early volumes of the Weimar edition of Luther's works. Through his many-sided work, German Protestantism remained closely in touch with its founder and original basis.

Another dimension to the nineteenth-century Protestant encounter with the Reformation developed, however—one more complex and perhaps ultimately more significant—the thoroughgoing re-examination of the Reformation heritage in light of the major philosophical changes stemming from the Enlightenment. Ironically, most of the key figures in nineteenth-century German philosophy emerged from Lutheran backgrounds, yet the overall effect of their recasting of philosophical ideas was to undermine the accepted basis of most theological work since the Reformation and radically question the relationship of contemporary Protestantism to its historical roots.

Immanuel Kant (1724—1804)

The refutation of rationalistic epistemology by Immanuel Kant, although specifically directed against the philosophical trends of his day, proved equally destructive of orthodox theology. Some Protestant scholars defiantly adhered to traditional patterns of thought, but the more flexible among them searched for a fresh nonrationalist basis for theology. The German idealist philosophers—Fichte, Schelling, and above all Hegel—developed the implications of Kantian epistemology into a comprehensive metaphysical system which, although it affirmed the primacy of spirit (*Geist*) in human existence and was thereby open to religious perspectives, essentially undermined the basis of most key Christian doctrines.

Fichte's development of Kant's definition of religion into ethical pantheism, Schelling's doctrine of God as the "world-spirit" (*Weltgeist*) and Hegel's generalization of the doctrines of the Incarnation, Crucifixion, and Resurrection into a universal pattern of nature and history left theology with the alternative of adapting its concepts to the Hegelian system or striking out in new directions. The first response came from F.C. Baur, D.F. Strauss, and the Tubingen school. The second was evident, in radically different ways, in the German Protestant theologian Friedrich Schleiermacher (1768-1834) and the Danish philosopher Soren Kierkegaard (1813-1855).

Schleiermacher, profoundly influenced by Romanticism, defined religion as the feeling of unconditional dependence, and he restructured theology on that basis. Kierkegaard rejected Schleiermacher's aestheticism along with Hegelian intellectualism and Kantian moralism in favor of the absolute "leap of faith". Schleiermacher appealed to the experiential dimension of Luther's thought and Kierkegaard, more plausibly, to Luther's notion of faith, yet each had a highly ambivalent attitude toward the Reformation, and their obvious subordination of historical analysis to the philosophical-theological task places heir work more clearly in the history of theological task places their work more clearly in the history of theology than of historical scholarship.

Albrecht Ritschl (1822-1889)

The most significant contribution of Protestant scholarship to historical understanding of the Reformation came from Albrecht Ritschl and the "Ritschlian school", whose most direct intellectual dependence was on Kant. The Ritschlians tended to interpret Kant as the philosopher of Protestantism because he rejected the identity of divine and human and insisted on human finitude. Hostile to all forms of mysticism, and indeed to any theology based on "experience", their scholarly program had a twofold basis—theology based on Kant's moral imperative and commitment to genuinely historical research opposing dogmatism of all kinds. The narrowness of their theological perspective has tended to preclude adequate recognition of their historical scholarship. Yet it was this very restriction of theology, and the consequent abandonment of any total intellectual system, which freed them to pursue historical inquiry with genuine openness.

Ritschl and those who followed him were avowedly Protestant but stood firmly for fair historical scholarship as the pathway to intellectual understanding. Accordingly, Ritschl's major work on the doctrine of justification and reconciliation was conceived in two parts, with historical study forming the basis of a dogmatic construction. He thereby reversed the almost universal tendency of Protestant scholarship to examine the Reformers' thought through their creeds and confessions and chose to approach dogmatics through history. This led him, for example, to question on strictly historical grounds the basis of Mohler's comparative symbolics by indicating the fundamentally different purpose of doctrinal statements in Protestant and Catholic theology.

In his theological analysis of the Reformation, Ritschl's strictly historical approach enabled him to anticipate by many years some insights of recent research. At a time when faith tended to be seen in subjective terms and the Reformation seen as an expression of individualism, Ritschl identified the essence of Lutheran faith as a conjunction of two elements—justifying faith, a frame of mind essentially determined by the historical appearance of Christ, and an objective conception of the Church as a divinely founded community of believers. Ritschl's stress on Luther's catholicity, commonplace today, was remarkable in his time. On the other hand, the major historical weakness of Ritschl's analysis was his tendency to treat Luther without reference to his inheritance from late medieval thought. Nevertheless, Ritschl showed a fine sense of the similarities and differences among Luther, Calvin, and Zwingli and of the modifications in their traditions since the Reformation. Moreover, his insight into the nature and origins of Anabaptism led him to articulate clearly views often thought to have originated in the 1930s.

Adolf von Harnack (1851-1930)

More influential than Ritschl in the long run was his pupil, Adolf von Harnack who, although primarily a patristic scholar, wrote extensively on the Reformation. Harnack's father, Theodosius, was the most significant representative of traditional Lutheranism, which had stayed aloof from the disturbing currents of nineteenth-century thought. He wrote the most influential book on Luther's theology published in the nineteenth century, and his son remained influenced by this tradition, despite his clear rejection of it. The younger Harnack's distinguished academic career took him from Leipzig to Giessen, Marburg, and finally Berlin. His lectures on the nature of Christianity, which articulated his view of Protestantism as a reduction of religion to the essentials of the Word of God and faith, were widely read and extraordinarily influential.

Yet Harnack's most imposing work was his massive *History of Dogma* (1886), which analyzed the development of Christian dogma from the new Testament to the Reformation. The study of Luther with which this work concludes is especially impressive and derives much of its power from the way it relates Luther to the entire tradition of Christian thought. To Harnack, the rise of dogma evidenced the triumph of the Greek spirit in Christianity, and his judgment on Luther was highly ambivalent. On the one hand, the Reformer had liberated religion from ecclesiasticism and moralism; on the other, he had strengthened the structures of Catholic dogma in which it was cast. Harnack's task, as he conceived it, was to apply to dogma the same liberating critique which Luther had applied to religion; and although this implied that Luther's Reformation had not gone far enough, Harnack also asserted that Luther had gone too far in rejecting some abidingly valid aspects of the Catholic tradition, such as the doctrine of sacrifice and monasticism.

Ernst Troeltsch (1865-1923)

The ability of some Protestant scholars to criticize their own tradition was even more clearly displayed in the work of Ernst Troeltsch (1865-1923), who belongs to the history of nineteenth-century theological scholarship as much as to the beginnings of sociology. Despite an early interest in jurisprudence and classical philology, Troeltsch had turned to theology because of its unique ability to unite metaphysical and historical questions. He served as professor of theology at the University of Heidelberg from 1894 to 1915 and subsequently as professor of philosophy in Berlin until his death. Never an "ivory-tower" academic, he held political office concurrently with his academic post during the early years of the Weimar republic, a testimony to his conviction about the close relationship of theory and practice, knowledge and ethics, past and present.

Troeltsch's views were expressed most directly in a major essay on Protestantism, although they also informed his massive and influential study *The Social Teachings of the Christian Churches* (1912). Unlike Ritschl and Harnack, he made no independent study of the primary sources and was content to reflect on others' findings, which made him vulnerable to scholarly attack. His mind was as committed to the present as Ranke's was to the past, and accordingly he approached the Reformation as a means to understanding his own time.

This posture led Troeltsch to challenge the widely held assumption that Protestantism represented the dawn of the modern era and that modern Protestantism was an authentic development of Reformation principles. To him, the Reformation was essentially a reshaping of the medieval idea and proposed new solutions to essentially medieval problems. In offering new solutions it was a genuine reshaping, yet it kept intact the basic features of the medieval system: the preoccupation with individual salvation, the ideal of a total Christian culture, the notion of the Church as a divine institution, and acknowledgment of an absolute authority. The result of the Reformation, therefore, was a second blossoming of medieval life for two centuries and a devitalization of the secular culture which had begun so tentatively to emerge.

Troeltsch, to be sure, recognized that Luther's key ideas were essentially destructive of the medieval system, but he insisted that their impact remained limited to the religious sphere and brought no basic change in social life. Change, in his view, was made possible by the Enlightenment, with its assertion of human autonomy carried forward by the alliance of the secular state with the secular study of science. Further, unlike other liberals, who argued that nineteenth-century neo-Protestantism was a legitimate development of the Reformation, Troeltsch could see only complete contradiction between the two. The neoorthodox Protestants of the next generation would share this view, although they would draw from it opposite conclusions.

J.H. Merle D'Aubigne (1794-1872)

In Continental Europe during the nineteenth century, no country rivaled Germany in vigor and vitality of scholarship on the Reformation Scandinavian research had as yet made no substantial impact outside the region. France, which had exercised such a pivotal role in the age of Bossuet and Bayle, had produced no successor of their stature, and French scholars who considered the Reformation at all remained largely preoccupied with local or national issues. However, a history in the French language by a Swiss Evangelical, J.H. Merle D'Aubigne, who had worked in Germany and the Low Countries, was translated into many languages and became more widely influential than any other single Evangelical contribution, especially in Scottish Calvinist circles, where its unstinting support of Reformation doctrine found a ready response.

If German preeminence was challenged anywhere, it was in Britain, where a vigorous scholarly debate on the Reformation continued throughout the nineteenth century. This debate was less insular than has often been assumed, for its links with German scholarship—particularly through books, translations, and personal scholarly contacts—were both extensive and profound. Nevertheless, British scholarship on the Reformation preserved distinctive characteristics and preoccupations arising out of its unique inheritance from the Reformation period. Spokesmen of the established Church of England were confronted by opponents in the Roman and dissenting traditions, powerful and articulate despite their continuing social and political disabilities. More significantly, these spokesmen could not even agree among themselves on whether the Church of England was a legitimate child of the Reformation, and whether the reformation it had undergone was a renewal or a perversion of the true faith. Consequently, the interweaving of historical judgments and contemporary preoccupations—never absent from scholarly debates--was in nineteenth century British studies of the Reformation particularly acute.

Perspectives of Church history

The Tractarian movement in the Anglican Church preserved its estimate of Anglicanism's integrity by driving a wedge between the English and Continental Reformations, holding up the Anglican Church as a *via media* between the superstition of Rome and the sectarian divisiveness of Geneva. It saw the Church of England seeking to unite true interpretation of Scripture with preservation of the apostolic succession. The Anglican Church, as Walter Farquhar Hook (1798-1875) put it, was "one and the same Church before and after the Reformation", which was "not a beginning but a turning-point". Tractarians were generally willing to recognize the sincerity of Luther's reforming intentions, but had no doubt about their lamentable outcome, not only in religious disintegration but in their supposed social and political fruits in the English and French revolutions. They were not, however, all of one mind on the details. E.B. Pusey (1800-1882) had originally asserted that error had been introduced not by Luther but by his successors, who had progressively lost his Christian inspiration and debased his doctrine of Christian freedom. Later Pusey argued that the crucial error lay in the schism and the Lutheran churches loss of the apostolic succession.

John Henry Newman (1801-1890), however, was already convinced during his Anglican phase of Luther's fundamental theological errors. In his *Lectures on justification* (1838, 1840), he attacked the heart of Luther's theology, accusing him of denying the unity of Scripture and treating faith as an end in itself, thereby leaving Christians in bondage to their feelings. Luther's problem was not so much what he taught as what he left out or denied, for a partial and unbalanced view of truth was to Newman the very essence of heresy. Newman, it must be said, had little direct knowledge of Luther or the Reformation, but centered his reflections on the history of the early Church, which he used as his measure.

At the opposite extreme of the spectrum, the Evangelicals saw themselves as spiritual heirs of the Reformers, although that consensus guaranteed neither the uniformity nor the reliability of their interpretation. Evangelicals were divided in two ways: ecclesiastically between adherents of the established Church and those of various dissenting traditions; and theologically between Calvinists, who identified Reformation theology with scriptural truth, and Arminians, who believed that the early Reformers had remained under the spell of Augustinian scholasticism. Yet all Evangelicals were at one in their anti-Romanism and their vision of an "evangelical succession" of true faith through the Christian Era derived from the traditions of the *Magdeburg Centuries* and John Foxe.

This notion received its clearest statement in the work of Joseph Milner (1744-1799), his brother Isaac (1750-1820), and John Scott (1777-1834). Joseph Milner's *History of the Church of Christ* (1794-1797) traced the story to the eve of the Reformation; Isaac Milner dealt with the first half of Luther's life, depicting the Reformer as God's instrument to reestablish the true basis of Christian faith. Scott continued their work, and at the time of his death had reached the death of Calvin, although a planned volume on the English Reformation never eventuated. Together, these works formed the standard evangelical account until superseded by the translation of D'Aubigne's book.

Universal conviction among Evangelicals about Luther's divine mission in no way preserved the Reformer from criticism. Henry Stebbing (1799-1887), an Anglican condemned Luther for his intolerance of Karlstadt; the Baptist Augustus Cox (1783-1853) regarded his sacramental theology as a superstitious remnant of Romanism. Luther's defects of character and personal behavior were widely and clearly indicated, though generally excused in view of his divine mission. Other common Evangelical themes included stern criticism of Erasmus for offenses ranging from weakness to apostasy and emphasis on pre-Reformation figures such as the Waldensians, Wycliffe, and Huss as Luther's spiritual fore-runners in the "evangelical succession."

Involvement of scholarship on the Reformation in the ecclesiastical controversies of the day resulted paradoxically in some major scholarly achievements, including the Parker Society's edition of the English Reformers' works and the Calvin Translation Society's fifty-two volumes of Calvin in English. Neither was a labor of disinterested scholarship: the first reflects the Evangelicals' determination to remind an English origins; the second reflects the Scottish Free Church's confidence "that the days of latitudinarian belief and ecclesiastical subordination to the temporal power were over". In the second half of the century, the scottish Free Church provided the most notable writers on Reformation theology, James Buchanan and William Cunningham, whose uncompromising Calvinist orthodoxy embodied the triumph of dogmatic tradition over genuinely historical analysis. In England, by contrast, Evangelicalism tended to decline into narrow fundamentalism and antiintellectualism in the face of challenges from both Rome and secularism.

The 1883 celebration of the 400th anniversary of Luther's birth provided some redirection of Evangelical energies in the face of these challenges, although Anglicans were divided about whether or not to observe the event. More significant than the celebrations was the stimulus they provided to informed and critical analysis of the Reformation, of which the outstanding products were Henry Wace and C.A. Buchheim's *First Principles of the Reformation* (1883) — a translation of the Ninety-five Theses and the Reformation treatises—and the translation of Kostlin's great biography of Luther.

Between the Tractarians on the one hand and the Evangelicals on the other, English liberal Protestants were broadly committed to a scriptural religion in which ethical concern took precedence over narrow dogmatism. Among the large group of broad churchmen, this standard tended to govern attitudes about the Reformers. Not surprisingly, Erasmus was accorded a better reception; and Zwingli, as the disciple of Erasmus and the Reformer most free from the scholastic inheritance, seemed more in line with the critical spirit of the times than either Luther or Calvin. Isaac Taylor (1787-1865) and John Tulloch (1823-1886) both criticized the Reformers for having compromised scriptural religion by their continued adherence to metaphysical dogma. They saw in this failure to transcend the dogmane spirit seeds of the Reformers' ultimate inability to carry the movement through to its proper conclusion.

The most comprehensive attempt to set this perspective in the full context of church history was provided by Henry Hart Milman (1791-1868)) in his *History of Latin Christianity* (1855). Milman accepted unequivocally the notion of progress and regarded Christian history as an incomplete historical development. The Reformers were in his view men of destiny who set the Church on its future course although they remained burdened by past legacies. The Reformation needed a Luther rather than an Erasmus to carry it out, although in the long run Erasmus's ideas were closer to the Christinanity of the future.

Another circle of liberal protestants owed much to the influence of the Anglican cleric and Christian socialist leader F.D. Maurice (1805-1872), whose reaction against narrow dogmatism was directed as much toward recovery of a deeper sense of the infinite as toward concrete social reform. For Maurice and his circle, contemporary liberal rationalism was no better than its scholastic ancestor; both made man the measure of religion and morality instead of aspiring to the absolute. Accordingly, Maurice responded warmly to Luther's passion for God, his great spiritual depth, his ability to litt man outside himself, and the hatred of formalism and definition which distinguished him from the other Reformers." In striving for the infinite, Luther had captured one half of Christianity admirably, although he had neglected the other half, the message of social renewal.

From Maurice's circle energed probably the most substantial and impressive work on Luther in nineteenth-century British scholarship, Julius Charles Hare's *Vindication of Luther against his recent English assailants* (1852). Hare (1795-1855), who was archdeacon of Lewes and brother-in law of Maurice, attacked a variety of opponents from the liberal critics William Hamilton and Henry Haliam to the Catholics Newman and W.G. Ward. All, he believed, were guilty of prejudice, selective quotation out of context, and reliance on second hand information. Moreover, they showed themselves unable to grasp Luther's spirituality because of their coldly rational attitude toward religion. Hare's point-by-point refutation of his opponents owes its strength to his direct and intimate acquaintance scholarship. But his criticism attained a deeper level. A great admirer of Ranke, Hare pleaded consistently for broad historical thinking about the Reformation as an alternative to submission to the exigencies of nineteenth-century Anglican polemics. In this respect, he had no more time for the Evangelicals' support of Luther than for the attacks of his detractors, because the Luther they had created in their own image—the individualistic proto-Evangelical—was equally a falsification of history. In his positive treatment, Hare showed an unerring sense of Luther's priorities. He insisted on the centrality of the doctrine of justification and much of his defense of Luther focuses on proper interpretation or that doctrine. He also insisted on Luther's positive and complementary relationship to the Anglican Reformation, which had added to Luther's concern for fundamental theology of gift for practical application.

English Roman Catholic scholarship in the eighteenth century had manifested virtually no interest in the Continental Reformation, and the first substantial treatment of it for some time appeared in the fourth volume of John Lingard's *History of England* (1819-1830), as an extended aside to the main theme. Writing a balanced Catholic account of the Reformation in the years leading up to Catholic emancipation was a sensitive and delicate assignment. Lingard (1771-1851), trained at Douai and influenced by its Gallican tendencies, eschewed the obvious distortions of the polemical tradition and wrote in such a spirit of fairness that some Catholics considered his work unduly conciliatory. He freely admitted the prevalence of corruption in the late medieval Church and attributed much of its to the apostasy of the papacy. Although Lingard acknowledged some admirable qualities in Luther, the Reformer emerges from his work essentially as a self-seeking opportunist, grossly intemperate and subservient to princely interests, one who in destroying regard for authority had become the father of sectarian division despite his bitter opposition to the sects his movement spawned. Lingard's account of the English Reformation is notable for its heavy emphasis on the impact of the Henrician divorce, its assessment of the reign of Edward as a time of confusion and anarchy, and its gross misjudgment of Cranmer as despicable.

Toward the middle of the century, in an essay attached to the English translation of the Tridentine decrees, James Waterworth gave a picture—similar to Lingard's and anticipating Jamssen's—of Luther as a learned but undisciplined scholar launching a reckless attack on a Church which despite its problems and abuses, remained fundamentally peaceful. The predictable recurrence of traditional Catholic perspectives did not indicate, however, a uniformity of view about the Reformation's place in the development of Christianity from medieval times. Some Catholics expressed a naive and romantic idealization of the Middle Ages and identified Protestantism with the evils which had borne fruit in the nineteenth century. On the other hand, scholars like Charles Butler and Sylvester Mahony, each of whom attempted to rehabilitate Erasmus as the proponent of wisdom and enlightenment, explicity rejected the medieval scholastic tradition as barbaric, anticipating Newman's stance on the side of Renaissance classicism against a Gothic barbarism which he saw extended in the Reformation." Lord Acton gave further proof that being a Catholic idealized Middle Age or opposition to the contemporary world.

John Emerich Edward Dalberg-Acton (1834-1902) brought to his historical studies an unusual background and training. Born in Italy of an aristocratic Catholic family, he grew up in a cosmopolitan environment, studying in Paris, Edinburgh, and Munich (where he was a pupil of Dollinger); acquiring a sound knowledge of major European languages; traveling widely through Europe and to America. He knew nothing of the political and social restrictions under which many of his coreligionists had labored in England, and his remoteness from them was only accentuated by his friendship with Gladstone and acquisition of a peerage, on Gladstone's recommendation, in 1869.

Acton remained, nevertheless, highly conscious of his Catholicism and deeply preoccupied with the relationship of Catholicism to the contemporary world, which became an important concern in the third quarter of the century and culminated—despite the best efforts of scholars like Acton and Dollinger—in the Church's resolute stance against modernity. From 1858, when he began his close association with the *Rambler,* Acton popularized a conception of the Catholic Church as the natural ally of freedom through its role as liberator of humanity from the tyranny of the antique state. Unafraid of historical truth and critical scholarship, Catholicism in this view contrasted sharply with Protestantism, which was naturally illiberal, fearful of critical scholarship, theologically barbarous, and tied to current creeds of political tyranny. The Reformation represented a narrowing of the European spirit after the freedom of medieval civilization. Yet this liberal and optimistic vision of Catholicism was shattered by promulgation of the doctrine of infallibility. From that point Acton's role in Catholic intellectual life diminished, although his commitment to unbiased historical scholarship as an expression of his Catholic faith only became firmer.

From around 1875 to 1900, British scholarship among Catholics and Protestants alike exhibited signs of increasing specialization. Apologetic motives often lay behind this trend, as was clearly the case with Abbot F.A. Gasquet's work on the dissolution of the English monasteries, an impassioned defense of English monastic life on the eve of the Reformation as healthy, vigorous, popular, and beneficent, and an account of its destruction through the greed of Cromwell and his supporters. Gasquet (1846-1929) also republished William Cobbett's *History of the Protestant Reformation* and was much influenced by its romantic conception of monastic estates as the "patrimony of the poor." In Gasquet's eyes the Reformation was a revolution of the strong against the weak, and—here he echoed Janssen—a blight on a society in which religion was "the bloom upon the choicest fruit." Far from being quintessentially English, as Froude had claimed, the movement had been a foreign import of "false and poisonous teachings." Gasquet's strength and originality lay in his setting of institutional history in a rich social and intellectual context, and this was certainly a healthy corrective to biased Protestant views of the dissolution. On the other hand, he was flagrantly inaccurate in his transcription and citation of sources, too much inclined to fill gaps with unsubstantiated conjecture, and, despite his foreign ancestry, stubbornly insular.

Scarcely less insular was the Anglo-Catholic version of Reformation history published by Canon Richard Watson Dixon of Carlisle (1833-1900), who triumphed over his remote situation by short, intensive visits to the library of the British Museum. Dixon severely criticized the Reformation's achievements, especially the dissolution of the monasteries, which he regarded as a vulgar profiteering. He insisted, nevertheless, that there had been no break in the continuity of the English Church during the Reformation. Although corrupted, robbed, and sized by alien influences, it had remained the true Church of the realm. In line with this perspective, Dixon began the history of the English Reformation with the 1529 parliament, and saw the religious revolution as the result of a tragic combination of circumstances (Including the king's divorce) without which the Church would have beaten off the Protestant challenge while absorbing healthy new influences from humanism. In his neglect off Lollardy and the earliest manifestations of Protestantism, Dixon reflected the characteristic attitudes of late Victorian High Churchmen. His prejudice mingled with chauvinism, leading him to attribute most evils to sinister foreign influences, which had their way for a time until the firm actions of churchmen like Gardiner managed to preserve the Catholic principle and save the old religion from heresy while dispensing with the Roman tyranny. Notwithstanding its prejudices, Dixon's conscientious six-volume *History of the Church of England* (1878-1902) retains a distinct value, especially in its close analysis of the Henrician statutes and its aspiration to describe the Reformation's social and economic consequences.

The upsurge of Protestant fervor in the celebrations of 1883 met a predicable response from Catholic circles in the form of a series of pamphlets rekindling the old fires of confessional prejudice. Yet the manturing of historical scholarship could not but affect church historians writing at this time. Although most scholars' personal religious stances remained abundantly clear, the trend toward historical realism and objectivity was no less apparent.

Henry Wace (1836-1924), dean of Canterbury and formerly professor of ecclesiastical history at King's College, London, complemented his point work on Reformation documents with some significant interpretive writings which, despite their moralizing tendency, are valuable for their stress on the positive relationship between the Continental and English Reformations and their placement of the Reformation in the context of late medieval spirituality and scholastic theology.

With his multivolume *History of the Papacy* (1897), Mandell Creighton (1843-1901), professor of ecclesiastical history at Cambridge and later bishop of London, demonstrated a clear commitment to Rankean principles of scrupulous objectivity and provided a most informative survey. On the other hand, his fifth volume, which deals with the Reformation, affords a somewhat superficial view of the German movement and scant understanding of its major ideas.

Charles Beard (1827-1888) was a Unitarian scholar, personally commutted to evolutionary science and empirical reasoning, and this profoundly shaped his distinctive—some would say perverse — view of the Reformation as a movement for free rational inquiry which had broken the authoriarian system but arbitrarily stopped short of its goal. Yet this rather narrow perspective did not prevent him from demonstrating a remarkably broad understanding of historical variety. Sympathy with the more radical trends of Reformation thought and a conviction that the path of the future lay with Erasmus rather than Luther in no way prevented Beard from recognizing Luther's profound spirituality and indispensable contribution. Meanwhile, Lord Acton, in his maturity as Regius Professor of Modern History at Cambridge, continued to be preoccupied with notions of liberty. Most of his work appeared posthumously as collected essays and lectures, but he did enunciate some genuine in sights, among which his recognition of Luther's essential conservatism deserves particular mention.

The outstanding British historian of the Reformation in this period was undoubtedly the Scotsman T.M. Lindasy (1843-1914), who not only summed up much of the best of nineteenth-century church historical scholarship but in a number of ways broke genuinely new ground. A minister of the Free Church of Scotland he was professor of church history from 1872 and from 1902 principal at a theological college in Glasgow; he wrote extensively on the Reformation for more than thirty years.

Lindsay's first major contribution was an article on Luther for the ninth edition of the *Encyclopaedia Britannica,* in which he united a firm grasp of Luther's central religious insight of justification by faith and spiritual freedom with a critical judgement about its inadequate social and political realization in Germany, for which Lindsay held Luther in part responsible. The Swiss Reformers were seen as having more fully part into practice the implications of Reformation doctrine, although there is no doubt that Lindsay regarded Luther's forceful enunciation of the Reformation's spiritual basis as the linchpin of the whole movement. In *Luther and the German Reformation* (1900) and in his chapter for the second volume of the *Cambridge Modern History,* Lindsay broke tree of the narrow confines of ecclesiastical history and academic theology, setting Luther squarely in his social context and arguing that the

Reformer's central insight sprang from the religious understanding of the common people from whom he had come. Luther thus became spokesman of the popular spirit against a sterile and lifeless theology.

In Lindsay's last major work, the comprehensive two-volume *History of the Reformation in Europe* (1906-1907), he maintained his interest in popular religion and argued that Luther's teaching succeeded because it presented no startling novelties to the people, but "something which they had always at heart believed, though they might not have been able to formulate it." The first volume gains much of its strength from detailed study of social, economic, and religious background, which forms the basis for Lindsay's account of the German Reformation up to the Peace of Augsburg. The second volume, treating the Reformation outside Germany, is especially notable for its demonstration of the author's sympathy for movements as diverse as Calvinism and Anabaptism. Particularly significant is his recognition—some decades before the revival of Anabaptist studies—that these sectarians had been unfairly treated by historians. Lindsay paid tribute to their high moral qualities, the learning of many of their leaders, and their pioneering commitment to religious toleration. In short, Lindsay provided the clearest Indication that sincere confessional commitment need not preclude historical writing which transcends party allegiances. The thoroughness and professionalism of his works make them not only definitive for their day but enduringly valuable to students of the Reformation.

The trend toward greater professionalism in British studies of the Reformation, of which Lindsay's work is the outstanding example, was not yet so evident on the other side of the Atlantic, although there were significant exceptions. The academic environments of the two major Engilish-speaking nations in the late nineteenth century had little in common, and a comparison in instructive.

Despite its geographic remoteness, the United States had maintained a more intimate connection which the European Continent than had Britain through a continuing stream of European immigrants and their descendants, who generally retained their linguistic and religious traditions. In particular, the strong complement of German and Scandinavian Lutherans in the United States had no counterpart in Britain. On the other hand, American religious life had as yet done little to foster scholarship on the Reformation. Nineteenth-century American Protestantism was characterized by either a narrow, inward-looking confessionalism or a proliferation of new denominations which owed more to contemporary American ideals than to an awareness of religious traditions. The Luther jubilee of 1883 brought to America, as to Britain, a heightened consciousness of the Reformation heritage, but most of its expressions were anything but scholarly. Celebrated as a folk hero and champion of American ideals of civic and religious freedom, Luther also became a focus for Protestant suspicion of a Catholic Church which was not only advancing theoretical claims but making its presence felt through large-scale immigration to major urban centres.

The celebrations, however, also bore positive fruits. Kostlin's activities as a writer, organizer, and editor were even more influential in America than in Britain, aided by a strong Lutheran confessional tradition and persistence of a large German-language reading public. These initiatives stimulated significant academic enterprises in America, including the first critical edition of the Lutheran confessions in English and the large St. Louis edition of Luther's works.

Moreover, when most American scholars remained bound by their confessional horizons, there was one who made a distinctive and enduring contribution to international scholarship of the Reformation. Philip Schaff (1819-1893) was anything but typical of American Protestantism and perhaps for that reason personified the best of its intellectual traditions. Born in Switzerland and educated in Germany, where he was deeply influenced by August Neander and the Tubingen school of Hegelian historians, he developed an intense commitment to his adopted country. A supporter of the Prussian Union Church, which had united Lutheran and Reformed traditions in Germany, he maintained wide contacts across denominational boundaries in his new homeland and progressively sought a less restricted constituency for his academic work.

After two decades in a Reformed denominational seminary in mercersburg, Pennsylvania, Schaff moved to cosmopolitan New York and the ecumenical setting of the Union Theological Seminary, where he became affiliated with the Presbyterian Church, a body predominantly British in origin. His career embraced New Testament studies, chairmanship of the American committee for revision of the English Bible (which involved close contact with the parent committee in England), editorship of a major religious encyclopedia, coeditorship with Henry Wace of an edition of the church fathers, and a leading role in founding the American Society for Church History.

Schaff's reputation, however, was based chiefly on his historical work, which displayed an unusual blend of confessional and ecumenical concerns. As early as 1845, in *The Principles of Protestantism,* he claimed that catholicity belongs to the Reformation rather than the Roman Church. That church had exchanged true catholicity for Roman particularity; by contrast, the Reformation was "the legitimate offspring, the great act of the Catholic Church," and hence truly catholic. The same preoccupation informs Schaff's *History of the Christian Church,* which covers from the Apostles to the Reformation era and was completed in six volumes in 1892. It is an antisectarian but by no means anticonfessional work. Schaff's ecumenical aspirations enabled him to appreciate and give full weight to the strengths of various confessional traditions without regarding any of them as final. This work remained for some time the most substantial account of the Reformation in English, and much of it is still valuable, although in some respects dated by its strong emphasis on Hegelian notions of development.

Schaff's vision of church history is embodied concretely in the substantial book *Creeds of Christendom* (1877), which assembles the bulk of the confessional writings of both Catholic and Evangelical churches with a massive and detailed analytical study. In thus introducing Americans to comparative symbolics, Schaff was highlighting confessional differences, but he made clear in the preface that this was an integral part of the ecumenical and historical process. In what amounts to a statement of his philosophy as a church historian, he declared that "honest and earnest controversy conducted in a Christian and catholic spirit promotes true and lasting union. Polemics looks to Irenics—the aim of war is peace.

Fitting though this may be as an epitaph for Schaff's work, early twentieth-century developments in the Roman Church would show that polemics might be used for a purpose far removed from irenics. The manifest progress of Catholic and Protestant historians of the late nineteenth century toward a more critical and historical approach was not likely to be permanently reversed. Yet the work of two scholars whose writings dominated Roman Gatholic research on the Reformation in the first two decades of the 1900 underlines the unpredictability of historical scholarship and the complete relationship between polemical and historical interests. Heinrich Denifle and, to a lesser extent, Hartmann Grisar manifested a spirit of bitterness difficult to parallel in the history of Catholic thought; yet, paradoxically, much of the power of their attack derived from the wealth of genuine sources on which their writings were based.

Heinrich Denifle (1844-1905) was a distinguished medievalist whose lifetime study of the problems of the late medieval Church ultimately led him to Luther. After five years' painstaking research in German, Austrian, and papal archives, he published *Luther and Lutheranism* (1904), which burst through the confines of the learned world to become a subject of debate in press and government circles. The work's staggering impact was a result not merely of the author's ferocious style, but of his claim that its only sources were Luther's own writings. This was no idle claim; he had made extensive use of sources previously available and unearthed in the Vatican library a copy of Luther's early *Lectures on Romans*, previously inaccessible to historians. These provided an arsenal with which Denifle attempted to discredit Luther as a creature thoroughly corrupted by his sensual nature and an ignoramus, incompetent to handle theological issues.

Several aspects of Denifle's historical outlook deserve note, specifically his implicit rejection of Janssen's idyllic picture of the fifteenth-century Church and his recognition of its deep and unresolved crisis. Yet the real importance of Denifle's work lies not in any specific historical judgments but in its attempt--virtually unparalleled at the time—to place Luther squarely in his historical context: ecclesiastically, by relating him to patterns of church life in the fifteenth century, and intellectually, by showing his dependence on a particular stream of medieval theology. Its inadequate analysis by no means negates the importance of this development in historiography. Denitle's failure to capitalize on the possibilities of this approach is attributable not merely to a passionate hatred of Luther, which overwhelmed all objectivity, but to his ultimately greater interest in philosophical patterns of history than in particular phenomena. Luther the man, the theologian, the reformer, was lost in the delineation of Luther the decadent type, the incarnation of that evil current running through the late medieval Church.

This fundamentally unhistorical aspect of Denifle's treatment did not escape the more astute Protestant critics, who were thrown on the defensive by such a savage indictment. The distinguished medievalist had exposed, if nothing else, the appalling ingnorance of many of Luther's admirers about the medieval world from which the Reformer had emerged. If the immediate effect of Denifle's attack was a mixture of outrage and panic, in the long run it forced Protestant scholars to re-examine their approach to Luther. The seninal work of scholars like Karl Holl and Otto Scheel originated largely from the challenge Denifle posed. By a strange irony, therefore, this archenemy of Luther became, indirectly and unconsciously, one of the major impetuses for the "Luther renaissance" of the early twentieth century.

That Denifle also substantially influenced contemporary Catholic scholars was to be expected. Yet it is remarkable how severely he was criticized by his fellow Catholics and how swiftly his most distinctive emphases were drastically modified or discarded. Such changes were facilitated by the appearance of another major Catholic work on Luther with a recognizably different perspective. Hartmann Grisar's three-volume study, published in 1911-1912, was also the product of years of scholarly research and centrally concerned with Luther's inward life as the key to the Reformation. Yet Grisar (1845-1932) openly rejected some of denifle's basic conclusions, especially the notion of Luther's submission to sensuality, and traced the Reformer's intelectual and moral decline to profound pride and egoism, rooted in a deep-seated psychopathic illness.

Grisar's work displays an impressive erudition. He was profoundly influenced by the school of Ranke, and he consciously aimed at an objectivity which he believed Denifle lacked. In many parts of his work, where he analyzed specific issues of historical interpretation in close detail, his talents are shown to good advantage. Yet few scholars could credit his work as a whole with that basic fairness he sincerely believed to it have. This was because Grisar's achievements were invariably balanced by failures. If he boldly refuted a number of palpable fables and groundless calumnies against Luther, he revivified just as many and left standing by innuendo others, which he acknowledged in the telling as unproven. He exhibited throughout a deep hostality and partiality, which led most scholars—both Catholic and Protestant—to conclude that his differences from Denifle were, in the last analysis marginal.

It is true that Grisar's analysis permitted a certain softening of the picture of Luther. He dwelled on the Reformer's favorable personality traits, credited him with the best of motives, and showered him with the sympathy appropriate to a diseased soul where Denifle could manage only scorn and contempt for a degenerate wallowing in his bestiality. Yet many Protestants found Grisar's condescending pity more offensive than Denifle's open hostility. Nevertheless, Grisar's work, based on such solid if selective research, continued to force scholars back to the sources to question unexamined assumptions and poorly founded conclusions.

Revolutions in scholarship can rarely be dated with precision, yet the four hundredth anniversary of the posting of the Ninety-five Theses, in 1917, saw the appearance of two major essays—one Protestant, one Catholic—each signaling something of great importance in the history of research on the Reformation. Karl

Holl's essay on Luther's understanding of religion has long been regarded as central to the Luther renaissance of the twentieth century. Franz Xaver Kiefl's shorter and less known essay on Luther's religious psyche" has more recently been recognized for its pioneering significance in Catholic scholarship. Yet more than mere scholarly caution warns against ascribing too much significance to particular dates. Seminal essays generally derive their power as much from favorable conditions as from their inherent qualities, and such was certainly the case with these two. Holl's work, for all its originality, is arguably the descendant of nineteenth-century scholarship, inconceivable apart from the historical traditions of the Ritschlian school and the textual research which from 1883 bore fruit in the monumental Weimar edition of Luther's works. Yet Holl's significance is equally illuminated by comparison with another group of Protestant scholars who began, from the second decade of the century, to reappropriate the Reformers' theological insights.

The theological revival led by the Swiss pastor and theologian Karl Barth (1886-1968) and somewhat misleadingly known as *neoorthodoxy* arose in opposition to the anthropocentric and humanistic theology of the Ritschlians and sought to reestablish theology as an authentic discipline in its own right, not dependent on changing patterns of philosophy or the spirit of the times. Although he was a product of the Reformed tradition, Barth pursued no narrow confessional bias, but used both Luther and Calvin, and indeed the whole tradition of historical Christianity, in a creative manner. Over a long career—as professor of theology at Gottingen, Munster, Bonn, and finally, when expelled from Nazi Germany, at Basel—Barth never wavered from his original goals. His thinking was oriented, above all, to a rediscovered biblical theology, yet it could equally well be regarded as a repristination of Reformation thought, stressing revelation over reason, the righteousness of God over religious experience, and divine grace over human works.

There can be little doubt that Barth and his circle recaptured authentic accents of the Reformers thought which the liberals had lost by refracting Christian doctrine through the prism of Kantian moralism. Moreover, as Barth moved beyond the prophetic criticism of his earlier writings to the positive reconstructive task, the Reformers' thought continued to play a decisive role in his dogmatic reformulations. Such was the power of the reorientation Barth offered that he dominated Protestant thinking for decades, and even theologians who took widely divergent pathways, such as Dietrich Bonhoeffer, Paul Tillich, and Rudolf Bultmann, were demonstrably dependent on him and shared some of his orientation to the Reformation. Yet if the Barthian movement of the early twentieth century helped revive interest in the Reformation, it was not without its threat to historical study. Barth's work could scarcely be regarded as a return to traditional orthodoxy, because he accepted the principles of critical biblical and historical study. Yet he did in effect reestablish the priority of dogmatics over history and reduce church history to a lesser role than it had exercised under the Ritschlian school.

The scholarly work of Karl Holl (1866-1926) can be seen as an important alternative to Ritschlian liberalism on the one hand and Barthian theology on the other. Holl's research was impeccably historical in the best ritschlian traditions, based on exact historical and philological scrutiny of sources. But, precisely through his historical study of Luther, Holl brought to attention those profound religious themes which Barth had appropriated dogmatically, but which the Ritschlians had tended to ignore. In particular, he demonstrated the signficance of the doctrine of conscience and its essentially theocentric character.

Holl, therefore, made possible a genuine rediscovery of forgotten dimensions in Luther's thought, yet without any sacrifice of a scrupulously historical method. This was especially important because Denifle's and Grisar's attack on Luther, based on historical sources, required something more effective than a dogmatic counterblast. Holl's studies of Luther address the kinds of questions the catholic polemicists had raised. He had the breadth of historical knowledge to answer Denifle's charges about Luther's ignorance of the medieval tradition, and he also took up the question of ethics, showing in a major essay how Luther's doctrine of justification—far from ignoring ethical considerations—involved precise moral principles capable of wide application in social life.

Holl's pioneering work on Luther was significantly complemented by other scholars. The exhaustive documentary studies by Otto Scheel (1876-1954) provided the basis for much interpretive discussion of the Reformer's thought. Heinrich Bornkamm (1869-1927) produced a major—and still valuable—biographical study of the young Luther. Through scholars like Walter Koehler (1870-1946), the Luther renaissance soon spread its influence beyond studies of Luther to work on Calvin and the other Reformers, and even into some important preliminary investigation of Reformation radicalism. Its results became accessible to English-speaking readers through the substantial works of James Mackinnon (1860-1945). As a scholarly movement, it has been as much concerned with the edition and publication of texts as with issues of interpretation, and, if its early provenance was chiefly theological, its implications for historical scholarship have been far-reaching.

The essay published in 1917 by German Catholic scholar and churchman Franz Xaver Kiefl (1869-1928) bears scant comparison with Holl's in scope, depth, or impact, yet it was, in its restricted circle, an important contribution. Kiefl brought no new sources to light and offered no original insights, yet his attempt to understand Luther's religious stance not only provided an interesting parallel to Holl's approach, but opened new possibilities for a Catholic scholarship still closely attuned to the harsh accents of Denifle and Grisar. Kiefl's willingness to take a fresh look at Luther was influenced, as he freely acknowledged, by the German war experience, which had forced the nation as a whole to come to terms with its deep religious cleavage, and forced Catholics in particular to reconsider their views of the man who, although a religious enemy, was a national hero. Yet Kiefl also pointed to an influence which was less obvious but ultimately more enduring: the advances in research which Catholic scholars could not afford to ignore and which provided an environment favorable to informed discussion and inhospitable to attitudes based merely on prejudice.

Kiefl differed from Catholic writers of the previous century not so much in his basic method as in the context of his interpretation. Dollinger, Janssen, Denifle, and Grisar had, after all, tried to interpret the Reformation through an understanding of Luther's inner life. Kiefl thought along similar lines, but found his subject fundamentally motivated not by violence, lust, or psychic illness, but by genuine and profound religious interests. His recognition of Luther's integrity and sincerity, however, in no way eroded his conviction about the Reformer's heresy. Indeed, basic doctrinal differences were stressed precisely because they were acknowledged to be rooted in fundamental divergences of religious perspective rather than trivial or external circumstances. To take Luther seriously as *homo religious* one could not dismiss his doctrine as the ignorant or misguided aberrations of a sensualist or psychotic. Like Mohler a century earlier, Kiefl provided the basis for a reasonable discussion acorss the lines of religious division, while highlighting the breadth and depth of that division.

Recognition of Luther's fundamentally religious motivation remained the keynote of much subsequent Catholic scholarship in Germany; in 1931 Hubert Jedin was able to report the end of Denifle's influence. But the newer approach made no substantial inroads into non-German scholarship. British and american Catholic writers perpetuated had abandoned them. French scholars like Jacques Maritain, Jacques Paquier, M.J. Lagrange, and Leon Cristiani added a dimension of xenophobia. One who stood out from the rest was Pierre Imbart de la Tour (1860-1925), who, though influenced by Grisar in his view of Luther, provided a more sympathetic portrait of his compatriot Calvin. In ways only fully recognized in recent years, he broke genuinely new ground, especially with his rich and subtle analysis of *evangelisme*—the world of Lefevre and Marguerite of Navarre—in the early decades of the sixteenth century.

The new direction of German Catholic scholarship on the Reformation found further expression in 1929 in a book of essays by both Protestant and Catholic authors, edited by Alfred von Martin. Scholars such as Sebastian Merkle, Johannes Albani, and Anton Fischer combined an exploration of Luther's religious piety and churchmanship with a critical discussion of the problems of the Church which made a Reformation necessary yet inhibited a positive Catholic response. If any Catholic writer summed up the state of Catholic work on the Reformation in the mid-1930s, it was Konrad Algermissen, whose massive study of Christian denominations, published in 1935, attributes to the Reformation the stuff of tragedy because of its juxtaposition of noble religious motives with dire theological error. But the views of scholars from Kiefl to Algermissen had no apparent influence outside Germany and limited impact within, because they were usually expressed in occasional essays or a few paragraphs of larger works. To this point, no Catholic scholar had provided a full-length, comprehensive, coherent statement of the revisionist view comparable in scope with the works of Denifle and Grisar.

That deficiency was remedied by Joseph Lortz (1887-1975), who shared Kiefl's general approach but went much further in providing a comprehensive history of the German Reformation (1939-1940), which attained as definitive a status in Catholic scholarly circles as Janssen's had earlier. The extent to which Lortz's work represented a revolutionary change in Catholic historiography has at times been exaggerated. His raw judgment that "Luther *was* the Reformation", although qualified in actual exposition, was symptomatic of a tendency, shared with writers like Denifle and Grisar, to exaggerate the undeniably crucial personal role of Luther in the outbreak and early development of the movement. Likewise, Lortz's theological assessment of Luther's heresy loomed large and similarly discredited the Reformation.

Nevertheless, Lortz's differences from these polemicists were more than variations of emphasis. His judgment of Luther's heresy was clear and unequivocal, but he understood it as the product not of base motives, moral depravity, or psychic collapse, but of a one-sidedness born of an earnest and godly spirit. According to

Lortz, Luther had distorted a crucial and neglected part of the Catholic tradition by isolating it from the whole. Moreover, this error was no mere personal failure; it reflected a basic lack of clarity in the late medieval Church about the Church's teachings. Here was a far more serious problem than the alleged moral corruption emphasized by earlier Protestant writers.

An especially interesting aspect of Lortz's approach in his attribution of a large share of blame for the Church's intellectual confusion to the disintegrating effects of Erasmian humanism. Essentially a restatement of a view first voiced by the sixteenth-century papal nuncio Aleander, this judgment places Lortz in line with Janssen, but sharply at variance with other contemporary Catholic historians, such as Imbart de la tour and Gasquet. Underestimating Erasmus constructive demand for a theology closely based on the New Testanient, Lortz considered him a "half-Catholic", a born relativist and individualist. By contrast, he paradoxically viewed the rebel Luther as a contender for Catholic truth against the corrosive tendencies of Renaissance humanism. Luther's error arose not from false doctrines but from an unbalanced emphasis on true doctrines. Lortz's assessment of Luther's one-sidedness and subjectivism was influential with a generation of Catholic scholars, but his delineation of the intellectual uncertainty of the pre-Reformation Church achieved far more general acceptance and helped direct attention away from the barren process of moral charge and countercharge, characteristic of many Protestant and Catholic writers, to a more fruitful study of the bewildering intellectual ferment in the early sixteenth century.

No less important than Lortz's constructive synthesis was the devastating critique of Catholic historiography pursued concurrently by Adolf Herte (b. 1887). Herte's subject was not Luther himself but Catholic interpreters of the Reformation, and his major work demonstrates that virtually all Catholic interpretation of Luther from the sixteenth century to the early decades of the twentieth, was dominated by the baneful influence of Cochlaeus's *Commentaries*. He argued that, with few exceptions, Catholic scholars, even those like Denifle and Grisar, who worked to a large extent with genuine historical sources, had derived their understanding of Luther directly or indirectly from Cochlaeus. Herte's critique was motivated by a positive desire to clear away centuries of interpretation based on malice and prejudice, as much for the sake of historical truth as for confessional harmony.

Although Lortz's work has rightly been recognized as an important turning point in Catholic scholarship, developments since 1940 moved far beyond his vision. Some significant work was done on other aspects of the Reformation, but the focus remained primarily on Luther and the German Reformation. Notwithstanding the continued influence of Grisar in some circles, Lortz's view of Luther as *homo religious* has been the fundamental starting point for most Catholic scholars' attempts to interpret the significance of the Reformation. Johannes Hessen provoked considerable controversy when in 1947 he published a small book which cast Luther in the role of a prophet, on the pattern of the Old Testament prophets. Erwin Isserloh, a pupil of Lortz, initiated a lengthy debate by denying the historical basis for the posting of the Ninety-five Theses on All Saints Eve, 1517. Iserloh, like Lortz, interpreted Luther as at that moment essentially conservative in his aims, a self-consciously loyal son of the Church who sought only a proper redress of errors by appeal to the duly constituted authorities. Most Protestant scholars remained unconvinced by Iserloh's arguments and saw in them a form of special pleading, but his painstaking dissection of the evidence stimulated close study of the events of 1517, which undoubtedly enlarged knowledge of the immediate circumstances and their broader implications. As in earlier generations, confessional concerns proved capable of advancing historical understanding.

Nowhere was the subtle interconnection of confessional and historical interests more clearly demonstrated than in the study of Luther's theology, which took over from historical biography as the main focus of Catholic research and in which the most significant advances beyond Lortz were made. In his major work on the

Reformation, Lortz had characterized Luther's thought as an "inchoate flood" and denied that he could be properly described as a theologian. Although he later modified this view somewhat, the most he expected from the study of Luther's thought was confirmation of the judgment that Luther had rejected a Catholicism that was not fully Catholic. Scholars since Lortz have expected, and obtained, far more.

A number of studies published in the 1960s demonstrate that Luther had considerable familiarity with Thormist thought through passages quoted in the writings of Gabriel Biel. Otto Pesch asserted, on the basis of a comparative study of Aquinas and Luther, that there was a surprising degree of basic agreement, obscured chiefly by sharply contrasting but potentially complementary styles of doing theology—Aquinas was a "sapiental" and Luther an "existential" thinker. Parallel works by other scholars examine the influence of Augustine, Gregory of Rimini, and Saint Bernard on Luther's thought. Harry McSorley's exhaustive study of the controversy with Erasmus on freedom of the will asserts the fundamentally Catholic content of Luther's theology of salvation.

The ecumenical spirit which pervaded the writings of this generation of Catholic scholars was strikingly evident, especially in the years following the Second Vatican Council, yet their confessional orientation was no less clear. They sought, on the one hand, genuinely Catholic elements in Luther's thought and action and, on the other, explanations for his deviations from Catholic orthodoxy by reference to the confused state of Catholic thought at the time. Yet in many Catholic writings on Luther these confessional limitations were increasingly abandoned and his thought was considered on its own terms and subjected to the scriptural test Luther himself acknowledged rather than to rigid dogmatic criteria emanating from the magisterium.

The result of this trend has been not only to blur the formerly clear boundaries of Roman Catholic research on the Reformation, but also to add to the debate a dimension of internal Catholic argument. Scholar accustomed to assessing "the Catholic view" must now reckon with a range of widely divergent perspectives. Frido Mann, Jan Aarts, and Wolfgang Schwab, for example, offered highly positive assessments of particular aspects of Luther's theology. Daniel Olivier, in a work on Luther's faith, presented the Reformer to Catholic readers as a "teacher of the Gospel" par excellence. On the other hand, Riccardo Garcia Villoslada's biography of Luther in Spanish, subsequently translated into Italian, breathes again the spirit of Grisar. Theobald Beer's weighty study of Luther's theology is so comprehensive in its negative judgments that it aroused much critical comment in Catholic circles.

Works of this character have been rare, however, and in the years leading to the Luther quincentenary in 1983 a variety of books from Catholic scholars notable for their balanced assessment appeared. These included biographies by Peter Manns and John Todd, a study of Luther and Erasmus by the Belgian scholar Georges Chantraine, a comprehensive guide to Luther's thought by Otto Pesch, a collection of essays by Yves Congar, and a biographical and theological assessment by the American Jesuit Jared Wicks. All in different ways present Luther from a perspective still recognizably Catholic, at times judiciously critical, but always fundamentally appreciative.

Scholarship on the Reformation in Protestant circles since the Second World War exhibited, as earlier, a close interaction with Catholic research and many parallel developments. Germany never abandoned its role as the originator of new trends and interests, but scholars in other countries increasingly made genuinely original contributions. Scandinavians in particular pursued a style of scholarship on the Reformation which has become very much their own. Nathan Soderblom and Einar Billing, both of the University of Uppsala, were among the pioneers of a fresh approach to Luther in the early years of this century, and their work was followed by a continuous tradition of research on Luther closely tied to a particular method of theological inquiry yet rigorously historical in its approach to the sources. The "Lundensian" theologians Anders Nygren and Gustav Aulen used study of the Reformation as an auxiliary aspect of a more fundamental interest in systematic theology. Regin Prenter, Lennart Pinomaa, and Gustav Wingren, working respectively in Denmark, Finland, and Sweden, were principally concerned with the historical exposition and contemporary relevance of Luther's doctrinal and ethical positions.

Continued preoccupation with Luther in the Scandinavian countries was virtually guaranteed by the presence of large national churches bearing his name. In England, where no significant Lutheran Church existed and Luther had been overshadowed since the sixteenth century by the more pervasive presences of Calvin and Zwingli, Methodist scholars like Gordon Rupp, Philip Watson, and Rupert Davies did most to revive interest in studies on Luther from the 1950s. Yet, notwithstanding some excellent work on the Continental Reformers, English scholarship has understandably maintained its preoccupation with the complex history of its own Reformation tradition, both at home and overseas.

French writers on the Reformation characteristically showed a special interest in the peculiarly French dimensions of the movement, and in their native son John Calvin. Protestant scholars in particular explored the movement exhaustively, aided by the industry of the long-standing Societe de I'Histoire du Protestantisme Francais. In postwar writings the balance has been redressed, and a number of notable studies of Luther have been made by scholars such as Richard Stauffer and Marc Lienhard. In the same period general works on the Reformation moved away from narrow "church historical" interests. Emile Leonard's *History of Protestantism* (1961), for example, although in many ways a traditionalist work, presents Protestantism as a complex, living reality embodying not only ecclesiastical structures but social groups and individual responses.

Scholarship in Germany continued to show na propensity for exhaustive and extended debates about precise historical issues, such as the controversy about the posting of the Ninety-five Theses and the vexed question of dating Luther's evangelical "breakthrough", but such exchanges took place in an increasingly broad and diverse range of historical and doctrinal investigations, made possible by the wealth of source material now open to scholarly investigation. Of particular significance was the inquiry undertaken at Tubingen by Heiko Oberman into the complex intellectual background of the Reformation: a fresh approach to questions which had been on the agenda since Carl Ullmann's publication in the 1840s of *Reformers Before the Reformation.* Ullmann had dealt in particular with the mid-fifteenth-century reformists, sometimes called Augustinizers, cited and edited by Luther—John of Wesel, John Pupper of Goch, and Wessel Gansfort—and with John Huss, who had assumed a parallel role, at least from the year 1520—when Luther read his *De Ecclesia* and had it printed, urging Germans and Bohemians to drops their old feuds and work together to further the Gospel. On the same general theme, Gerhard Ritter had contributed an article in 1927 entitled "Romantic and Revolutionary Elements in German Theology on the Eve of the Reformation", showing that so-called Augustinizers derived their views directly from Scripture, which they sometimes cited to contradict Augustine.

Oberman's specific concern was the Nominalist tradition, which Catholic controversialists like Denifle had used to discredit Luther. In a major study of Gabriel Biel, intended as the first part of a trilogy linking the later Middle Ages and the Reformation, Oberman employed the image of a "harvest-time" to argue for the health and vigor of the Nominalist tradition. In the second volume of the trilogy he studied late-fifteenth-century theological development through focus on the University of Tubingen; the third is intended to discuss Calvinism. Meanwhile, in biography marking the quincentenary of Luther's birth, Oberman focused on the Reformer "not as a desk-bound research scholar but rather as a man besieged by and responsive to the conditions and convictions of his day and age."

Although we will refer to Oberman's professed desire to develop a "social history of ideas", his major contribution to studies of the Reformation is undoubtedly on the theme of intellectual continuity. In this respect his immensely learned and detailed trilogy should not obscure the more straightforward contribution of his *Forerunners of the Reformation* (1967), a superb collection of pre-Reformation texts with illuminating comments and an incisive essay on the "problem of the forerunner". Oberman was also instrumental in the publication by others of many detailed studies of late medieval scholars, theologians, and preachers, which has continued to enrich our understanding of the early Reformation intellectual environment. These range from highly specialized monographs to the useful collection edited by Steven Ozment *The Reformation in Medieval Perspective* (1971), which brought together European and American contributions on the general theme of continuity.

The emergence of american scholarship to a prominence rivaling that of Germany was signaled as early as 1946 with the foundation of the American Society for Reformation Research, and that society's collaboration with its German counterpart to revive the journal *Archiv fur Reformationsgeschichte.* The United States had been well served for a generation or more by scholars in theological seminaries and universities, many of whom explored the traditions of their respective religious confessions. But more often, in a country as ecumenically minded as it is confessionally diverse, narrow denominational barriers were ignored. J.T. McNeill's studies of the Calvinist tradition characteristically look outward. Roland Bainton showed himself equally at home interpreting Luther, Erasmus, and the radical sectarians. Wilhelm Pauck set his primary study of Luther in the context of the protestant movement as a whole. One needs only to place the articles in the American-edited *New Catholic Encyclopedia* (1967) beside their counterparts in the original *Catholic Encyclopedia* (1907-1914) to see how deeply these expansive attitudes influenced Catholic scholars.

The establishment in 1957 of the Foundation for Reformation Research in St. Louis, with its ambitious program of archival acquisitions, was only the most obvious example of using modern technology to expand the resources available to scholars. Research on the Reformation not only was a lively interest in the theological seminaries but found an equal welcome in the graduate schools of american private and state universities. The mobility of faculty and students at that time and the flourishing of professional societies combined to stimulate wide overlapping of scholarly interests and creative application of historical research in contexts as diverse as arcane points of theological interpretation and the study of sixteenth-century urban society.

Protestant and Catholic scholarship has clearly traveled a long way since the first were exchanged. Once partisan and myopic, it has become ecumenical and genuinely international; once limited to theological and ecclesiastical concerns, it has, without losing this primary focus, become increasingly interdisciplinary and concerned with the fullness of historical experience. Once preoccupied exclusively with great leaders and broad sweeps of history, it has come to share the fascination of general historical scholarship with lesser-known figures and the largely anonymous multitude who brought the Reformation what success it achieved in the towns and countryside of Europe. Discovery of a large neutral territory in social history has been as important as ecumenical sentiment in enabling Protestant and Catholic scholars to find common ground.

The religious commitment so many of these scholars brought to the study of the Reformation over four and a half centuries has been both a strength and a problem. At its best, it has engendered the enthusiasm without which historical study readily becomes lifeless; at its worst, it has falsified the past. The historian can only be thankful, in retrospect, that the cruder forms of bias by which devout scholars reinforced self-righteous prejudices have been eradicated. Yet it is difficult to escape the conclusion that the involvement of deeply committed partisans produced much of the tangible progress in historical research in this field. They may have been hell-bent on some private or group theological triumph, but in the process they uncovered lost sources and provoked inquiry into neglected subjects. Leopold von Ranke's supposedly objective history stimulated Dollinger to bring forth materials Ranke had passed over. Denifle's violent attack on Luther proved a major motivation for Protestant scholarship to abandon its complacent hagiography and seriously explore the Reformation's intellectual roots. Even since the Second Watican Council, when Catholic scholars have chaired seminars and delivered papers to international congresses of research on Luther with ecclesiastical blessing, some of the more productive historical work has originated in confessional commitment. Religious interests can raise genuine historical questions which might not otherwise be investigated, and even unhistorical questions need not be antihistorical.

Where Catholic and Protestant scholarship failed to advance understanding, that failure was not so much the result of confessional commitment as of the unnecessary tyranny such commitment exercised over historical judgment. The problem, which has its parallel in political affairs, is exacerbated when any group of scholars is obliged by overt, covert, or self-imposed restraint to work in a narrow intellectual environment. A solution is, however, less likely to lie in the pursuit of a chimerical ideal of pure objectivity than in the breaking down of situations in which bias runs rampant because it is unchecked by counterbias. The clearest evidence of the historical maturity of Protestant and Catholic study of the Reformation is the distance it has already traveled along that road.

2

The Fundamental Theology

Introduction

The apologetical approach forms the basis of all genuine Christian theology. As an attempt to justify or defend Christian hope, it is as old as Christianity itself and he controversy in which the Christian religion has always been engaged. One basic experimental aspect of theological reasoning is clearly visible in fundamental theology, namely that it is concerned with experiences, insights and theories with a theological character that cannot always be ascertained in advance because it has to be rediscovered again and again in a historical, experimental synthesis. It is not purely by chance that nontheological definitions (concepts) are always available in fundamental theology, which is obviously in a permanent state of being systematically reconstructed if this experiment of theological reasoning is found to be present in its structure.

For a long time it has been recognized that the classical division of fundamental theology into three parts (religion, Jesus Christ and the Church) and the inner structure of each of those three parts had been determined by historical factors. The form and content of the treatise on the Church, for example, are still to some extent conditioned by the controversies of the post-Reformation period. Most of the questions in the treatises on religion and Jesus Christ are still reactions to the controversy about the metaphysical and historical foundations of Christianity that was current during the period of the Enlightenment. Indeed, almost the whole repertoire of classical concepts and problems to be found in fundamental theology (or theologies) today can be traced back to precisely that period and its radical self-questioning. The concept of religion and the distinction between religion and revelation and the problem of natural theology that are both connected with it are all questions originally asked during the post-Reformation era. They can all be grouped under the heading of the question of the possibility of and the conditions governing revelation as such that is based on a rationality outside history and independent of subjects. This rationality that is presumably outside or above history is nonetheless conditioned and made relative by history and, although it has always determined and still determines the structure of fundamental theology, it does not necessarily lead directly to the heart of those questions with which contemporary fundamental theology is confronted.

Apologetics did not emerge as an independent theological discipline until the end of the Enlightenment, when it came as a reaction to the problems that had been raised during that period. In the immediately post-Reformation period and the Baroque age, the disputes that took place were almost exclusively interconfessional and concerned with what we now call controversial theology (the period of the great arguments with the *gentes,* as represented, for example, in Thomas Aquinas *Summa contra gentiles,* had passed long since). These disputes also took place within a cosmos that was recognized on both sides to be Christian. The Enlightenment, however, introduced two important changes in the situation of the Church and its theology. On the one hand, the identity of faith and religious consciousness, which had hitherto been accepted more or less unquestioningly, ceased to exist. Christian faith found itself confronted with a universal critical concept of religion and challenged to justify or defend itself. On the other hand, the unity of religion and society, which had similarly hitherto been accepted without question, also broke up, beginning in France during the early period of the Enlightenment. Christianity began at that time and in that place to appear, in relationship to its social environment, for the first time as a particular aspect of an all-embracing historical and social connection with the world that could determine the universal consciousness of man more and more fully.

It was, at that time and in that way that the requirements for a form of questioning and criticism of religion that is still of great importance today were evolved. This questioning mainly takes the form of a criticism of ideology. In other words, it tries to place the Christian religion in a connection with the social processes of the world that might determine it and to expose religion as a function (or ideological superstructure) of certain relationships or certain subjects in society. The religious subject came therefore to be defined as the conscious social subject that is not yet adequate for itself or as the social subject with a false consciousness.

In what follows, I shall therefore, attempt to check theology against its ability to take the so-called Enlightenment as an epoch-making event seriously and to deal with it critically. It the first section below, I shall examine the ways in which such themes as tradition, authority and reason, which were carefully considered by the philosophers of the Enlightenment, were debated (or not debated) by the theologians of the periods preceding, during and following the First Vatican Council. In the second section, I shall look at the attempts made by more recent theologians to overcome the thinking of the Enlightenment in the light of German idealism or the principle of secularization.

In the third part of this chapter, the attempts made firstly by the apologetical approach and secondly by the new theology to break through the influence of Enlightenment thinking are critically considered together with the aim of establishing whether what has taken place politically since the Enlightenment has in fact been realized in theology and the Church of the First and Second Vatican Councils. The aim, in other words, in this third section is to ascertain whether the Church has been able not only to make use of the questions considered by the Enlightenment, but to recognize those questions as rooted in the rise of a new kind of man—the citizen or middle-class subject—and his relationship with religion and faith. The third section is of special importance in connection with my attempt to define a practical fundamental theology today. It is also inevitably bound to lead to certain changes in our attitude towards the apologetics of Vatican I and the new theology of

Vatican II. It will also make me correct to some extent the contribution that I have so far made to the formulation of a political theology. Finally, it forms a preparation for a renewal of the debate with the Enlightenment that is undertaken in the third chapter of this part of the book ('Political theology of the subject as a theological criticism of middle-class religion'). Section 3 of this chapter and the third chapter of Part I should therefore, be seen as a single argument.

The apologetical front

The Tubingen school can certainly be regarded as an exception to the general pattern of apologetics in the Catholic Church during the nineteenth century. From the end of the eighteenth century onwards, its members (including J.S. Drey, J.B. Hirscher, J.A. Mohler and J.E. Kuhn) engaged in brilliant theoretical apologetics which constituted what was in the best sense of the word a theology of response which was at that time not, as was later the case, isolated from all other systematic and historical concerns in the sphere of theology. On the contrary, the apologetics of the Catholic members of the Tubingen school arose directly out of those other concerns. As F.A. Staudenmaier has said, 'the only true Christian apologetics are a direct self-representation of the spirit of Christianity.'

The apologetics of the Catholic Tubingen school were in no sense isolated from the philosophy and science of the period. Indeed, the weakness of these aggressive and interdisciplinary apologetics was above all to be found in their being based on the conviction of the members of the school, who were fully acquainted with nineteenth-century scientific progress, that the problems of the Enlightenment had already been overcome, or would soon be overcome by the idealism and romanticism of the age. In so doing, the Tubingen theologians gave too little attention to the central problem of the enlightenment that Kant had approached and Marx had later explored in depth with important consequences--the primacy of practical reason.

a. Roundabout the middle of the nineteenth century, however, a second attack was made against the foundations of Christianity by thinkers such as Feuerbach, Marx and Nietzsche and religion was radically criticized under the guise of a criticism of ideology. At the same time, with rather tragic consequences for the history of theology, the powerful light shed by the apologetics of response of the Catholic school at Tubingen began to grow dim and was replaced by another form of pure apologetics which was isolated from contemporary historical and philosophical concerns. This is the period of what is usually known as neo-scholasticism. This theology predominated in the Catholic Church during the second half of the nineteenth century until as late as the nineteen-thirties.

Neo-scholasticism has lest a lasting impression on apologetical theology as a whole and indeed on every attempt that has been made from the mid-nineteenth century until the present time to provide a theological response to all contemporary questions. Although they are not at all easy to assess, I shall discuss the achievements and the important figures of neo-scholastic theology later in this book. In the meantime, however, I am bound to point out that it was in certain clear ways a regressive movement. It retreated from contemporary philosophical and related problems and, at a time when the safe foundations of theology began to shake, sought refuge in the past and revived earlier traditions. Kleutgen, a leading exponent of neo-scholasticism, called his work a 'theology of antiquity' (*Theologie der Vorzeit*) and the title is very revealing.

The cognitive and political isolation of neo-scholasticism is fully in accordance with the spirit of Catholic Christianity at the time when this theology was formulated. During this period, Catholics, rather feebly imitating the great Corpus Christianum of the High Middle Ages, had retreated into a to-some-extent political stronghold which might be called a nineteenth-century *Corpus Catholicum.* Apologetics became polemics in a very far-reaching sense, even embracing social action (Bismarck's *Kulturkampf* is the classical example of this). During the first phase of apologetics, the mutual relationships that existed between Catholicism and Protestantism were very fruitful, but these soon deteriorated into defensive attitudes, isolation and even aggressive denial. The aim was above all to achieve a new stability.

Neo-scholastic apologetics also remained isolated from theology as a whole and moved in the fringe areas of the consciousness of and teaching about faith. It was above all a theory of the *praeambula fidei.* It was a concept not of mediation but of defence. One of the most important consequences of the neo-scholastic approach was that theology was threatened with division into two separate spheres of assertive and defensive thinking. Dogmatic theology and apologetics tended to exist side by side without touching. Theologians specializing in the first discipline were not conscious of any need to justify Christian faith, while apologists lost sight of the living content of faith and were consequently in the long run unable to defend it in accordance with its content and its immanent intelligibility. One result of this attitude was that neo-scholastic theologians often discussed aspects of faith objectively in order to protect them from the critical questions raised by the contemporary world with the inflexible weapons of apologetics.

These apologetics were deeply marked by a defensive attitude and proved to be incapable of constant honest self-criticism and correction of the kind that ought to arise from the very heart of Christianity. As a consequence, the neo-scholastic apologists looked more and more outside Christianity itself for the causes of failure in theology and the Church.

b. Religion and society became more and radically separated as a result of the Enlightenment and this led to a loss of plausibility, universality and normativity in theology and the Church. The relationship between religion and society, which had, until the Enlightenment, been unquestioningly accepted in dogmatic theology, therefore became a problem, on the assumption that *Doctrina christiana* (or *Doctrina catholica*) could not provide the basis for giving consent to social action. In the course of the nineteenth century, the Church attempted to make up for this loss of universality and normativity by evolving its own social teaching, which is to be found in the papal encyclicals that appeared in the nineteenth century and the Roman pronouncements about social and political questions of the time.

This social teaching of the Church also formed part of the apologetical syndrome. Neo-scholastic apologetics raised a protective wall around Catholic dogmatic theology to defend it against the historical, philosophical and general scientific questions that attacked it. In the same way, a relief attach was made against the political challenge of the times in the social teaching of the nineteenth and early twentieth-century Church. In other words, the fight against civil democracy, liberalism in the nineteenth century and finally Marxism was carried on just in front of the fortress Church, on the territory of pure social ethics. In this attempt, the theological and dogmatic content of the Christian message was as far as possible kept out of the controversy about social matters. It was therefore an indirect attempt to deal with the basic problems of faith and theology while bypassing the controversies of the period. (Those problems were, of course, always 'political'.)

What is important, however, to bear in mind is that controversy with political and economic ideas and the theoretical systems of any period cannot be carried on by means of apologetics or in the fringe areas by means of neo-scholasticism or the Church's social teaching. It has rather to be carried on by using the very substance of Christian faith. This conviction forms the basis of the political theology that is developed in this book.

c. The political phenomenon, which is also concerned with theology and the history of the Church and has usually been known as traditionalism, can be regarded as a prototype of the apologetical front described above.

Traditionalism was a theoretical movement connected with the state and society in France at the end of the eighteenth and the beginning of the nineteenth centuries, that is, immediately following the French Revolution. It took the form of a radical criticism and generally also a rejection of the political form of Enlightenment thought that was current during the Revolution. The most prominent representatives of this movement in France were de Bonald, Lamennais and de Maistre. The movement also had lay exponents in other European countries, notably the political philosopher Burke in England, Donoso Cortez in Spain and three outstanding germans, J. Gorres, F. von Baader and the young Pilgram.

The traditionalists differed from the neo-scholastic theologians or the exponents of the Church's social teaching in that they believed that the identity of the Christian religion could not be considered, let alone saved, outside the social context in which it was placed. For this reason, any attempt to mediate aspects of faith such as original sin, divine authority and providence socially was also regarded by the traditionalists as an attempt to save its substance.

The traditionalists threw doubt on the knowledge gained through natural reason (pointing again and again in this context to the weakening power of original sin) and stressed how unsuitable natural reason was as a means of providing access to the idea of God or revelation (referring repeatedly in this instance to the need for what they called a primitive revelation). In so doing, the traditionalists played the part of adversaries in the theology of the nineteenth century and the Church of the First Vatican Council. The Fathers of that Council were clearly opposed to traditionalism in their teaching about the relationship between *ratio* and *fides* and their pronouncements about revelation and man's knowledge gained through revelation.

Later, in the third chapter of this part of the book, I shall be able, by dealing with a number of questions which will become clear at the end of this examination of the progress of fundamental theology, to recognize what is legitimate and indeed theologically indispensable in traditionalism and to see its achievements in the field of apologetics in a different light. At present, however, I must confine myself to criticizing traditionalism as a social and political aspect of apologetics.

The traditionalists' rejection of reason and the general public use of reason has to be seen as operating within a directly political context. They rejected reason because they wanted to invalidate its claim to criticize the prevailing authority of the state and those who held that authority and to overcome systematically the idea of democratic self-government that was regarded as the capital sin of the French Revolution. This process was very problematical because it contained the danger and clearly recognized fact of making the Christian religion and its dogmas move in the direction of a restoration of an earlier system. The traditionalists' denial of the primacy of reason, then, did not operate within a primarily theological context. It was, on the contrary, almost exclusively interested in making the idea of a powerful monarchy prevail over that of middle-class democracy (the latter was, of course, based on the concept of universal autonomy which had its roots in the primacy of human reason). The traditionalists therefore, made use of theological data and gave these a relative value in order to emphasise political ideas and systems and to keep the mass of the people, who were thought to be insufficiently mature to hold political power, in a state of subjection.

An even more basic process, however, can be seen in this aspect of traditionalism—the hypostasization of political power or an attempt to trace political authority back to religious authority with the aim of giving politics the stability and immunity possessed by religion. This is, however, not primarily a theological question concerned with the way in which political authority is related to the authority of God. If authority could be shown to be an expression of God's plan, the traditionalists believed, then the monarchical idea of political authority could be safeguarded and made unassailable.

This theory of sovereignty clearly had an influence on the practical ideas of primacy and infalliability at the First Vatican Council, although the Council in fact condemned traditionalism, or rather those of its teachings which were dogmatically immediately identifiable (the need for a primitive revelation and the denunciation of natural reason). The disastrous aspect of the division between dogmatic theology and social theory as described above is made quite clear here. The dogmatic aspects of traditionalist teaching were condemned by the First Vatican Council, but the social teaching of traditionalism was validated in the practical self-understanding of the highest authority of the Church.

The breakthrough of the apologetical front by the new theology

In this section, I shall discuss very briefly and simply the path followed by the new theology in its breakthrough of the apologetical front and its attempt to defend Christian faith by means of a constructive association with recent traditions. In the previous section, I drew attention to the theological movements that were active in and around the First Vatican Council. In this section, I shall be dealing with the theological changes connected with Vatican II.

The new beginning made with Vatican II was preceded by several decades of preparation on the part of French and German theologians especially working in the nineteen twenties and thirties and elaborating their ideas immediately after the Second World War.

a. The neo-scholastic ghetto, with its defensive attitude towards the philosophical and scientific traditions of the modern world, was broken through. Catholic theologians came to understand that this modern consciousness was really representative of the historical mediated totality of the modern world, on the basis of which a critical theological concept had to be elaborated if they were to talk about God and his dealings in history with men. The dialogue conducted in the nineteenth century by the members of the Tubingen school with the great traditional representatives of modern thinking which had been more or less completely broken off was resumed. The dialogue with the world continued, not in a defensive way, but with the aim that had characterized earlier periods of Christian theology,, namely of assimilating critically and productively what was of positive value in those great traditions.

Characteristically, the new theology began almost exactly where neo-scholasticism had left off—at the debate with the philosophy of idealism and especially with Kant, who was regarded as the precursor of idealism, and his criticism of pure reason. I am bound to point out in this context that it was the transcendental Kant whose thought was considered by the new theologians working before and after the Second World War, not the Kant of the philosophy of history or the Kant of practical reason. German idealism was therefore, considered by the new theologians along the path of certain clear (Hegelian) traditions, embracing phenomenology, existentialism and personalism, to such an extent that present-day systematic theology and apologetics still seem to be determined by the philosophical forms within the tradition of German idealism, even when the latter is not explicitly taken into account.

Not only apologetics in the narrower sense of the word but the whole of systematic theology have been affected by this development in theological thinking. This has not come about purely by chance. It is a remarkable feature of the twentieth-century breakthrough in Catholic theology that apologetics have regained a more genuinely theological character and have come to be a theological discipline in the narrow sense of the word and are no longer used as they were in new-scholasticism as the front line protective forces of dogmatic theology with certain tasks allocated to them. In other words, one clear result of the new theology has been that apologetics have become fundamental theology and are now concerned not simply with strategic defence, but also with the fundamental problems of Christian faith.

One of the most important elements in this twentieth-century penetration of neo-scholasticism by the new theology was the movement known as immanentist apologetics, which developed as a result of the work of the French philosopher Maurice Blondel and the controversy with various French representatives of the Modernist movement. In the German-speaking countries, on the other hand, the most significant result was that fundamental theology came to be regarded as a kind of investigation of theological principles or simple as a fundamental theological discipline. The leading exponents of this kind of fundamental theology in the German-speaking world are G. Sohngen, B. Welte and H. Fries, each of whom has, of course, a different emphasis. It is, however, Karl Rahner who has been responsible for the clearest and most lasting exposition of this tradition in Catholic theology of apologetics and fundamental theology, in the distinction that he has always made in his dogmatic teaching between formal and fundamental theology. According to Rahner, the formal structures of dogmatic theology are dealt with in fundamental theology, which is to some extent formal dogmatism. Dogmatic theology can also only continue to be meaningful if it is a material fundamental theology, that is, if it expresses the contents of dogmatic theology that it presents in the context of the questions raised by the contemporary world. it is only possible to be a true hearer of the Word in the strictly theological sense if one at the same time hears the objections raised by the world of one's own time and shares the problems of that world. The name of Rahner, who has always insisted on the legitimate function of classical apologetics and the rational and historical apologetical form of argument, is therefore, always associated with this new phase in Catholic theology, in which the contents of Christian faith have been mobilized for a critical justification of that faith, in other words, for the apologetical task of theology in the strict sense of the word.

b. I am bound in this context to point to the ecumenical significance of this new beginning in Catholic theology. The reformulation of apologetics and renewed understanding of the part they played in theology as a whole led above all to a marked decrease in polemics and confrontation between the different Christian confessions.

It is also important to mention another development in apologetics. After the penetration of neo-scholasticism by the new theology and the resumption of dialogue with contemporary ideas, the Enlightenment once again came to occupy a central place in the minds of Catholic theologians, who began to suspect that the ideas of the Enlightenment had not been sufficiently well understood by the idealists, the romantics and their successors, the phenomenologists, the existentialists and the personalists. This problem, which had been either forgotten or suppressed by the representatives both of the Tubingen school and of the new theology of the twentieth century, became one of the most important themes in fundamental theology.

This acute and complex problem of a criticism of metaphysics and Christianity that is not based on idealism is still unresolved today. It has not yet been fully understood and many aspects of it have not yet been discussed. Yet this positivistic or Marxist criticism of religion is, in all its contemporary variants, now clearly shaking the very foundations of theology and Christianity as a whole.

To begin with, an attempt was made by the new theologians to do justice to the autonomy of reason and the world, which had become historically conscious of itself in the Enlightenment, in the so-called secularization argument. Special attention has to be given to this theology of secularization in any examination of development of fundamental theology. This is important not only because it is something which concerns all the Christian confessions and is therefore a valuable ecumenical aspect of the new Apologetics, but also because it is, according to the theological arguments based on the transcendental approach, existentialism or personalism, the theoretical aspect of the new theology that has been most discussed and has in one way or another received the greatest measure of consent.

There is, of course, one version of the theology of secularization in which Christianity appears not as a victim or as an opponent, but rather as the originator of the process of secularization. This is the incarnation, in which God's acceptance of the world in his Son is interpreted as the most radical release of the world to itself, with the result that the principle of incarnation becomes the principle of secularization. In the incarnation, Christian faith sets the world free to itself, releases it from the immediate normative claims of the religious traditions and thus brings about its fundamental secularity. It pays for this by means of a special kind of freedom from the world. At the same time, however, it can only remain closely connected with these processes of secularization by virtue of the fact that it has also constituted them historically.

In my *Theology of the World,* I moved clearly in the direction of a theology of secularization, but at the same time criticized it explicitly in the political theology that I formulated in the book. I asked, for example, whether the secularization argument in the form in which I have described it above could really lead to a constitution of theological reason in the contemporary situation or whether it would not invalidate it or else lead to a purely privatistic choice. I also asked whether, if the pre-condition for secularization was faith's freedom from the world, the critical and liberating power of Christianity with regard to history and society was not forgotten or at least obscured. I came in this way to see the argument of the new political theology as increasingly plausible, namely that the idea of a faith that was quite free from the world could be viewed with suspicion for several reasons. It might, for example, become on the one hand, because of its privatistic isolation, an ideological climax or a symbolic paraphrase of every single historical or social process in the world. On the other hand, its secularity might be basically no more than a novel way of immunizing Christianity and therefore, simply a bad form of apologetics in the most sublime sense of the word.

Another form of theology of secularization grew out of the traditions of the liberal theology of the nineteenth century. This liberal theology of the world had an influence on many more Christians than simply the supporters of the nineteenth-century liberal theology and it is still of importance in Protestantism today. It can be summarized in a few words. What was regarded by the thinkers of the critical age of the Enlightenment as rational is, according to this liberal theology of the world, fundamentally Christian. The Christian and theological interest is identified in this movement with such contemporary historical interests as emancipation, freedom and man's coming of age. The Christian element consists in the affirmation of these contemporary processes. Secularization is regarded as Christianization.

In my opinion, the energetic forward-looking form of apologetics leads (and has indeed already led) to the theological reason being absorbed in the abstract emancipative reason of the modern era. Its creed is based on the canonization of developments that have in fact taken place and the tendencies that were in fact manifested during the enlightenment. Theological understanding of the Enlightenment seems to consist of an ultimate acceptance of the triumph of the Enlightenment over the Christian Church or of the replacement of Christianity by the Enlightenment.

What is hardly recognized at all is that there is an inner dialectical tension in emancipation, Enlightenment and secularization and that the Enlightenment has, therefore, given rise to problems over and above what it has itself raised to the level of a problem, has put as a question on the order of the day and has enabled to be discussed. This knowledge, it has to be admitted, has not been present from the beginning in the new political theology and one of the most important aims of this book is to formulate it.

A Pyrrhic victory over the Enlightenment

a. In the progressive liberal Christian apologetics described at the end of the preceding action, the tables were turned completely against the apologetics which the neo-scholastic theologians, the exponents of the Church's social teaching and the traditionalists used as a defensive front against the Enlightenment and contemporary thought generally. The Enlightenment is no longer regarded as the quintessence of anti-ecclesiastical and anti-theological provocation. It is treated as a *locus theologicus*, a place, in other words, where Christianity becomes universally rational and, therefore, at the same time historically universal. In one form or another, almost all theologics that have in their own time been regarded as modern or progressive have been filled with satisfaction with regard to this late victory. Whereas the earlier Catholic apologists had defended tradition and authority, the liberal theologians pleaded, with the restrained pathos of the Enlightenment, for democracy, public life, honesty, freedom of conscience, autonomy and freedom to express one's opinion in the Church. Their plea was to a great extent justified, but it should not be forgotten that, when they took up the weapons of the Enlightenment, these liberal apologists also took over the difficulties.

The weapons of the earlier apologetics, with their strong opposition to the Enlightenment, could, of course, obviously be used against the arguments of the liberal and the new theologians, both of whom have emphasized emancipation, freedom and so on. But the latter have not allowed themselves to be defeated or even persuaded to follow the anti-Enlightenment path, which they have recognized as wrong.

It has, however, proved necessary to re-examine the Enlightenment itself and to throw a new and radical light on the Enlightenment in the form of a political and theological enlightenment of the processes of the modern era. These are not simply the same as the new concepts used in contemporary reflection about the Enlightenment and made more precise in the course of time. What is more important than these new concepts themselves is the process by which they become rooted in the new man's understanding of himself. In other words, the subject who articulate themselves—and assert themselves—in these concepts are more important than the concepts themselves.

I shall discuss this question of the subject in greater detail and in many different contexts in the following chapter. In the meantime, however, I would like to draw attention to a few important aspects of this theme. In the first place, a new man, the citizen, arose in the Enlightenment and came to assert himself in the processes of the modern era, during which he was made absolute. Secondly, this new man or middle-class subject has become established through the liberal and the modern theology, both of which have made use of the ideas of the Enlightenment (though with a different emphasis). Finally, and perhaps most important of all, a middle class concept of praxis has to a great extent replaced the authentically Christian concept of freedom and praxis that is critical of society. In other words, it has reduced the Christian concept to the level of the private subject existing without problems in society and to that of individual moral righteousness.

It is, therefore, obvious that there is an urgent need for a practical fundamental theology that will continue along the path of Christian apologetics, restore the radically Christian concept of praxis and place it at the disposal of the subject who is not yet established (as a middle-class citizen), that is, at the disposal of the state of all men as subjects and the process by which they become subjects.

b. A new light is thrown from the vantage point of practical fundamental theology on the work of those apologists who acted with the right conservative instinct in combatting the Enlightenment and the emergent middle class as enemies of Christian faith. Because they did not do this consciously and consistently, however, they were quickly defeated by their middle-class opponents. What is more, the new liberal theologians treated Christian apologetics in their defeated state with a scorn that revealed the naivety of the trifling way in which they had dealt with the inner crisis of identity in Christianity created by the Enlightenment and the middle-class subject.

Christianity has had to face a challenge of enormous proportions in the presence of the middle-class citizen. This new man can be defined as the subject who is in control and at the same time in need in society. His ability to control new has hardly any remaining receptive aspects and he is already able to dominate almost everything in the natural world and in human history. His practical understanding is orientated almost exclusively towards models that are based on this control of nature and on the satisfaction of his own needs. His other practical patterns of behaviour as a subject are disappearing and losing their effectiveness.

The seriousness of this challenge is bound to lead the Christian to respect the attempt made by the neo-scholastic theologians to combat the tendencies outlined in the preceding paragraph, although it has to be admitted that they did not succeed in finding suitable critical means. Their tendency to immunize Christianity is understandable, although it is difficult to understand why they were prepared to risk everything in the Church and theology in the face of middle-class power and to define the essence of Christianity according to the dictates of middle-class plausibility. I stress this because I am convinced that these points which marked the failure of neo-scholasticism in the past form the central problems of present-day apologetical theology.

Resistance to the privatization of Christianity by the middle-class subject is clearly reflected in the Church's social teaching generally and the papal encyclicals dealing with social teaching since the time of Leo XIII and Pius XI. What is regrettable is not so much that forces have emerged in opposition to the middle-class movement and liberalism or that the absorption of the social praxis of Christian faith by the purely private moral praxis of the middle-class Christian has been opposed, but rather that this resistance has been too little the result of radical Christian faith itself. It was therefore possible for the resistance offered by those practising the Church's social teaching to be so misinterpreted that it came to be seen in the end, at least in the German-speaking world, simply as a defeatist defence of the middle-class attitudes of late capitalism.

The militant nineteenth-century apologists were both clear-sighted and blind to the truth at the same time. This is particularly true of the French traditionalists who, as lay theologians, developed the most carefully reflected and most suitable form of theology as far as social questions were concerned that was available at the time. We would be seriously understimating the theological and political importance of this movement if we were to maintain that it was no more than a cynical and arrogant rejection of the ideas of the Enlightenment. The traditionalists were, after all, aware of the great danger inherent in the cult of abstract reason and in handing down a rationality that was independent of subjects. They were also conscious of the perversion of political power that occurred when politics became subject to a similarly abstract concept of freedom and reason. Traditionalism also draws attention to another consequence of the abstract nature of middle-class reason and its dissociation from history and the human subject. It is that the rejection or destruction of tradition and memory does not simply lead to increased freedom and autonomy. On the contrary, it usually results in a new form of stultification, in which man is easily manipulated or corrupted.

The traditionalists were mistaken not so much in their attack against middle-class religion as in their conviction that it could be replaced by a movement back into an earlier, supposedly utopian form of Christianity. The level of the traditionalists criticism of the Enlightenment and the middle-class subject should not be lowered, nor is it possible for theology to return to a period before the middle-class revolution.

Only if the Enlightenment is scrupulously questioned and re-examined (partly in the light of the resistance offered by what we have called the apologetical front in the nineteenth century), theology will finally be able to respond to the challenge presented a long time ago by Marxism in its struggle for a new subject. This challenge is accepted in particular by practical fundamental theology as a political theology of the subject, in an attempt which will go beyond its debate with the post-idealist thinkers in their criticism of religion and ideology, since this debate has too often been disassociated from the human subject and therefore conducted at too abstract a level.

3

The Middle-class Religion

Introduction

Far from being diametrically opposed to present-day theology, Enlightenment or contemporary thinking certainly has a right to be domiciled in theology, even though that right may perhaps be vague and difficult to distinguish. The right to domicile does not mean that its criticism of the Church and theology will always be understood or even heard or that it will have, in modern theology an equal partner in debate. Much that was called into question in the Enlightenment is still waiting for an answer in theology What, however, is firmly established in modern theology—and, what is more, in the theological thinking and the different theological positions of all the various Christian confessions— is the formal Enlightenment or contemporary principle of the subject. The deepest level of theology has in fact been reached in this principle of the subject and attempts have been made to reconstruct it as a specifically religious subject. going back beyond the Enlightenment, in Protestant circles to the Reformation and in Catholic circles to mediaeval theology. It is, however, worth pointing out here that the supermacy of the subject in theology in the abstract sense has not become more easily distinguishable in the process. By this I mean that it is difficult to distinguish, in the enlightenment itself the validity of speaking about mean as such and his reason, autonomy, freedom and other abstract attributes. No real, critical clarity existed here with regard to the concrete subjects intended and defended in the idea of man or the subject, in other words, with regard to the social reality expressed in this concept. A most important achievement made in the debate with religion and the criticism of ideology is that problems should not be discussed without reference to the human subject or independently of their social and political background. This is an important aspect of the so-called enlightenment of the Enlightenment, which is constantly required and without which neither contemporary thought itself nor those who receive it can remain rational and subjects can remain subjects.

In this perspective, it is necessary to question what is really meant, in the sense of actual social subjects, by such theological abstractions as man, existence, person or subject in modern theology, which is obviously able to include and deal with the Enlightenment and contemporary thought as a purely theoretical intellectual process dissociated from the human subject. Does modern theology know, in other words, what is taking place when it defends, as a specifically religious subject, the subject of the modern era, whose problematical social situation it does not always necessarily take into account?

This is perhaps the time to summarize briefly what has to be discussed in this chapter, as opposed to the preceding chapter. Although the Copernican revolution did give rise to a crisis in theology and the Church, which was recognized and eventually overcome so that it is no longer a crisis, this was not the cause of the extreme crisis that has continued to be felt in Christianity. This crisis in theology and the Church, which has not yet been grasped in its real proportions, let alone overcome, is due to the breakthrough at all levels of the new man or middle-class citizen with reservations towards, and what one might call a 'division of labour' relationship to the Church. This new man emerged in the Enlightenment. He is the subject in the subject. he is concealed behind the rational. autonomous man who has come of age in the modern era. He is finally also the creator of that form of religion which is used, as it were, to decorate and set the scene, freely and in private, for middle-class festivals and which has for a long time been current even in normal Christianity. Theology, which believes that it is bound to defend the contemporary human subject uncritically as a religious subject, is, in this perspective, simply a late reflection of this middle-class religion *('burgerliche Religion')*. It is not my aim to make this religion an object of scorn by examining it so intensely. The aim is rather to elucidate what is meant by the fact that religion no longer belongs to the social constitution of the identity of the subject, but is rather added to it.

I shall, therefore, attempt in the following sections to throw a little more theological light on the Enlightenment and its consequences. In this, I shall try to avoid the common practice of German scholars in the past, who believed that it was possible to overcome the effects of the Enlightenment by means of political restoration and a return to periods of human consciousness which preceded the modern era and had been superseded. My attempt will take the form of a theological enlightenment of the Enlightenment and its subject, the middle-class citizen. The latter does not present us with a theological problem in his origin. This theological criticism is only necessary in the citizen's self-assertion and absolute value. We know, after all, from the dialectics of the Enlightenment that the process of liberation ceases at the point where it becomes an unconscious and mechanical self-defence.

We have therefore, to go back to the Enlightenment, not in order to define the reaction of theologians or the Church more precisely or critically, but rather in order to acquire a batter understanding of the crisis itself that has come about as a result of the Enlightenment and the middle class or perhaps as a result of the gradual disappearance of the Enlightenment into the middle class. This imporved understanding of the crisis will inevitably be directed above all to wards theology and the Church.

In the following six divisions of this chapter, then, the central elements of the crisis caused by the Enlightenment will be examined and subjected to theological analysis. These include the phenomenon of privatization, the loss or tradition and the crisis of authority. the reduction of reason to rationality and of tradition and the crisis of authority, the reduction of reason to rationality and of religion to sphere of private religion. The concluding section contains a number of indications pointing to the need for a political theology of the subject.

Privatization

Privatization, the most important phenomenon in the crisis caused by the Enlightenment and therefore the first to be discussed here. had its origin in the conflict between the Church and the State that began in the late Middle Ages and became more acute during the period of the religious wars and divisions. The two confessions which were in conflict with each other at that time were in no sense private religions. They were both above all sovereign expressions of the social life of their period. This conflict made it increasingly impossible for the political unity of the state to be based on religion in those parts of Europe where it was no longer possible to enforce religious and confessional uniformity. If the state, then, was to have a chance of survival and was to carry out its tasks of creating unity and guaranteeingg freedom, it had to be emancipated from religion. Even before the widespread process of privatization took place in the Enlightenment, then, this home-made from of privatization already existed in the Christian religion.

A distinction was always made in the Enlightenment between the private and public spheres as one of the fundamental conditions for a humane society and I do not intend to question this good aspect of the Enlightenment phenomenon of privatization. I am only concerned here with what is in my opinion the continuing problem of the subjects of that process of privatization.

The way of life of the middle-class citizen is ultimately contained within the concept of 'private.' The middle class is no longer sustained by any all-embracing traditions, let alone religious traditions. It owes its existence and survival largely to an economic and political struggle against social systems and economic structures, such as feudalism and absolutism, that were sanctioned by religion. It is supported by a new principle which regulates and underpins all social relationships—the principle of exchange. Production, trade and consumption are all determined by this middle-class principle of exchange. All other values, which may have had a decisive effect on society in the past, but which no longer directly contribute to the functioning of the modern middle-class society of exchange, have receded into the sphere of private individual freedom.

From the economic point of view, the property of the middle class citizen forms the basis of and safeguards his freedom to dispose of materials, services, technical processes and so on. From the political point of view, this results in his claim to self-determination and self-government on the one hand and a precarious separation between private and public interests on the other. Religion has become a private matter. It is possible to make use of it to satisfy cultural needs, but it is no longer necessary to have it in order to be a subject.

Religion is no longer the expression of a primary need. Pascal was aware of the rise of this new man and was passionately opposed to it. It was not the fact that men would have found different answers to the ultimate questions from those provided by Christianity, but rather that they could live without having or even seeking any certainty with regard to those questions that made them so difficult for Pascal to understand. Indeed it was this life without ultimate certainty that made him call the phenomenon of the middle-class subject, which had hardly made its appearance and which he did not really know himself, 'monstrous.'

I have in this context to correct an error that is frequently made in theology: namely, that the Reformation was the period when the new middle class and the principle of privatization emerged. Luther was not the middle-class citizen who sustained the processes of the Enlightenment and impressed them with his personality. His question about the certainty of salvation was quite different from the questions asked by the new man of the Enlightenment. It is possible that a pre-middle-class subject appeared at the time of the Reformation, but what certainly did not appear then was the phenomenon of middle-class, privatistic subjectivity which led to the crisis in Christianity and the Church and which can, therefore, not so easily be given theological honours.

The Crisis of Tradition

I have already alluded to the crisis of tradition caused by the Enlightenment. I must now discuss the extremely important and legitimate aspects of that crisis. The Enlightenment was not, after all, a process in which man ultimately became practical in his freedom in the face of the direct constraints of tradition.

In the Enlightenment, tradition undoubtedly lost its power to determine human activity and to direct man's life. It also became an object of historical knowledge or a storehouse of information to satisfy the needs of reason in the Enlightenment. This technical association between history and tradition was given scientific expression in historicism. Obligation and normativity can no longer be based on historical reason as a medium of tradition—historical knowledge is a medium by which history is made relative and less important. As a result, what lessing called a 'horribly wide ditch' has appeared between the origin of religion, and especially the Christian religion, and its present, historically mediated claims.

Theology could certainly be usefully occupied with a study of tradition and its loss of power to determine human action and to direct a consensus, a loss that was observed by Lessing, and it is true to say that it has indeed been concerned with this question from the time of Kierkegaard onwards. Karl Barth and the representatives of existential or transcendental hermeneutics have studied it. There is, however, a more profound reason for the need to make even greater efforts to understand this question theologically (it has become again and again clear that theology is impotent in the sphere of hermeneutics). The reason is that Lessing's difficulty remains because it cannot be understood and overcome purely as a theological problem. Its existence compels theology and the Church to enter into dialogue with the subject of historical reason—middle class society.

The Enlightenment criticism of tradition can only be properly understood in the light of the phenomenon of the rise of the new man, the middle-class citizen, and the society of exchange that was fashioned by him. It can be understood above all as endangering what has no exchange value. One of the greatest dangers of middle class life is that everything that does not conform to calculating reason and the laws of profit and success is left to individual and private choice. By making religion a purely service religion to which he turns as a private individual, the middle-class citizen has also made tradition a value of which he makes use as a private individual. The 'culture industry' (Horkheimer's and Adorno's term) is a recent expression of a process that began in the Enlightenment.

The citizen is, however, generally regarded as favourably disposed towards history, traditional and, in that sense conservative. If my analysis is correct, on the other hand, and what I have said about the growth of the middle-class consciousness is true, then this common view of the middle-class subject must clearly be corrected and he must be seen as conservative only in a very limited, partial and privatistic sense. He will, in other words, subordinate everything, including his own love of the past and of tradition, to the rules of the exchange game.

This ought to make the Church, which apparently regards the citizen as reliable in this respect, think. This loss of tradition can, moreover, perhaps be seen most clearly in our attitude towards the dead. There can, of course, be no relationship of exchange with the dead. According to Kierkegaard, our live and mourning for the dead is the only form of live that cannot be included within the framework of a society based on exchange and the satisfaction of needs. For this reason—and that is why *Kierkegaard* made this criticism of the middle-class Christiantity of his own period—community with the dead has been thrust further and further into the background. It has lost its importance and has become privatized. There is in modern society a rapidly increasing loss of power and value in traditional values such as friendliness, thankfulness, attention to the dead, mourning and so on for which there is no corresponding counter-value and for which one gets nothing in return. In the firmly established Socialist societies, there is really no human solidarity of a totally new kind, simply the perpetuation of earlier middle-class society with all its inner tensions. One symptom of this situation is the fact that in those Socialist societies people are still, as in the West, forbidden to show any sign of mourning. No prohibition have even been publicly issued, but the socially accepted ban on mourning has for this reason continued all the more obstinately.

In view of this act, the frequently expressed opinion that our contemporary concept of tradition originated in the Reformation and that the Enlightenment criticism of tradition was already present in and anticipated by Luther's criticism is, in my opinion, naive and even wrong. It is true, of course, that the practice of going back to Scripture is in certain respects a criticism of ecclesial and theological traditions, but it should always be subject to the condition that this tradition has a normative effect on Christian life and action. An appeal to Scripture is ultimately in itself an appeal to a particular tradition.

Since the Enlightenment and the rise of middle-class society, tradition has clearly become less important. Yet it forms a constitutive element in religion. For this reason, theology is bound to have an interest in overcoming this loss of historicity in the case of the middle-class subject and therefore in this sense in overcoming the Enlightenment itself.

What, then, at first appears to be a process of liberation from the anonymous oppression of unknown traditions in which the new longing for freedom is not expressed conceals a radical danger, not only for the existence and identity of traditional religion, but also for the identity of man and his state as a subject.

However well-founded, legitimate and necessary the Enlightenment criticism of traditions may have been, we are bound, if we follow its development into the present time, to recognize that memory is not only the object (which is gradually losing its objectivity), but the inner element of the critical consciousness that is trying to gain clarity about its interests and the direction of its own criticism. This topic will be discussed in greater detail later in this book. In the meanwhile, I must consider the problem of the loss of authority which has accompanied the loss of tradition.

The crisis of authority

Together with tradition, authority, which cannot derive anything from reason, is also in a state of crisis. In his well-known attempt to define Enlightenment (*Die Beantwortung der Frage: Was ist*

Aufklarung? 1784), Kant said: 'Enlightenment occurs when man leaves the state in which he has not yet come of age and which he has brought about himself. This state is marked by a lack of ability to make use of his intellect without the guidance of another person. Man brings it about himself if the cause is not a lack of intellect, but rather a lack of decision and courage to make use of oneself without the guidance of another. This definition of Enlightenment is obviously critically aimed at the state in which man is prevented from coming of age by an authority which cannot be tested or questioned with regard to its legal status. This kind of authority was diametrically opposed to the Enlightenment principle of equality. There is also an inevitable tendency that it will go on producing or reproducing new inequalities and new forms of tutelage.

The authority of the Church is particularly endangered by this spontaneously critical aspect of the Enlightenment. A continuous insistence on an authority which is no longer universally convincing and has ceased to be socially plausible can easily assume the character of coercion and authoritarianism. When this occurs, criticism inevitably intensifies.

There is always a temptation in the Church and theology to reject criticism or religious authority on purely theoretical grounds, while at the same time preserving what is often authoritarian in the Church and decisionistic in theology. What is generally overlooked, however, is that the middle-class subject or middle-class society has been concealed behind the Enlightenment criticism of authority. Its characteristics must be investigated critically if the Enlightenment criticism of authority is to be rejected successfully by theology.

The equality of the partners is, at least in principle, assumed in the middle-class concept of exchange. This equality is assumed so that society, which is based on exchange, will function smoothly. For this reason, authority, as a principle of inequality and subordination, almost automatically loses social plausibility. It has come to be regarded as a relic of feudal society and its patriarchal and hierarchical structure that have been successfully overcome by the middle class. The aspect of authority that is retained and can still command the respect of middle-class reason is competence, which can be described as authority in the form of knowledge.

As authority increasingly becomes part of (calculating) reason, both the feudal survivals of authority and what is authoritarian in authority on the one hand and the saving aspect of authority on the other disappear, as in the case of tradition. Authority cannot be separated from tradition. It is the force of tradition, its persistence and urgency, with which it remembers and must be sued. Insofar, however, as tradition is a constitutive part of critical reason, the latter must always have elements of authority. Without them, it has no power to liberate.

In middle-class society, authority is threatened as a precondition and inner aspect of critical and liberating reason. What is threatened, in other words, is that authority to which men give their consent when they affirm their own state as subjects or the possibility of others being subjects. This authority is the authority of freedom and justice on the one hand and suffering on the other. This kind of authority can never have much exchange value. This is why it can hardly ever be regarded as competent by the forum of calculating reason.

This authority, which can and should be defended by theology and which cannot be interpreted by the criticism of ideology as an alienated form of knowledge, enters the state of crisis that is synonymous which that of the religious subject whenever the latter is unquestioningly absorbed by the contemporary subject. In other words, this crisis occurs when the religious subject ceases to be proof against the middle-class imagination.

At this point, I make a brief aside, which is nonetheless closely connected with what I have said so far about the Enlightenment criticism of authority. The problem confronting authority in religion and the Church is above all that, when that authority has not assumed authoritarian aspects, it tends to reveal aspects of that form of authority which are both permitted and produced by middle-class society and which also constitute a great danger to religion. These aspects include routine, bureaucratic forms of authority, the worst forms of hierarchical authority, overgrown with administration and unapproachable, and authority as a management of truth without any social basis.

It is not possible for authority in the Church to avoid this danger altogether, but it should certainly not be completely absorbed by these forms of authority. A form of authority which was legitimately required by the Enlightenment should, therefore, develop within the Church's praxis. This is authority based on competence. This competence is not an administrative or a legal competence of the king that is prominent in middle-class society. It is also not a purely cognitive competence which presupposes the silent absorption of authority by knowledge (this would be the king of competence required by a liberal theology, based on a false understanding of the Enlightenment). The type of authority needed is one that is based mainly on religious competence. In so far as this kind of authority is really competent, it would be able to learn from the Enlightenment and, in so far as it is not purely functional, but really religious, it would be able, at least to begin with, to overcome the effects of the crisis in which authority found itself placed by the Enlightenment and middle-class society.

This authority based on religious competence could be a critical and liberating authority in middle-class society today. A new kind of authority based on being authority rather than having authority would gain in importance as political and social life approached the model of a complex administration more and more closely. It would become more and more significant as all functions in society became increasingly structuralistic, anoymous and divorced from the human subject and as the relationships between responsibilities became less and less distinct. It might also be one of the central places where the unconditional demands of the authority of freedom, justice and suffering could always be expressed on behalf of the majority. It could be a means of saving Enlightenment reason from banality and collective obscurity.

The Crisis of (Metaphysical) Reason

The Enlightenment led to the creation of a new community of mutual consent that was not based on the metaphysical reason that formed the silent and unquestioned basis of mutual consent on which feudal societies were founded. The Enlightenment was, after all, a consistent criticism of classical metaphysics.

The Reformation was, of course, also a criticism of metaphysics, that is, the metaphysics of scholasticism, but this criticism took place on the basis of a completely Christian community of mutual consent. The process of the social differentiation of reason, which was at the heart of the Enlightenment criticism of metaphysics, had not begun at that time.

The appeal made for the first time during the Enlightenment to reason the subject and praxis points to a totally new process. This is that reason was, also for the first time, no longer thought of as independent of the subject and its practical aspects. Whereas the metaphysical use of reason concealed the question raised by its social and political context, the Enlightenment threw light on the background to this abstract use of reason. In other words, the usurpation of metaphysical reason for a definite power that remains in the background and functions as a social subject is revealed. What has taken place is the acceptance of universal reason by a control that is on the one hand ecclesiastical and on the other political.

According to Kant's definition of Enlightenment, the man who has the freedom 'to make public use of his reason in all things' has come of age. I shall examine this idea later on, but in the meantime I would point out that it has primarily the value of a moral appeal. It is not in the first place a call to create new social conditions of freedom. On the contrary, it is directed to what already exists and to those who already have—perhaps latently and perhaps partly openly—the social power to come of age and who only need to be set free. As Kant himself said in the same essay of 1784 : 'Laziness and cowardice are the reasons why so many men, even after nature has set them free from alien guidance, still do not come of age throughout the rest of their lives and why others find it so easy to become their tutors and guardians. It is so comfortable not to come of age.' To whom is Kant referring in this passage? He is not really saying that mankind as a whole, which has not yet come of age, should achieve freedom from tutelage. He is rather referring to a particular subject who is in danger of being 'lazy,' 'cowardly' and 'comfortable.' This subject is the propertied citizen who lacks the moral strength to make use of his own intellect and to become politically what he has already been both socially and economically for a long time.

It is, course, true that the pathos of the Enlightenment was certainly directed towards making all men come of age as subjects of the use of their intellect. Without distinction, knowledge and knowing more, education and being more educated were proclaimed, encyclopaedias were published and indeed what Lessing called the 'education of the human race' could be regarded as the basic programme of the Enlightenment. At the same time, however, the language used in the Enlightenment should not deceive us into thinking that the Enlightenment aim was to make the propertied citizen the bearer of political reason. Nor was the coming of age of the Enlightenment a coming of age for those without property, the population living on the land or the peasant classes, who were almost all illiterate at the time when the great encyclopaedias were written. What asserted itself, then, in the criticism of metaphysical reason and the emphatic affirmation of coming of age and the subject was ultimately a new elite or a new aristocracy. In other words, what was given prominence in the Enlightenment was in a reversed image in the mirror, so to speak, precisely the same phenomenon against which the Enlightenment was fighting.

The characteristics of this middle-class elite, however, also entered into Enlightenment reason itself and its concept of praxis and the subject. In the logic of this reason, praxis developed not as a praxis of liberation, but a praxis of control, which was not control in the earlier, direct sense of the word, but a control of nature in the interest of the market.

That is why the reason that supports the subject in his control of nature is a universal nature is a universal theme in the middle-class society which was first reflected and first became conscious of itself in the Enlightenment. This is, then a technical reason which at once reduces everything to the level of an object and makes it marketable and profitable. If this is forgotten and reason, praxis and the subject are used in the abstract sense in theology, without also taking into consideration the middle-class society of exchange that is expressed in these three concepts, the consequence might be that the middle class may imperceptibly be given those theological, religious and ecclesiastical honours which were denied to it in the beginning because a better instinct prevailed and which will now help it at this late stage to justify itself.

Religion in a State of Crisis

The criticism of metaphysical reason which was initiated in the Enlightenment must become a criticism of religion when religion and metaphysics condition each other. If metaphysical reason, which is divorced from the subject, loses its (political) innocence in the light of the Enlightenment, then religion, which also makes use of this abstract metaphysical reason to justify its universal claim to validity, at once becomes suspect. The criticism of religion that was undertaken in the Enlightenment at first on the basis of a completely different title (the criticism of tradition or the criticism of authority) is deeply rooted in this phenomenon.

Initially, then, the criticism of religion in the Enlightenment was a criticism of ideology. This was more clearly the case in France than in the German Enlightenment. It was in France that religion was traced back by the 'atheists' of the Enlightenment to self-seeking deceit on the part of priests and it was Voltaire who on the one hand rejected religion in itself, but on the other recommended it because of its socially useful function in stabilizing the *status quo* in society and preserving private property.

The Enlightenment did not simply criticize religion in the sense of providing a criticism of ideology. It, above all, affirmed religion, although this affirmation was not the same as that a positive religion in Christianity. It was also in no sense indebted to the Reformation criticism of religion. The religion of the Enlightenment, in critically rejecting the idea of revelation, was *religio naturalis*—a natural religion or a religion of reason.

This natural religion of the Enlightenment was at first thought of as the rational religion which was in accordance with all men's needs and which could be justified on the basis of the history of mankind. This understanding of natural religion was accepted into many liberal theologies, in which religion was—and sometimes still is—generally described as a feeling of simple dependence (Schleiermacher) or as the expression of the numinous depth of existence (Tillich).

This general summary of the religion of the Enlightenment is, however, misleading, because the so-called natural religion of reason which apparently applies to all men is as elitist as he enlightened reason itself. It is in fact only applicable to the new man of the Enlightenment, the citizen, as the subject of reason. The natural religion, then, is an extremely privatized religion that has been, as it were, specially prepared for the domestic use of the propertied middle-class citizen. It is above all a religion of inner feeling. It does not protest against or oppose in any way the definitions of reality, meaning or truth, for example, that are accepted by the middle-class society of exchange and success. It gives greater height and depth to what already applies even without it.

The concept of a natural religion is, therefore, in no way neutral or historically innocent. It is no more neutral than the middle-class citizen himself. It is therefore impervious to experiences and testimonies both of the biblical and of the non-biblical religions. It could hardly be used as a leading concept for an encounter and a dialogue between religions.

It is here that the element of truth that is present in the criticism of religion made by 'dialectical' theologians (Barth especially and, even more radically, Bonhoeffer) is revealed. The distinction made by these theologians between faith and religion is, in my opinion, problematical for several reasons. They have, however, possibly in opposition to their basic intentions, managed to save the very concept of religion that they rejected in their terminology. They have above all recognized what is deeply middle-class in religion and have drawn attention to the danger in which Christianity would be placed if it were to be absorbed by the weakest level of liberal religion as left behind by the enlightenment and the middle class. There is a great deal of contemporary theology in which only the natural and rational elements in Christianity are accepted as valid and a great deal in the Church of today, which, at least in Germany, is too closely identified with middle-class religion, that points to the fact that this process of absorption has already begun to take place.

The Need for a Political Theology of the Subject

This assessment of the process which took place in the Enlightenment and which can be summed up as a process in which religion became a private affair of the middle class can certainly be said to have a bearing on the concept of a practical fundamental theology of the subject. According to the latter, the Enlightenment cannot be received or inherited in a purely abstract form and the subject, the person and existence should not be taken over uncritically by theology as a result of the modern era and its process of privatization.

The private middle-class reality which resulted from the Enlightenment and characterizes the modern era cannot be completely identified with the subject, the person or existence in a way that is strictly relevant to religion or theology. What we have here, then, is the process of atrophy that takes place in the state of all men as subjects in the presence of God, a state which is the concern of any political theology and which is only possible if religion is not simply added subsequently to the social constitution of the subject.

It would certainly be wrong to use such direct contrasts as private and public, inward and outward realities, theory and praxis or mystical and political as a means of illustrating the significance of a political theology of the subject. It would be equally wrong to apply in a rather condescending way the categories of public, outward, practical and political to it. This distinction is in itself the result of the very process of Enlightenment of which a political theology inevitably tries to be critically conscious. Whenever this critical consciousness is lacking, theology is bound to continue to exist without reference to the subject. Alternatively—and this amounts to the same thing—it will try to conceal, by speaking very generally about the subject—or the contemporary subject—all the contradictions which go to the very heart of the Christian identity and which are the result of the socially differentiated history of the subject in the modern era. Theology will in that case hardly be able to develop any critical means for the defence of the middle-class subject (the source of the various crises of identity in Christianity that were revealed in the Enlightenment) as the really religious subject.

I am bound to stress here, and I shall later discuss systematically, the fact that this theological criticism of middle-class religion will certainly not result in an abstract negation of the individual, including the middle-class individual. All that the theologian can do here is to question whether the middle-class principle of individuation is the only valid one and whether it is strong enough to carry out the task given to it by religion. The religious task here is to stand up for all men as subjects in the face of violent oppression and of a caricature of solidarity in a violent absorption by the mass or an institutionalized hatred. This theological criticism of middle-class religion does not in any sense amount to an abstract devaluation of middle-class values. All that it does is to question whether these values can be saved and defended simply and solely by means of the middle-class principle of individuation.

4

The Political Theology

Introduction

Like every other new theology, the new political theology had problems in establishing its legitimacy and authenticity and still has them. We may apply what Walter Benjamin has said in another context to these problems and say that the political tendency of a political theology can only be accepted as valid if its theological tendency is valid. The reverse is not true. A political theology must be consistently orientated in this direction and must recommend this criterion to all theologies, because none can, without practising self-deception, regard itself as being entirely without a political tendency or as politically innocent. A political theology of this kind is therefore able to expose and combat every prejudice that is active in theology and the praxis of the Church, according to which a theological tendency is valid if its tendency in politics is more or less right wing and conservative in the usual sense of the word.

The present chapter plays a central part and deals with the task of working out the theological structure of this approach and of correcting earlier attempts at political theology and introducing considerable differentiations. In this practical fundamental theology, the main concepts are *praxis* and the *subject*. In the first section, I shall attempt to throw light on the meaning of the primacy of praxis or the practical foundation of all Christian theology. This practical fundamental theology will then, in the second section, be presented as a political theology of the subject and its claim to authenticity will be justified in the strictly theological controversy about direct theologies of the subject and in the wider dispute concerning man's ability to be a subject. As a direct consequence of this, the importance of the religious subject in the historical struggle for man will be discussed in Section 3. Finally, in the last section (4), I shall suggest a theological definition of faith. This section is, like the book itself, entitled 'the faith of the Christian in history and society.' My definition of this faith will, I hope arise out of the approach made in the earlier sections. In it, faith will also be defined, in a nutshell, in such a way that its theological validity need not be gained by obscuring the contrasting social experiences and positions by means of which it can be cancelled out or made to disappear nowadays.

The Practical Foundation of Christian Theology

The term 'practical fundamental theology' is in itself unusual and may surprise many readers. I use it, however, to draw attention to the fact that theory and praxis are not dealt with here in the usual order of priority, in which praxis is regarded as the continuation, implementation or concrete application of a previsouly defined theory. Practical fundamental theology is, on the contrary, directly opposed to a non-dialectical subordination of praxis to theory or the idea. In it, great emphasis is placed on the intelligible force of praxis itself, in the sense of a dialectical tension between theory and praxis. To that extent, it is a theology that operates subject to the primacy of praxis.

What, then, is the situation here? It is something more than simply an emphatic, overlegitimized and therefore extremely abstract use of praxis? Or will a theology that is made subject to the primacy of praxis not inevitably be thought to be uncritical and divorced from theory? We are, however, bound to ask in the context of this question what 'critical' and 'theoretical really mean here. The starting point for a practical fundamental theology is that all attempts made to base theology on pure theory or absolute reflection must be regarded as uncritical or only apparently theoretical. Practical fundamental theology does not appeal primarily to an understanding of theory and criticism which is valid outside the sphere off theology and according to which all pure theories are seen within a wider context of communication and action, with the result that they cannot be critical without reference to praxis. On the contrary, practical fundamental theology is based on the practical structure underlying the logos of Christian theo-logy.

a. The Practical Structure of the Logos of Christian Theo-logy

In itself, the Christian idea of God is a practical idea. God cannot be thought of at all unless this idea irritates and encroaches on the immediate interests of the person who is trying to think of it. Thinking about God is a review of interests and needs that are directly related to ourselves. Conversion, metanoia and even exodus are not simply moral or educative categories—they are also and above all noetic categories. Stories of conversion and exodus are therefore not simply dramatic embellishments of a previously conceived 'pure' theology. On the contrary, they form part of the basic structure of this theology. This practical structure of the idea of God is the reason why the concept of God is basically narrative and memorative. (Narrative and memory are not added as a ornament to a 'pure' idea of God).

This practical structure applies with particular clarity to our Christological knowledge. The praxis of imitation forms a constitutive part of Christo-logy, if the logos of the Christology, like that of Christianity itself, cannot ultimately be united with the logos of Greek philosophy which has to be regarded as pure and for which Christ was always 'folly.' It is true of any Christology that Christ has always to be thought of in such a way that he is not simply thought of. All christology is nourished, for the sake of its own truth, by praxis and particularly the praxis of the imitation of Christ. It is, in other words, expressed in a practical knowledge. In this sense, then, all Christology is subject to the primacy of praxis. This might be called Christological dialectics or the dialectics of imitation. These dialectics are not in any sense idealistic conceptual dialectics expressing a tension between two ideas (divorced from the subject). They are rather dialectics of theory and praxis or dialectics of subject and object. It is only when they imitate Christ that Christians know who it is to whom they have given their consent and who saves them. This Christo-logical dialectical tension can be clearly recognized in the accounts concerning the imitation of Christ in the New Testament. There is, in those accounts, no adequate distinction between narrative and commandment, with the result that the listener is able first to hear the stories of Jesus and then reflect about the consequences that he may or may not draw from them and apply to himself. These New Testament stories of the imitation Christ are in themselves appellative and imperative. They attempt to change the listening subject in the telling of the story and to make him ready to imitate Christ. Christological knowledge, then, is not handed down primarily as a concept, but in such stories of the imitation of Christ. It therefore has, as the theological idea of Christ itself also has, a narrative and practical character. I shall try to show in the following pages the extent to which this Christological knowledge in its practical aspect is and must be, in accordance with theological thinking as such, political.

In the meantime, however, it is important to indicate the constitutive part played by such practical concepts as imitation, conversion and exodus in the structure of theology as such. This also automatically raises the question of the status of praxis or the specific relationship between theory and praxis in fundamental theology.

In my earlier considerations concerning an approach to a political theology, my point of departure was the primacy of praxis, to such an extent indeed that this primacy of praxis or the relationship between theory and praxis that was expressed in this primacy became the key concept in my approach. In the perspective of the debate about the foundations of theology as such, we may say that the so-called hermeneutical problem of theology was not really a problem of the relationship between systematic and historical theology or between dogma and history, but rather a problem of the relationship between theory and praxis or between the understanding of faith and social praxis. The concept 'praxis,' however, had too great a content and this led to misunderstandings and equivocation, with content and this led to misunderstandings and equivocation, with the result that it was necessary to introudce differentiation into the concept. Karl Rahner's theology was influenced by Kant's transcendental teaching and his question about what conditioned the possibility of knowledge generally. Unlike Rahner's theology, political theology was, to begin with, more emphatically orientated towards the traditions of the practical philosophy of history and society, in other words, towards Kant's teaching about the primacy of practical reason and the dialectics of theory and praxis in Marxism. The constant point of departure for political theology was that the change to the primacy of praxis in philosophy (Kant, the Enlightenment—Marx) should be regarded as the real Copernican revolution in philosophy and that it was therefore very important not only to solve the basic problem of theological reason as it were this side of idealism, but also to try to do theology on the other side of idealism.

The praxis that was central in Kant's teaching and on the basis of the intelligible force of which practical reason was built up in moral praxis (this has already been explained in some detail in the preceding sections). Kant's practical philosophy of history and society was therefore developed above all as ethical teaching. From then onwards, there could be no critical logos which was not practical in its intention as ethics. No differentiation, had, however, as yet been made between moral and social praxis or, to express this in another way, social praxis was the same as the moral praxis of the subjects who had already achieved power in the social sense. Social praxis was, in other words, identical with the moral praxis of the citizens. Individual moral imperatives in Kant's teaching replace the question of social action and conceal the fact that coming of age is a question not only of the moral exertion of the individual, but of social structures and relationships. It was Marx who first made it clear that individual moral praxis was not in any sense socially neutral and politically innocent and that the so-called purely ethical interpretation of social praxis always worked with substitutions. Reference is made to 'man,' but what is meant in each case is the socially established subject. Although this cannot be discussed in detail here, the same obviously also applies to Kant's categorical imperative.

I did not make a clear enough distinction in my early attempt to formulate a political theology within the concept of praxis between moral and social praxis. In so doing, I placed the teachings of Kant and those of Marx too much at the same level. The political statements made in his theology were therefore often purely moral, in the nature of an appeal or an exhortation. They were therefore able to be used in widely different contexts.

It is theologically important that moral praxis not be socially neutral and politically innocent. If the primacy of praxis in theology is taken seriously, this has a bearing not only on moral praxis in the narrower sense, but also on social praxis. This can be illustrated by reference to Kant's postulate regarding coming of age. Kant was able to describe coming of age as a moral task, because he had in mind only people who had been of age for a long time in the social and economic sense, that is, people who already existed as socially powerful subjects. There is, however, clearly a situation in which man has not yet come of age and is impotant and oppressed which is not simply due to the moral weakness of those who have not yet come of age or are impotent and oppressed. And who can doubt that this socially conditioned failure to come of age, this impotence and this oppression—in a word, this poverty — forms an important object of Christian praxis? Who would deny that Christian praxis must inevitably be concerned not only with man's state as a subject in the presence of God, but also with the fact that men can become subjects and can live as subjects rising from misery and oppression?

I may conclude this section by saying that the practical structure of theology, as outlined here, includes not only moral, but social praxis. In other words, the forms of behaviour such as metanoia, exdus and the imitation of Christ which are constitutive in my idea of God and Christological and eschatological knowledge in general have a social and political structure. This understanding points clearly to the very deep meaning and significance of my idea of a political theology.

b. The Practical Hermeneutics of Christanity

It is clear that Christian praxis as social praxis ought to be more precisely defined. It should therefore be discussed within the framework of practical hermeneutics of Christianity of a kind that could be described cautiously as practical and dialectical hermeneutics, since it does not simply have its object, Christian praxis, outside itself.

We must first define these practical hermeneutics more precisely with regard to other theological attempts to define practical Christianity, in other words, with regard to universally historical, eschatological and transcendental hermeneutics.

We must, for example, ask, in the light of the approach that has been elaborated here, whether, in his extremely valuable attempt to develop universally historical hermeneutics. Wolfhart Pannenberg's anticipation of a total meaning in history is not too little interrupted or irritated by what is described in the apocalyptic tradition as a universal catastrophe, in other words, as the reign of the Antichrist. According to Pannenberg, praxis is of secondary importance and subordinate or else it is in danger of becoming a praxis that is orientated towards a previously conceived totality of meaning. But does history really follow its logical course in this sense? And, if it is really uninterrupted in its course, does it then (as Max Horkheimer, for example, correctly asked) fulfil its human destiny?

Jurgen Moltmann's concept of an eschatological hermeneutics of Christian praxis is very close to my own ideas about a political theology and for this reason I am bound to point to a clear difference. His book, *The Crucified God,* was in many respects quite splendid, but since its publication Moltmann has used the concept of praxis increasingly to describe a theology in which the history of the suffering of the Son and the world is rooted within the Trinity. Praxis, which can only prevent the danger of speculative gnosis in such an approach, is no longer an intelligible principle in Moltmann's theology. On the other hand, this intelligibility is required in the attempts made to find a narrative and practical approach to Christology and steriology and indeed in the idea of a practical fundamental theology as such.

These hermeneutics of Christian praxis have, however, to be clarified with regard to theories of action that are outside the sphere of theology. It is clear that both theories of action which work analytically and scientific and linguistic theories are ultimately social theories which owe their alleged autonomy to a social division of labour that is not reflected in the analytical approach to knowledge. They have therefore to be examined within the framework of a theological theory of history and society. What is more, these theories are, in my opinion, characterized by a non-dialectical logic of development and I shall consequently have to question them and narrow down their theoretical status again and again in the course of my reflections.

Here I shall confine myself to a brief outline of the most important aspects of this practical and dialectical form of hermeneutics which will then remain normative for the two following sections (2 and 3), where this praxis will be characterized as having solidarity and liberating in the interest of the process by which all men become subjects.

1. Christian praxis as social praxis—also in view of what I have just said about Kant's teaching — remains ethically determined. This is because the demand for the social conditions and constellations of moral action to be considered does not have as its aim a process by which moral praxis is simply interpreted as social praxis and the moral subject is also made simply relative. A consideration of the social dependences of moral action can be regarded as a necessary condition, but not a sufficient one, in determining Christian praxis. The consequence of this ethical determination of the Christian's social praxis is that this praxis cannot lead to an abstract or a violent negation of the individual. This moral determination of social praxis also makes possible and guarantees the fact that it will become really practical as a criticism of violence or of the

recording of violence continuously by means of a logic of hatred, so that it becomes possible to overcome violence only by further violence.

2. Christian praxis as social praxis continues to be determined by an excess of historical determinations that are the non-inferred function of the prevailing social totality. This is where the hermeneutics of memory as a dangerous phenomenon or as subversion and rebellion plays an indispensable part. Every utopian concept of liberation which questions and breaks through what is currently held to be plausible is ultimately rooted in this kind of memory, which is in turn not simply a reflection or reproduction of the contemporary factors determining society and economics. Otherwise, from what source could interests and norms be gained that could be applied to the practical task of criticizing existing relationships? A materialism based on the conviction that society is determined strictly by economic factors could never be revolutionary unless it unreasonably demanded of matter itself a kind of teleology of freedom.

It is here, however, that the idea of narrative plays a part in heremeneutics, insofar as it determines praxis on the basis of dangerous stories which call the social conditioning of human activity into question and which are directed against a kind of history in which, under certain structures and systems, the subject, who can never be accurately calculated by anyone, is made to disappear. It is precisely this excess of historical determinations that are communicated by memory and narrative which can prevent new forms of praxis from being purely sporadic, from standing simply symbolically for a new reality and not raising this up and therefore from being re-absorbed too easily by the existing system. Innovatory praxis must therefore be accompanied by a making present of a collective historical memory.

3. Christian praxis as social praxis is guided by an understanding of praxis that also takes what may be called the pathic structure of this praxis into consideration. In other words, praxis is seen not

simply as action — which means that it is regarded as the subjection and contract of nature—but also as suffering. Sorrow, as a category of opposition to the prevention of sorrow and melancholy by a society of achievement and triumph, and joy, as a category of opposition to man's increasing inability to celebrate the meaning of life, are both examples of the pathic or suffering structures of human praxis that can be regarded as forms of opposition to the prevalent apathy of society. Another example of a pathic structure is solidarity as openness to past suffering, in other words, as solidarity with the dead and those who have been overcome. The claims made by this pathic or suffering structure of social praxis are outlined in 'The future in the memory of suffering', in which I also make clear that an emphasis placed on this pathic structure of human praxis does not in any sense lead to a paralysis or a calming down in the sphere of political action. On the contrary, it can only liberate praxis from its exclusive orientation towards an anthropological mode, according to which man is viewed one-sidedly as a subject exerting control over nature and human history, the later being regarded as a non-dialectical history of progress and triumph or conquest. At the end of this process, man is bread back to nature and his status as a subject ceases, because his control of nature is ultimately exercised with the help of a model of knowledge and action which is itself orientated towards natural processes that lie outside the sphere of history.

It is obvious that the category of memory — in the form of a memory of suffering — and the category of narrative — as a linguistic identification of the stories of human suffering, which escape the system of the history of progress and triumph is given greater importance here. Similarly, the category of solidarity in its extended sense of anamnesis or the memory of the sacrifices of history also gains in importance. In the same way too, these categories are, in the various arguments used directed against any attempt to interpret the history of suffering in terms either of evolution or of dialectics and indeed against all attempts to define the subject only on the basis of his actions, not on the basis of his suffering.

This, then, concludes my introductory clarification and differentiation in the concept of praxis in the idea of the primacy of praxis. In Section 2 of this chapter I shall try to define it more precisely. In the meantime, however, it is important to deal at once with two questions that arise in connection with the idea of the practical foundation of Christian theology.

c. The Question of the Subjects and the Functions of Theology

In addition to the question of the relationship between the subject and praxis, which is of fundamental importance and will have to be discussed in greater detail, there is also the question of suitable and competent subjects of theology, in other words, who is competent to do theology? In a truly practical fundamental theology we should above all be conscious of the fact that theology should not simply elaborate and pass on themes without reference to the subject, but that it must again and again be interrupted by praxis and experience. The important questions to be asked by theology, then, are : Who should do theology and where, in whose interest and for whom? Is it sufficient in this context simply to point to the usual division of labour within the Church? Is it, in other words, enough, to have recourse to the standardized subjects of theology (professors, teachers and specialists in theological studies), places (universities, seminaries, colleges), the normal forms of communication (books, lectures, discussions) and interests (the Church's teaching mission)? It is important that theology itself poses these questions and that they are not imposed on theology from outside, in the spirit of a criticism of ideology.

In this context, we are bound to consider very briefly an objection to the new political theology. Overemphasising the word 'political', the objection is made that there is a rather dubious attempt in political theology to place lay people in a position of tutelage in the Church by means of a professional, official theology. What is often overlooked when this criticism is made is that this political theology in fact looks forward to the emergence of a new subject of theology. It is in no way assumed that the only adequate exponent of this political theology is the professional theologian or the one who, as it were, specializes in God because of his office. On the basis of the intentions of this theology, the distinction between official and lay theology ceases to exist. Indeed, it is possible to say that the abolition of this distinction is to some degree a presupposition of this whole approach, one the basis of the theory of knowledge. In other words, political theology transcends, in its intentions, the narrow sphere of professional theology, whether this is practised by official representatives of the Church or lay people.

d. The Question of Truth Within the Primacy of Praxis

We must now briefly consider the very important question of the meaning of truth within the primacy of practical reason. What, in other words, is the position of truth in a practical fundamental theology? Is truth in this context not simply made subordinate to praxis? Is truth not re-interpreted as relevance? And does this re-interpretation not simply conceal (because it is in fact a semantic deception) what really happens, namely the liquidation of the concept of truth, insofar as a truth that is orientated towards praxis is no longer truth?

In a practical fundamental theology, the difference between truth and relevance is in no sense simply a mater of personal discretion.

In such a theology, the idea of truth without reference to subjects is irrelevant and even dangerous, with the result that truth and relevance are bound to converge to the extent that truth becomes the type of relevance that applies to all subjects. In other words, in a practical fundamental theology, truth is what is relevant to all subjects, including the dead and those who have been overcome or conquered. I shall attempt to show in the following section how this understanding of truth is in accordance with the understanding of the subject in political theology.

It is only if truth is previously conceived as correlative with pure reason or theory or as the result of absolute reflection that this objection to practical fundamental theology and its supposed attitude towards truth can be sustained. The same objection could also be made to the biblical traditions. Towards the end of this book, when I deal with the categories of memory and narrative, I shall attempt to throw some light on the narrative and practical structure of knowledge and truth. This is analogous to the practical structure of the idea of God.

2. The Struggle for the Subject of Practical Fundamental Theology as a Political Theology of the Subject

If political theology, as a practical fundamental theology, is to avoid the danger of divorcing its praxis from the subject, it must be elaborated as a theology of the subject. I must, therefore, elucidate this essential aspect of political theology and define it more precisely, on the one hand because it is often suspected of obscuring the subject too much in the interests of history and society and, on the other, because the theologies that are often criticized by political theology are also regarded as theologies (of the subject of a transcendental, existential, personalistic or paradoxical and dialectical kind).

a. The idea of the God—Constituting the Subject and Forming Identity

The history of the biblical religion is a history of the way in which a people and the individuals belonging to that people became subjects in the presence of their God. In this sense, the word subject does not refer to the isolated individual, the monad who only afterwards made sure of his co-existence with other subjects. Experiences of solidarity with, antagonism towards, liberation from and anxiety about other subjects form an essential part of the constitution of the religious subject, not afterwards, but from the very beginning. The question about the relationship between the individual subject and other subjects is unreasonably expected and is the product of later abstraction. The universal solidarity that existed among biblical subjects, then, is a fundamental category in the political theology of the subject. It does not point to a subsumption of individual religious subjects at a later stage. On the contrary, it is the form in which those subjects existed in God's presence and through him.

The Old Testament and New Testament histories of faith cannot be added as a kind of superstructure, or accompanying phenomenon to mankind that has already been constituted in its subject state. They are rather histories of the dramatic way in which men were constituted as subjects through their relationship with God. Those men were called out of the anxieties and compulsions of archaic societies in order to become subjects of a new historical process. The terms of their state as subjects were dynamic—being called in danger, being called out of fear, the exodus, conversion, the raising up of their head, the imitation of their leader and so on. Religion was not an additional phenomenon. It was an active part of the process by which Israel became a subject. In the Old Testament, it was in the exodus that the people most clearly became subjects.

Their relationship with God was not an expression of slavish submission and weak subjection. It did not humiliate them as subjects, but compelled them again and again to be subjects in view of the extreme dangers of that state. Prayer therefore impelled the one who prayed to remain a subject and not to avoid his responsibility in view of his own guilt. It made him become a subject in the presence of his enemies and in the midst of fear to lose his name, his own face and himself.

This shows us, then, how essentially practical the biblical and Christian idea of God was and is. As such it is not an expression of a subsequent overcoming of the subject and his previously conceived identity by strange, alienating powers that are not understood. As such it is not the result of a projection of the endangered subject, who is impelled by archaic fears, into a state beyond danger and destruction. It is in no sense a superstructure onto an already formed identity of the subject. It is above all an idea that forms identity and enters deeply into the basis of existence. It is opposed to the formation of an identity of the subject that is orientated towards possessions and on the contrary constitutes the subject as solidly united.

In this idea of God, man's state as a historical and social subject is in no way suppressed or disregarded. On the contrary, it impels it into situations where it is seriously threatened. Just as this idea of God has, for example, to make itself responsible for guilt if it is to remain a subject, so too it has to oppose suppression and contempt of men if it is to become a subject. This can be expressed in a more dramatic way: the struggle for God and the struggle to enable all men to be free subjects does not operate in the opposite direction, but proportionally in the same direction. It is clear that this concept of a political theology has to be further elaborated, both theologically, in contrast to the so-called direct—and in my view abstract—theologies of the subject, and the secular perspectives, that is, in view of the historical struggle for the subject and indeed in the form of a practical criticism of a culture of hatred and a culture of apathy.

b. Against the Theologies of the Subject that are Divorced from the Subject

In my earlier attempts to formulate a political theology, I directed my arguments against the various theologies of the subject that dominate the theological scene today the thesis of deprivatization that was elaborated in it did not intend. In its use of the direct and in this sense abstract contrast between public and social on the one hand and private and subjective on the other, to move away from the subject and towards society (which is, if possible, regarded as independent of the subject). It was from the beginning determined by the impression that theology is in danger, because of the tendency to privatization, of failling to perceive the existence of the individual to whom it appeals. As I pointed out in my earlier work, any existential and personal theology that claims to understand human existence, but not as a political problem in the widest sense, is an abstract theology with regard to the existential situation of the individual. The thesis of deprivatization therefore attempted to criticize prevalent theologies (such as the existential theology of demythologization, the personal theology and the transcendental theology) in an effort to get away from privatistic categories and the long established abstract contrast between the subject on the one hand and history and society on the other and to move closer to a new theology of the subject, even if this proved inadequate. The problems, however, remained.

In so far as they are relevant in this type of theology of the subject, history and society only appear as anthropological reductions. They can be regarded only as variables of a subject or an anthropology which tries to keep the subject out of its historical and social struggles for identity, as it were almost *a priori*, by means of a late and diminished form of metaphisics and which compensates for its suspected dissociation from history by a weakened idea of the historicity of the subject. The thesis that is critically presented and renewed here, however, is that this theological understanding of man must inevitably become more and more atrophied in view of the role that is attributed to him, namely that of being the subject of his own historical and social processes.

It would not be difficult to demonstrate how the eschatology of the universe that is directed towards history and society has receded more and more and has become almost completely overshadowed by the eschatology of the individual and how this process has gone hand-in-hand with the anthropological reduction of history and society in theology. The same applies to apocalyptic studies, in which attention has for a long time been exclusively concentrated on individual situations of catastrophe in the death of the individual. The questions that are so deeply involved with the apocalyptic literature — to whom does the world belong? to whom do its suffering and its time belong? who is its Lord? — have been more successfully suppressed, it would seem, in theology than in any other sphere. They arise every day in a secularized form in the historical and social struggles for power which take place in our world and in which, it should be noted, the fate of man as a subject and particularly as a religious subject is ate stake. The anthropological reduction of history and society that I have criticized above also takes place not where a beginning is made with the transcendental experience of the subject, man's openness, the true nature of his existence or the paradox of meaning and suffering, but where the intersubjective I-Thou experience is approached. In this approach, the mystery of suffering in historical life is reduced to the problem of the obscure Thou in the encounter between men. The list of questions could, of course, be enlarged. The aspect that has to be stressed, however, is that these questions point to consequences of an abstract theology of the subject which is divorced from history and to which almost all modern theological approaches seem to be committed.

This reduction of history and society in the determination of man's state as a subject in the presence of God is resisted in the political theology of the subject. This does not mean that it makes the subject into a sliding function, a variable in historical and social processes. On the contrary, it tries rather to keep to a twofold structure that is constantly entire and to a mutual priority of subject and history-society. It can, however, only do this if it develops the theology of the subject as a theory of history and society, in opposition to the usual division of labour between systematic theology and theological teaching about society, and if it deals with and elaborates this theory as a practical one.

The most enduring of these theologies, because it has been elaborated with the most powerful arguments, and one which has an effect in all the Christian confessions, is the transcendental theology of the subject developed by my teacher, Karl Rahner. The questions of a political theology of the subject have partially been evoked by Rahner's theology, but they have remained captive in contradiction in it. Rahner's basic thesis of theology as anthropology cannot be simply repeated in a political theology of the subject, but it can be made more historically and socially evident in it.

I would like, however, to deal briefly here with the fundamental anthropological definition that is present in the transcendental theology. This can be expressed concisely in the following way; man exists as an anticipation of God and this anticipation conditions the possibility of his knowledge and his behaviour. I am overlooking the fact that it is difficult for a political theology of the subject not to recognize, in such a definition of man, the anthropology of a society which is basically still determined by religious aims and which is therefore only capable of consent when such social conditions prevail. The only question that I would like to ask in this context is whether this anticipation itself has anything to do with history, in other words, whether the anticipation has temporal structures. This question can be expressed differently in the following way; does this transcendental anthropology take into account the fact that man's anticipatory existence is historical existence?

The concept of experience that has been elaborated in the transcendental theology of the subject does not have the structure of historical experience. The social contradictions and mutually antagonistic aspects which form the basis of suffering in historical experience and in which the historical subject is constituted in fact disappear, in this transcendental theology, in the absence of objectivity of a previously known transcendental experience in which these contradictions are already reconciled in a non-dialectical way. The transcendental theology of the subject has the effect, then, of overlegitimizing the identity of the religious subject in view of the historical suffering of man.

If this safeguard of transcendental identity is abandoned, several questions are at once raised, for example, how can norms be obtained for the historical struggles for man's state as a subject? How can we be orientated and inspired to save his identity? How can we find a foothold in the turmoil of historical and social processes that are becoming more and more divorced from the subject if this can no longer be found by means of metaphysics or even by the late metaphysics of anticipation?

c. Memory and Narrative as Categories of Salvation

The categories that can be applied in order to ascertain religious identity and to safeguard norms are those of man's historical consciousness — memory and narrative. These categories have a different part to play in a political theology of the subject from the one that they may play in a transcendental theology of the subject. In other words, they do not have a deduced or inferred significance as pure categories. They have, on the contrary, a fundamental importance. They do not, for example, act as a decoration, filling in the details of a previously conceived idea. They are rather fundamental categories used in ascertaining and saving identity in the historical struggles and dangers in which men experience themselves and are constituted as subjects. Memory (and narrative) are not to be understood in this context as categories of defeatism and resignation — they are dangerous categories.

Here, however, I will confine myself to an indication of the universal meaning of memory as the category of the salvation of threatened identity. If this question is approached from the negative point of view, we see that the destruction of man's memory systematically prevents him from becoming or remaining a subject in the context of history and society. It is, in other words, as obstacle to identity. For example, the uprooting of slaves and their deportation helped to destroy their memories and at the same time helped to establish them successfully as slaves. The destruction of memory therefore led to the confirmation of their existence as slaves and their systematic deprivation of power in the interest of complete submission. The reverse is also true—identity is formed when memories are aroused.

The historical process by which a nation, race or class become subjects almost always begins with their breaking through the power of the official idea of history by exposing it as propaganda on the part of those who rule them. This idea of history is called, in various contexts in this book, the history of triumph or conquest. In this history of conquest, those who are conquered and oppressed are not remembered. Peasants, for example, have revealed their memory of suffering in their chronicles and citizens have made that memory visible in their art. In this way they have derived the power to resist the threat to their identity. Workers have similarly begun to discover that the current works of history are silent about their suffering and have become dissatisfied with the state of affairs. In this, then, memory operates above all as a category by which historical identity is found and as a category of liberation.

d. The State of all Men as Subjects

A political theology of the subject, for which memory, as a definite memory, is fundamental (this definite memory being that of men's process of becoming subjects in the presence of God), is bound to criticize the usual theological idea of man and the subject, especially when it becomes increasingly clear that this idea only acts as a camouflage for one definite subject (the central European) or when the idea of the modern subject in theology has the obvious aim of avoiding all the problems that have arisen in the last two hundred years.

The political theology of the subject will also keep to the idea of man and the subject with the help of the categories of historical identity and conscious of the concrete origin of these abstract concepts, since it cannot be concerned simply with an identification with some historical class subject or other.

A political theology of the subject which cannot, in the name of the memories that it tries to express, simply let the middle-class subject be a middle-class subject, will also not be able to let the comrade be a comrade. In other words, it will not be able to identify the socialist personality with the subject that it is seeking to express. With the help of its memory, which is neither absorbed by the existing structure of social relationships nor produced by that structure, the political theology evokes a subject that cannot be defined simply on the basis of antagonistic models of a class society, by the negation of whatever opponent appears at the time. When there is opposition (based on memory) to the refusal to allow man to be a subject, this opposition is not only to feudalism or capitalism, it is also to any form of suppression or institutionalized hatred. In this process, the God of this dangerous memory does not secretly become a political utopia of universal liberation. The name of God stands rather for the fact that the utopia of the liberation of all human subjects is not a pure projection, which is what that utopia would be if there were only a utopia and no God.

In this sense at least, the idea of God is indisputably political. It is moreover political in itself and not simply political in the sense of acting as a criticism of ideology, with the result that it is — as it would be in the latter case — not in continuous need of being set free from an association with particular power structures. It represents an option in favour of the state of all men as subjects — all men can be and must become subjects. The freedom of the

Christian memory with regard to existing relationships and structures therefore does not consist of its imagining, rather as art does, a fictitious counter-world. In this freedom of memory, the history of men as subjects in the presence of God is evoked and Christians are compelled to respond to the practical challenge of this history. In its praxis what will emerge, at least partially, is that all men are called to be subjects in the presence of God.

Will Christians succeed in this important task of making man's religious state as a subject socially and visibly incarnate in the struggle for man and his history? Those who are not aware of any problems in this task because they believe that they know what the proper subjects of Christian praxis are ought to ask themselves whether they can deal with the crisis of religion that has been brought about by the middle-class subject in any way that is not defeatist. This way of dealing with crises of this kind has so far at least achieved very little. Church life in the developed world is tending to develop more and more into two patterns— on the one hand there is the Church with the liberal touch serving the middle class in its need for celebration and, on the other, there is the anxious, traditional church as a sect. There is an increasing loss of deep inner conviction regarding faith in the official Church today, resulting in a corresponding loss of nerve and decisiveness. The life of the Church is characterized by a fear of powers and processes that are not understood. This anxiety has sapped the courage of Christians to take new steps, encourage the development of new, alternative forms of Christian praxis and to make new religious and political experiments. This anxiety has led to a quest for stabilization in past forms.

In my previous arguments, I assumed that religion and man's be coming a subject were inseparably connected. I could not appeal to a transcendental theology of the subject which presented man *a priori* as absolutely transcendent. I can, however, go beyond the developed ideas and refer to a historical anthropology based on the history of religion. This historical anthropology is certainly able to support the idea that man did not transfer his state as a subject to

God in human history seen as a history of religion, but that he only acquired identity as a subject and became the subject of his own history through religion, that is, in his relationship with God.

The connection has been made even more plausible today by the simultaneous occurrence of a fundamental crisis in religion on the one hand and a social crisis of the subject on the other. It is purely by chance that the idea of the end of history should arise at a time when the universal history of men ceases to be understood as a history of religion? Is it a pure coincidence that suspicion about the death and collapse of language should occur at the moment when religious language is becoming increasingly atrophied" Is it fortuitous that the announcement of the death of man should follow that of the death of God? Theodor Adorno proclaimed the 'end of the individual' — or at least that of the citizen — many years ago and noted: 'The horror, however, is that the citizen has not found a successor.' Is the subject dying out altogether, then? For determined structuralists, the death of the subject is already a fact. They regard man as an anthropomorphism and a 'remarkable invention of the eighteenth century.'

In its struggle for the 'new man' and the state of the oppressed class as subject, Marxist socialism is firmly opposed to this paralysis of historical subjects (even though it is, at least in its western forms, irritated by adaptation to structuralism). Where however, has this struggle succeeded to such an extent that we can see, in this 'new man,' the identity and solidarity of all men in their free state as subjects? I should like to be able to say that Herbert Marcuse is right, when he, who is reminded of Fascist praxis by the pure negation of the individual, including the middle-class individual, says that solidarity and community do not imply an abandonment of the individual, but are the result of autonomous individual decision and that this solidarity is a solidarity of individuals, not of masses.

From where, then, do the forces producing a new individualization that is not the outcome of repression of others come? How does the strength to resist a systematically distorted form of solidarity based on hatred or the massing together of people come about? How can we at the same time avoid abandoning true solidarity which offers us the opportunity to perpetuate individual identity and a human status as subjects not in opposition to other weaker and socially deprived groups and classes, but together with them?

3. Religion in the Historical Struggle for Man

It is the religious subject who is particularly required here? It is, if that subject understands the practical interest in the process by which others become subjects, that is, those who live in a state of oppression and collective obscurity, as a necessary, although perhaps not sufficient condition of his own state as a subject in the presence of God. It is also, if the subject realizes that the Christian Gospel is only political and politically committed by proclaiming the state of all men as subjects in God's presence and by paying no less a price for this state and subjects in God's presence than for the struggle against oppression and hatred of the kind that make it impossible for the mass of the populations in many parts of the world to become subjects.

An example of this is the contrast, to which I have already referred, between the rich industrial countries of the North and the poor countries of the South. Because the population of these southern regions is to a great extent traditionally Catholic, this contrast between North and South cuts right through the one-world Church and, for example, affects the relationship between the central European and North American churches on the one hand and the Church in the Latin-American subcontinent on the other. Just as the Gospel to which the church bears witness acts again and again as a challenge to political and social life, so too must the contrast between North and south become an irritation to the Church and make demands on it. How, then, can the one Church deal with the class contrasts that exist between the northern and the southern regions of the world, both of which are included in the same Church? How can these contrasts be reconciled with the living unity of the Church? How can they be brought into harmony with the Church as a eucharistic community of those who are called out and should raise their heads in order to be subjects of a new history? How can we deal with the fact that entire populations in the one church live in collective obscurity? Can the rich churches of the North only redress the balance between them and the poor churches of the South that has been destroyed by what has been recognized as the mechanics of exploitation and structural injustice by means of almsgiving? As long as the attempt made by theologians (especially in this case those responsible for the theology of liberation) to make sure of their point of departure by means of an analysis of the world situation is criticized as too general and suspected of being a concealed manoeuvre on behalf of foreign interests, there can be no real awareness in the Church of the extent of these problems.

The considerations should not be understood as an attempt to raise the kingdom of god to the level of politics and economics. They do, however, point to the fact that religion has been made guilty by its attempt to purchase its political innocence by not participating in the historical struggles for all men and their status as subjects. In the earlier considerations of political theology, which took the form of criticism of ideology, this presumed innocence and neutrality of the Church and its members were criticized almost exclusively. Now, however, political theology is also expressed as an option in favour of the state of all men in solidarity as subjects.

There is certainly religion in an authentic form even when there is oppression. The God of the Christian Gospel is, after all, not a God of conquerors, but a god of slaves. This would be the case even if middle-class theologians were not allowed to justify a strict division between 'person' and 'work' and thus to infer a completely interiorized state of man as a subject in the presence of God—a state that they patronizingly offer to all men and especially to slaves.

Whenever Christians bear this fact firmly in mind, they are able to express the principle of the religious individualization of man with conviction in the face of all opposition and conduct the struggle for God as a struggle for the process by which all men are able to become subjects in the face of any collective misunderstanding of man's new solidarity and of the creeping death of the individual in an evolving world.

The question of men's ability to become subjects in solidarity with each other and that of the religious subject are convergent. Here the reserves of religion to save identity are required more than ever. These reserves, which can resist apathy and a distorted collective life that is divorced from the subject, are, however, clearly not unlimited. They are dependent on the historical ability of living religion to resist and on faith in the state of all men as subjects in God's presence. This state as subjects in the presence of God is one of solidarity in a universal sense—not only with regard to those who are oppressed, deprived and needy, but also with regard to those who have been overcome or conquered and those who have died in the world's history of suffering.

One of the indispensable ways in which this solidarity is expressed—and this has to be stressed—is prayer. In this, religion is fundamentally different from that pure utopia to which no one prays and which is clearly only a promise for those who are still to come—a paradise for the victorious—but not for those who suffer unjustly and die. A society which has lost its interest in the continuing state of its people as subjects and which has abandoned its community of interest with the dead will invitably become weaker and weaker in the historical struggle for the state of the living as subjects and fall victim to evolutionary apathy. The God of the living and the dead is a God of universal justice who destroys the norms of our society based on exchange and the satisfaction of needs, saves those who suffer unjustly and die and therefore calls on us to become subjects, to help others to become subjects in the face of hostile oppression and to remain subjects in the face of guilt and in opposition to apathy and the massing together of people.

Surely the identity of modern man is extremely fragile. Fitted into the complex structures of contemporary society which function almost without reference to the subjects of that society, he is in constant danger of losing his face and his name (in the biblical sense) more and more. His dreams and imaginings are less and less frequently creative, but are, on the contrary, levelled down more and more. In the name of evolution and technological progress, he is increasingly subject to a process of back-breeding to the state of a very adaptable animal or a quietly functioning machine. From time to time he tries to raise up his state as a subject on the basis of those artificial 'great' subjects that are the most pitiful imitations of the state of being a subject in the face of the most radical danger that threatens it.

Responsibility, which is not sustained by structures, is a disappearing value. The state of being a subject in solidarity with others is weakening. The art of suppressing or banishing guilt and obligation to others is widely practised. Politics tend to be less and less successful and to give way to administration and power structures. Is it perhaps true that we are living in an age of apathy? It is certainly true to say that human apathy is as bad as hatred and as disastrous in its effects on the process by which men becomes subjects in solidarity.

4. The Faith of Christians in History and Society

I would like to conclude by attempting to define the faith of Christians in the light of a political theology conceived as a practical fundamental theology. I, therefore, propose the following definition: The faith of Christians is a praxis in history and society that is to be understood as hope in solidarity in the God of Jesus as a God of the living and the dead who calls all men to be subjects in his presence. Christians justify themselves in this essentially appocalyptical praxis (of imitation) in their historical struggle for their fellow men. They stand up for all men in their attempt to become subjects in solidarity with each other. In this praxis, they result the danger both of a creeping evolutionary disintegration of the history of men as subjects and of an increasing negation of the individual in view of a new, post middle-class image of man.

a. With an apocalyptical sting

This theological approach is strongly characterized by the primacy of eschatology and faith is primarily expressed in it as hope in solidarity. I have already justified and given meaning to an eschatologically-orientated theology in earlier reflections about a political theology and do not wish to repeat this discussion here. One new aspect of this eschatological orientation of political theology, however, can be mentioned in this context and that is its apocalyptical character. The theological primacy of an apocalyptically-directed eschatology has important consequences both for theology and for practical Christianity. In particular it affects both the practical and the temporal structure of Christian hope, which is here seen as imminent expectation. This hope could only be deprived of its temporal character by an (objective) semantic deception in respect of the biblical traditions and re-interpreted as the timeless existential aspect of being a Christian, in other words, as constant expectation. I shall deal in greater detail with the full scope of this attempt to express once more this apocalyptical aspect of Christian eschatology that has for so long not been considered in view of the present challenges facing Christianity. In the same chapter, I shall also try to show the extent to which Christian hope, understood as imminent expectation, can provide the practical basis for a criticism of an evolutionary understanding of time, in which God himself becomes more and more vague and eventually unthinkable and in which the way is prepared for the end of history and the death of man's state as a subject.

b. God of the living and the dead

On the basis of this theological primacy of an apocalyptical eschatology, there is one fundamental theological statement that includes all other statements made about God and his existence as creator. It is that God is a God of the living and the dead and a God of universal justice and the resurrection of the dead. This faith in the God of the living and the dead shares the Marxist socialist interest in the process by which man becomes a subject and in particular deprived and oppressed man's state as a subject and is opposed to a technological and scientific culture which produces apathy and in which the death of the subject, the destruction of language and the end of history are anticipated, at least in theory. This faith, however, also examines critically the teaching of historical and dialectical materialism, in which the reasons for the historical struggle for universal justice and the existence of all men in solidarity as subjects are to be found. It also questions whether the dialectics of freedom that are attributed to nature or matter are not in fact weaker than those of religion. An understanding of history as a dialectical process of liberation cannot, if it is divorced from or opposed to religion, remain uninfluenced by evolutionary thinking. This is, in my opinion, clear, in theory at least, in the remarkable hybrid form of structural Marxism. Is it not true to say that there is evidence here of the beginning of a victory of an (ultimately undirected) evolution over history as a history of freedom and of the disclosure of dialectical materialism as an evolutionary idea, the paralysis of man's consciousness of solidarity by a growing sense of apathy and the disappearance of historical subjects in administrative structures?

This same faith in the God of the living and the dead also questions post-theological theories of history and society, asking especially whether they do not simply bisect history and thus cause it to end. The dialectical version of these theories remains firmly tied to the historical unity of mankind, but gives a relative value to the idea of universal justice that qualifies this unity. It does so by applying this universal justice exclusively to future generations and not to the dead and the sacrifices of history. The dead, after all, also belong equally to the universal community of all men in solidarity with each other.

It is deeply inhuman to forget or suppress this question of the life of the dead, because it implies a forgetfulness and a suppression of past suffering and an acceptance of the meaninglessness of that suffering. Finally, the happiness of the descendants cannot compensate for the suffering of the ancestors and social progress cannot make up for the injustice done to the dead. If we accept for too long that death is meaningless and are indifferent towards the dead, we shall in the end only be able to offer trivial promises to the living. We are often told nowadays that there is a limit to the growth of our economic potential. This is, however, not all—our potential in meaning seems to have limits. It would seem as though our reserves of meaning are running low and as though there is a danger that the great words that we use to guide the course of our own history—freedom, emancipation, justice, happiness—will be leached and dried out until little meaning remains in them.

As soon as this faith of Christians in the God of the living and the dead, the God of universal justice, is critically introduced into the historical struggle for the state of all men as subjects in solidarity with each other, however, it is confronted with critical counter-questions. Where, for example, is the historical and social basis of the claim made by Christians to be the advocates of this universal and undivided justice? Where can concrete examples of the history of liberation be found in Christianity? Is the Christian promise of universal justice in the resurrection of the dead no more than an impotent idea without reference to human subjects? Is it not, in this sense, simply opium of the people? Does it not merely provide a soothing element in the historical struggle by which all men can become subjects? It is quite clear from these questions that the crisis in Christianity today is not primarily a crisis of the content of faith and its promises, but a crisis of subjects and institutions which do not measure up to the demands made by faith.

c.Hope in solidarity

In my definition of the faith of Christians, I spoke of hope in solidarity. Solidarity here should be understood in a strictly universal sense as a solidarity that has to justify itself not only with regard to the living and future generations, but also with regard to the dead. In this hope, then, the Christian does not primarily hope for himself—he also has to hope for others and, in this hope, for himself. The hope of Christians in a God of the living and the dead and in the power of that God to raise men from the dead is a hope in a revolution for all men, including those who suffer and have suffered unjustly, those who have long been forgotten and even the dead. This hope does not in any sense paralyze historical initiatives or the struggle for the state of all men as subjects. On the contrary, it acts as a guarantee for the criteria which men use again and again to oppose, in the presence of the accumulated sufferings of those who have been unjustly treated, the prevailing unjust structures and relationships.

d. Praxis again

Religion is not absorbed by existing structures and relationships, just as art, for example, is not absorbed in this way. Indeed, we may say that religion is not absorbed by any structures or relationships. God is not just an early, mythological name for what Ernst Bloch has called transcendence or for a transgression of existing structures. The name of God means rather that transcendence is not simply a symbolic paraphrase at a higher level or an impotent reflection of what simply happens, in other words, what ordinary historical events would have been if only they had been really transcendent.

We have, however, to pay a price for a statement such as this. If it is not to remain at the level of a pure assertion that is suspected of ideology, theology must be able to define and call upon a praxis in which Christians can break through the complex social, historical and psychological conditions governing history and society. What is needed, then, is a praxis of faith in mystical and political imitation.

5

The Christian Church

Introduction

That mass movements would result in the establishment of self-supporting churches has apparently been the hope of all missions associated with them. Records of mission meetings, correspondence between missionaries and their societies, and reports and diaries of missionaries from the beginning of each of these movements have contained clear, and some of them forceful and frequent, declarations of this hope, and of the purpose to promote its realization as early as possible.

In conceptions of the process by which this hope would be realized, in plans and programs for its promotion and in the time estimated as required, the records show striking differences between and within the missions. But, despite these differences, the experiences of the missions have been surprisingly similar, especially in their early stages.

Without a clear comprehension by anyone of what was happening, the converts in every area, in respect to their religious life and training, assumed the status of wards or dependents of the missions, or of individual missionaries and their local associates. These dependents in the course of time were to be made fit and able to assume the rights and responsibilities of church members. Men were recruited and trained to minister to them. From the beginning in every area, so far as we can find, these men were urged to prepare the converts for church membership, teaching them, among other things, to contribute to the support of the ministry. But, without exception in every area, a *status quo* was established in which the locally recruited staff served, not the body of converts functioning as a church and aided by the mission, but the mission, aided slightly by the converts, in a program designed by its makers to establish a church. The situation disturbed some missionaries who, being unable to change it radically, eased their minds by camouflaging it. They set up a skeleton organization which they called the church, not composed of the body of believers but of selected individuals from among them: this organization did not—perhaps could not—assume the responsibilities of functioning for these individuals in arranging for worship, a pastoral ministry, and discipline. These functions of the church were exercised by representatives of the mission.

This situation did not develop in exactly the same way in connection with all mass movements. But the foregoing represents in general outline the common experience in the first stages of all the movements we have studied.

Transition From Mission to Church

In such conditions transition from a system of mission-supported evangelists to a church-supported pastorate is extraordinarily difficult. It can be made possible only through the co-operation of the missionary, the evangelist, who is the potential pastor, and the body of converts, which is the potential church. The task is to induce the converts to accept the support of the pastor as one of their responsibilities. This step requires that they be both able and willing to provide his support. We shall shortly consider situations in which the ability is lacking, but must first look at those numerous situations in which the number and the economic resources of the converts are sufficient to make it possible for them to support a pastor.

We have not learned of a single group of mass-movement converts that has indicated a belief that it can get along without a spiritual adviser, a man who will teach the converts, lead them in worship, and give counsel concerning their problems. They have been accustomed to the idea of spiritual advisers and teachers of religion, and unquestioningly assume that in their new venture as Christians they require the help of a minister. But they do not assume that they should provide for his support. The evangelists have not come to them in the traditional guise of Indian religious mendicants but as men with financial backing. They have not been trained from childhood to give to an institution, nor to men of the type of the evangelist, and will not undertake the evangelist's support on their own initiative. They must be made to see the reasonableness and the necessity of supporting the man whose services they require. If the missionary and the evangelist co-operate wisely, with conviction and determined purpose, the converts may be convinced and induced to accept the responsibility.

As the Missionary Sees It

Let us examine the positions of the missionary and the evangelist. The former is handicapped by certain severe limitations. He does not understand the social organization of the people; many of their customs and characteristics puzzle him; he does not know how to appraise the strength and meaning of much of what he sees and hears. His knowledge of the language in which he converses with them is limited. Idioms and shades of meaning often escape him. Even if he has mastered the correct literary forms of the language, the dialects of the village people introduce new and strange forms.

He is oppressed by the poverty and the generally pathetic condition of the people. His experience in his own country has never brought him into touch with such need. Congregations he has known there, with fifty to one hundred times the resources of the people with whom he is now dealing, have received mission grants to enable them to maintain a church and a pastor. He wonders whether it is right to insist that the poor people give for the support of their pastor. Can they do so, he asks, without taking food from the mouths of their children? He thinks of the people of his church at home, and asks if it would not be more in accord with Christian principles for them in their strength to bear the burdens of the weak people with whom he is dealing.

Moreover, he is subject to the common human forces that

make for satisfaction in being able to spend money in a good cause. He appreciates the influence the spending of this money gives him and is eager to use it for the upbuilding of the church. But he believes that the future, if not the present, well-being of the church depends upon the acceptance by Christian converts of responsibility for maintaining that church, so he speaks frequently on the subject. He looks forward to a time when there will be other converts who will be better provided than those with whom he is now associated with the means to support a church in India. It is not surprising if he insists less than he might that the existing church shall at once accept responsibility for the support of the pastor.

As the Evangelist Sees It

Let us turn now to the mission-supported evangelist. His association with the missionary, his education, and his widening outlook give him a rising scale of needs. He sees little opportunity to get from the poor converts to whom he is ministering the means to provide what seems to him a reasonable, even an irreducible, standard of living. In moments of spiritual exaltation he thinks he will throw himself entirely upon the people whom he serves, taking what they give him and bravely enduring any privation that step makes necessary. But he is a married man and a father. He has obligations to a wife and children. "What will become of them"? he asks, and the answer that comes from his fears drives him back into a cautious mood. The easy way for him is to protect his mission salary. It is possibly the only way to assure that his wife and children shall not go hungry or be clothed in rags.

Unless he has come directly and recently out of the group to which he is ministering, he is likely to have an ingrained dislike of the idea of being known to the public as economically dependent upon these poor and,m in some respects, degraded people, who are held in contempt by the upper classes of the community. A pastor, who is supported entirely by a group of former outcastes in a rural pastorate, told us that his greatest difficulty in passing from mission-support to the present situation was this one that he had to meet in his own mind. When he was able to identify himself with a despised group of Sweepers, to the extent of being publicly recognized as dependent upon their gifts for the food that he and his family would eat and the clothes they would wear, his battle was more than half won.

In addition to the almost certain reduction in his income if he becomes dependent upon the local church for his support, the uncertainty and irregularity of the receipt of the reduced amount, and the fear of the loss of public esteem, the evangelist thinks of the humiliations that are likely to be heaped upon him by the converts themselves. He entertains no illusions about their saintliness. Although he may be ignorant of a psychological vocabulary he is acquainted with the facts that form the basis for our modern theories about inferiority complexes and reactions. He knows that a people who have long been oppressed are not tender in their dealings with folk who are dependent in any way upon them, especially when they recognize in those folk signs of advantages they have never enjoyed. One Indian pastor, who was an ardent Nationalist and very free in criticizing missionaries, told the writer that he would prefer to be paid Rs.20 a month by any missionary he had known than to collect Rs.30 a month from the Chamar converts he was serving, because so many of the latter would berate him and humiliate him when making their small gifts.

These difficulties of the evangelist all appear more formidable when regarded from the sheltered position within the mission budget than they do from the point of view of the men who have experienced them. Pastors who are being supported by their people discount all such difficulties and tell of compensations that make them prefer the support of their people. But we are now looking at the evangelist who is on mission support and trying to understand his relation to the call for a church-supported pastorate. It is not surprising that he does not often do all that he might to induce the body of converts to accept full responsibility for his support.

As the Converts See it

If we examine the position of the converts more closely, we

shall find another set of obstacles. We are considering particularly groups of converts from the depressed classes. *It should be recognized that these classes have been trained by centuries of exploitation and servility to avoid the acceptance of responsibilities that may prove burdensome, and to get all they can out of every situation, while obligating themselves as little as possible.*

Furthermore, these converted groups recognize a vast difference between the standards of living, the economic position of the missionary on the one hand and of themselves on the other. They understand that the missionary represents a large and prosperous company of people in his homeland, and assume that his potential resources are very large. They suppose that what he says about their duty to give is true, but they can think of a dozen reasons why they should not give, or should give only a little; moreover, they believe that if they do not give, or give just enough to escape the appearance of non-co-operation, the missionary's friends will come to the rescue. *The Hindu idea of giving to gain merit remains long in the mind of many Christian converts, and they think of the foreign supporters of the mission as being permitted to earn much merit by continued support of the evangelist who ministers to them.*

We must bear in mind that even those people to whom we have referred as being able to support their pastors are very poor. The need of some of them is desperate. Support of the church would necessitate for them an almost heroic devotion. If, for instance, all the expenditures for tobacco were stopped and the equivalent given to the church, a good many congregations would have enough from that source to pay their pastors in full. But if these expenditures were stopped, the money saved could be expended on additional food and still leave many families undernourished. In many homes it could be added to the amounts paid as interest to the money-lender and leave a part of the interest bill still unpaid.

If the extravagances connected with marriages were all stopped, and the money spent on the church, the pastors' salaries would be assured. If all the members should give a tithe of their income to the church, they could provide more than enough to pay the evangelists on their present scales to pay. But new converts are not much more likely to do any of these heroic things than are the members of the Church in Western lands, and they are far less able to pay the tithe of their income.

Missionary Funds Received in Every Area

When we turn to records of accomplishment the outstanding fact that faces us is that in no wide area have we found the Church fully supporting the program which its leaders have thought necessary for its proper development and extension. A grant-in-aid from foreign funds is being received for some part of the Church's program in each of the ten sample areas of our study, as well as in every other mass-movement area of which we have detailed information. But there are significant differences in the amounts of aid received and in the range of uses to which they are put.

In the United Presbyterian Church in the Pasrur area all of the ordained pastors receive their full support from the church, and no candidates for the ministry are sent to the theological school for training, or appointed after training, without a clear understanding that they will look for their entire support, throughout their ministry, to the churches they serve.

In the United Church of South India around Nagercoil, which is the field of the London Missionary Society, no man is ordained unless he has a call to a church that guarantees a minimum monthly salary of Rs.25.

But in both of these areas unordained evangelists, supported in part by the mission, minister to weak congregations that do not contribute enough to support pastors and which have not been able to link up with other congregations in the joint support of a pastor.

In the Church of India, in the area around Vidyanagar, collections for ministerial support far exceed the salaries of the ordained ministers assigned to pastorates, but a great deal of pastoral work is done by lay teachers and by catechists, for whose support contributions are received from the Church Missionary Society and from individual donors abroad.

Statistics Do Not Tell the Whole Truth

Statistics on the support of the church in India are even more misleading than statistics usually are. Comparisons are of little value because of the different processes followed in preparing the reports. Three illustrations will suffice to make the meaning of this statement clear.

1. Strong emphasis on stewardship and tithing led the preachers and their salaried lay assistants employed in one area to decide that a tenth of their salaries should be given each month to the church, being paid as a lump sum into the treasury. In the interest of efficient and easy collecting, these "gifts" were deducted at the source. In practice, therefore, the tithe contributed was based only on the grant-in-aid from mission funds. This resulted in a statistical increase of giving by the Indian Church whenever mission expenditures for salaries were increased, unless offset by decreases in giving by other members of the church; and a statistical decrease whenever mission salary expenditures were reduced, unless offset by increase in the giving of other church members. Thus, in a year when contributions from Indian sources really decreased, or were at a standstill, an encouraging increase might be recorded in the statistics because of a larger distribution for salaries of funds from outside India.

2. In one area standard salaries are fixed. A grant-in-aid is made on account of many salaries from centrally administered funds received from the Missionary Society. The preacher is supposed to collect the remainder locally. As the central administrative body escapes responsibility for paying the portion assigned to be raised by the people, it considers that portion as found locally, and statistics record it as given. "A's" salary is fixed at Rs.25 per mensem. The funds available for his support in the Central Treasury amount to Rs.15 per mensem. "A" is authorized to collect the remaining Rs.10. What he does not collect he has the privilege of giving. He draws Rs.15 each month from the Central Treasury and

the church is recorded in the statistics as having given the remainder. Actually "A" may have received from the church an average of only Rs.6 per mensem, in which case the statistics for the year are Rs.48 too high; or he may have received an average of Rs.12 per mensem, in which case the year's statistics are Rs.24 too low.

3. Much of the giving is not in cash but in commodities. When statistics are recorded, the cash value of commodity gifts is figured and included. In some areas a scale of values at which commodity gifts are to be figured is decided upon and sent to all who make the statistical reports. In others there is no central control or advice, but every reporter does what is right in his own eyes. Many rates for figuring these values are possible. Rice, for instance, sells fifty per cent higher at one season than at another, and either extreme rate, or some intermediate rate, may be used in the report.

According to church statistics in a certain area "B" was considerably better paid than "C". But when a detailed inquiry was made, it was found that "B" had translated his commodity receipts into cash values at a rate more than sixty per cent higher than the rate "C" had used. Actually "C" had been better paid than "B".

Some Advantages Gained by Support of the Pastors

When these mass movement groups support their pastors, great benefits accrue to them. The result is most stimulating. Their self-respect gains, and they value the ministry of their pastor more highly. This is not mere theory. We have the unanimous report of church-supported pastors in the Pasrur area that their people have been more responsive to their ministry since they began to provide their entire salaries. Pastors of self-supporting congregations in Govindpur and Nagercoil also testified to the same effect. There has been a notable development of Chritian consciousness. Discipline is more successfully and more easily enforced. The church is theirs, the people feel, since they pay for its maintenance. The pastor is their pastor and not merely an agent of the mission or the missionary. They are members of the church and not merely attached to it.

Success Dependent Upon United Effort

Enough has been written earlier in this chapter to make clear the importance of the personal qualities of the ministerial leadership, both indigenous and foreign, in bringing about the establishment of a church-supported pastorate. Wise and persistent effort, backed by clear thinking and firm conviction, can induce groups of converts to do what they would not seriously think of doing on their own initiative. In a great many places it has led such groups to accept full support for their pastors and in some places to accept additional responsibilities. There is every reason to believe that the same kind of leadership can produce like, or better, results in many other places. But weak missionary leadership can make it impossible for the Indian evangelist to produce any of these results, just as an unconvinced or non-co-operating evangelist can make it impossible for the missionary to achieve them.

Conditions that Determine the Possibilities in Pastoral Support

There are mass-movement areas where purely physical difficulties apparently make it impossible for a church-supported pastorate to be established at the present time. Perhaps this statement should take the more conservative form that the possibility of a church-supported pastorate, under the physical difficulties confronted in some areas, has not been demonstrated. Chief of these difficulties is the wide geographical distribution of Christians in several areas, making it apparently impossible to include the number of families necessary to provide the salary of a pastor in a parish that is not too large for him to care for effectively.

In the Nagercoil area 230 villages, in which Christians live, contain an average of 29.5 families. Only 96 villages contain less than 6 families each. All of these small groups are within two miles of large groups, many of them within a half mile. Parishes containing a minimum of 100 families can be organized so that no pastor has more villages to visit than he can reach with adequate frequency, with all the families within a reasonable walking distance of a regular Sunday church service.

In the Vidyanagar Deanery 17 villages contain a total of 320 families, an average of 18.8 families per village. Here the staff consists of a Deanery chairman, who is also principal of a boarding school, an ordained pastor, who visits all the villages, and 14 teachers, each of whom conducts services daily, including Sunday. Only 5 of these villages have less than a dozen Christian families and all are within easy reach of Sunday services.

In the Govindpur area 58 villages contain an aggregate of 655 Christian families, an average of 11.29 per village. Here also, pastorates that reach every village with the necessary home visitation and provide for Sunday services within reach of all have proved practicable, although the distances involved are greater than in Nagercoil or Vidyanagar. The missionaries in this section, with characteristic German thoroughness, taught the converts to attend church, even though they had to walk several miles to get there.

In the Pasrur area the average number of Christian families in four pastorates for which information was secured is 9.8 per village. Villages nearest the pastor's residence receive most of his service and pay most of his salary. But all Christian groups are visited several times a year. More pastors are needed before all the groups can be adequately ministered to.

The Complex Problem in the United Provinces

But when we come into the United Provinces, we find Christians in many areas much more scattered, and church-supported pastorates rare. The most difficult conditions reported from any area that has a large Christian community are in Moradabad District, in the field of the Methodist Episcopal Church. A survey of about two thirds of the district shows 700 villages and towns in which Christians live and an aggregate of 1,877 Christian families, or an average of 2.68 per village. Each of 306 villages contains only one Christian family. Three castes, Mazhabi Sikhs, Lal Begi Sweepers, and Chamars, have provided the village Christian population in this district. The first and second castes are widely scattered, and not frequently in the same villages. The third are more concentrated, but only a few groups have been converted. The Lal Begi Sweepers form the largest element in the church. In the social sense they form a mass, and they were converted in a typical mass movement, but geographically speaking they are a people broken into numerous small fragments.

Another unit of the work of the Methodist Episcopal Church, the Aligarh District of the Northwest India Conference, where Sweeper converts predominate but a Chamar movements is in progress, reports an average of 4.1 Christian families per village in which Christians live. In this matter of wide distribution Moradabad and Aligarh are typical of many districts of that church in the United Provinces, though fortunately not of all districts.

In the North India Mission of the American Presbyterian Provinces, of which the area at Etah is a part, and a number of isolated outlying districts, an aggregate of 5,357 Christian families are scattered through 1,757 villages, an average of 5.08 families per village. All but a few hundred of these families come from the Sweeper castes. Rural pastorates, locally supported, have not been successfully established in any part of this field.

Almost the whole of our study of the selected area around Etah was spent in a group of villages that were being ministered to by one unordained preacher, assisted for a part of the time by an American lady evangelist. This preacher's parish includes 48 villages in which Christians live. some of these villages are ten miles from his residence of Etah. They are widely scattered. To some of these villages he had not been for six months before his visit there with us. Very few Christian families have learned to go to other villages for services. However, this situation is by no means unique.

In the methodist Episcopal Church in the United Provinces, as one of a number of tragic results of a devastating series of reductions in missionary income in recent years, there are dozens of preachers trying to care for an even larger number of village groups and succeeding no better than this Etah area pastor in providing regular pastoral service for their people.

The church-supported pastors of the Pasrur area were unanimous in saying that at least 100 families are required to provide a minimum support for a pastor. Some pastors thought the minimum figure should be 150 families. In Nagercoil and Govindpur, where the average economic strength of Christian families is higher than around pasrur or in the United Provinces, the pastors estimated the minimum requirement as between 80 and 150 families. If the Pasrur standard of 100 families should be adopted for the United Provinces, pastorates in Moradabad District would have to include an average of 38 villages, and throughout the North India Presbyterian Mission an average of 35 villages. In the Aligarh District the average would be 25 villages. But in the Pasrur area pastorates containing a minimum of 100 families each would require only 10 villages, in the Vidyanagar area only 6 villages, and in the Nagercoil area only 4 villages.

The obstacles to the establishment of church-supported pastorates in areas where Christian families are distributed over such a wide territory are not confined to the difficulties of pastoral visitation and the conducting of regular services within reach of the Christians. A major obstacle arises from the effect upon converts of their isolation from other christians. There is little in their environment to re-enforce a Christian purpose or an appreciation of Christianity; there is much there to undermine both purpose and appreciation. The wonder is that these isolated families so generally continue to declare themselves Christians and to welcome the infrequent visits of their overburdened ministers.

A very much more hopeful situation prevails in a number of districts in the west of these provinces, where in addition to the Sweepers large numbers of Chamars have become Christians. The Chamars are more numerous than the Sweepers and live in larger groups. In areas where both they and the Sweepers have been converted the villages average as many as fifteen families of Christians. Around Ghaziabad approximately one third of the Chamars have been converted. As a result the concentration of Christians has risen to 11.21 per village. If the Chamar movement in this area should continue until the entire community is converted, it would be possible to set up many pastorates containing one hundred families each by combining only four or five villages.

How one Humble Lay Preacher Solved the Problem of His Support

A suggestion of the possibilities in this situation is provided by the experience of a very humble man trained at Ghaziabad, several years ago, to be a lay assistant to a pastor in this field. He worked for a short time on mission support. When news came of a further reduction of missionary appropriations, he was dismissed. But his heart was in his work, and he had a strong desire to continue telling people of Christ. He knew of two villages, located only a male apart, where groups of Chamars, a total of about twenty families, more prosperous than most, were eager to be instructed in Christian teaching and received into the church. He went to them, explained his situation, and asked them to provide for his support as their teacher. They gave him a house, a cow buffalo, the promise of fooder, and assured him of monthly offerings in cash and food. He opened a school for the children in which he and his wife both teach, and began holding regular and frequent services. A third near-by village group became interested and began to cooperate.

He had been among these people with his family about five months when we visited the main village, inspected his school. joined the congregation in worship, and interrogated him, his wife, and many of the people to whom they were ministering. Everyone was happy. The school was well established and had made an excellent start. The people had made remarkable progress. In creedal knowledge, in orderly worship, in comprehension of the meaning of Christianity, they impressed us as being more advanced than many groups that had been professing Christians for ten years or longer. The lay pastor and his wife are typical village people. They had had only a little better than an upper-primary education. Their needs are limited and they are happy with what these groups give them. A pastor, with sufficient education to qualify for ordination by any of the churches engaged in these mass movements, would demand and need more support than this lay preacher is getting, but he would provide reasonably well for the pastoral care of one hundred families who, with anything like proportional giving, could insure him a sufficient, though modest, living.

In the areas where Christians are divided into such small village groups and are so widely scattered as in Moradabad, Aligarh, and the North India Presbyterian Mission, the only hope of establishing a church capable of supporting an all-inclusive system of pastorates would seem to lie in winning other elements of the population. There are indications that the Chamars in many districts would respond encouragingly to a vigorous effort to win them. But missionaries and Indian ministers alike hesitate to try to win new groups when they feel that so much remains to be done to establish the Sweeper converts. When they cannot care for the groups whom they have encouraged to enter the church, they fear to accept new responsibilities.

Yet the conversion of groups of the Chamars might provide the resources to increase the staff and reduce each preacher's parish to workable size. There is also reason to believe that converts from one caste are helped in many ways by the conversion of members of another caste. The Oraon and Munda movements in Chota Nagpur have re-enforced each other, the Mala and Madiga Christians of the Telugu country have each been helped by the movement in the other caste. The Sweeper Christians around Ghaziabad have been heartened by the conversion of the Chamars, and have been helped to develop the necessary new consciousness as Christians by association with them in worship and church discussions.

Where Christian converts are unable to support their preachers, because they do not have sufficient resources, the attempt to force them to do so by withdrawing mission appropriations must end disastrously. For a mission to abandon these scattered groups after bringing them to confess Christian faith, because they cannot do what is apparently impossible, would be a tragic blunder. The reduction of missionary appropriations in the last few years in the Methodist Episcopal Church has gone so far, and so many preachers have been dismissed, that thousands of families, while nominally included in parishes that were already unreasonably large, are now virtually abandoned. Unless missionary appropriations can be increased very soon, sufficiently to add to the staff again, the superintendents in those areas will find it necessary to completely abandon thousands of families in order to care effectively for the remainder. Several superintendents have, in fact, already formulated plans for doing so.

The Necessity for Christian Leadership From Within the Groups

The support of the Church in mass-movement areas is linked closely to the problem of securing effective Christian leadership within the several groups. This issue is in turn linked with caste. In the areas where the Church is supporting its pastors the groups are effectively led from within by men who have been prepared for Christian leadership by intensive training. In the Pasrur area, in the Punjab, practically every village group has two or more elders who have passed examinations in courses designed to train them for their duties. They are honorary assistants of the pastor, helping to arrange for church services, to encourage attendance, to minister to people in trouble, to enforce discipline, and to collect funds. In this area the pastors, with a few exceptions chiefly recruited in recent years, have come from among the Chuhras, who form an overwhelming majority of the converts. These pastors have never hesitated to declare their caste origin and even those who have come from other castes, or from the Mohammedans, have identified themselves fully with the people of their pastorates.

In the Vidyanagar, Guntur, and Cumbum areas this trained leadership has been provided very largely by the school-teachers, at least one of whom has been located in nearly every village. They have come from one or the other of the mass movement groups and have given strong leadership within their respective group councils. They have never set themselves off socially from their people.

In the United Provinces, however, this leadership from within has not generally been secured. A considerable proportion of the preachers has been rectuited from converts from other castes, and many preachers who have come from among the Sweepers and the Chamars, in the process of their education and special training have broken away from their groups. The preachers in the United Provinces usually live in the quarters of the higher castes and work for and with their people from the outside. Elsewhere, they live with the groups to whom they minister work from within. In the United Provinces the preachers have often acquired a social prestige which has not benefited, but in some cases has actually harmed, the members of their congregation.

They have esteemed the privilege of living among the caste Hindus and to safeguard that privilege have cut themselves off socially from their people. Some who have come from the Sweeper caste have gone so far as to pose as converts from higher Hindu castes. Two groups of Sweeper converts known to the writer objected to proposals that young men from their villages go to a school to be trained as teachers in mission schools saying that if they went, they would be lost to the groups, for when their training was completed, they would be ashamed to acknowledge that they had ever been Sweepers.

A side-light on this situation is provided in the fact that in the Etah and Ghaziabad areas more than sixty per cent of the preachers and teachers reported that their father's birth-place was in some other civil district than the one in which they were working, but in no area outside of the United Provinces was the proportion reporting their father's birthplace to be in another district as high as ten per cent. In other words, Etah and Ghaziabad, unlike the more successful areas outside the United Provinces, do not have a ministry that has come out of the Christian population in their districts.

We must not judge these preachers and teachers too harshly.

It is hardly possible in the compass of this book to indicate what it would cost a man from the outside to go into a sweeper *mohalla* andidentify himself with its families, even though they be Christians. It is, in our judgment, more than can be asked of any man. But it is imperative that an able, trained, Christian leadership be provided for the converted Sweepers within their groups. Efforts in the past have generally failed because they have lifted the trained man out and left the group exactly where it had been.

Two lines of experiment are being conducted to meet this need. Dr. M.T. Titus, in the Moradabad District, has been in the forefront of an effort to train village leaders in a program of instruction built on the model of the elders' course in Pasrur. Selected men, often the village Chaudris, are intensively taught by the preachers in preparation for examination in the prescribed course, which includes, *inter alia,* a brief outline of the life of Christ, selected passages of Scripture, a form for congregational worship, a brief ritual for the burial of the dead, and a number of Christian *bhajans*. When these men have passed three sections of this course, if their conduct has been satisfactory and they are recommended by the church officiary, the superintendent may appoint them leaders of the Christians of their village, authorized to conduct services in the absence of a minister in their own or near-by villages, to bury the dead, and to perform other services as needed.

In the Ingraham Training Institute at Ghaziabad, the Rev. William Dye has developed a program for giving short-term courses (from three weeks to three months) to selected men, who on completion of the course are appointed honorary assistants to the pastor. A number of men have been trained and are said to be serving acceptably. They work on much the same program as that described above. Their training emphasizes the conducting of congregational worship in orderliness and reverence. Indian music is stressed and many of the men learn to sing, and accompany with typical village musical instruments, a number of Christian *bhajans*. These leaders must agree to oppose vigorously all idolatrous practices by the Christians of their villages, and of any other villages of which they are given oversight, to insist that all marriages of Christians in their villages be solemnized by Christian rites, to report cases of misconduct and to try to bring the offenders to penitence, and are held responsible for the records of their groups. The support of the pastor is much less difficult where an effective local Christian leadership is established.

Methods of Pastoral Support

There are three main plans of pastoral support operating in our ten selected areas. The most fundamental division in the discussion on the subject occurs on the issue of whether people should contribute to their pastor directly or to a central fund from which their pastor and others are paid. The United Presbyterians in the Pasrur area give us the best composite picture of a pastorate supported on a parish basis. The Church of India in the Vidyanagar area provides the clearest example of pastorates supported through a central fund. The United Church of South India in the Nagercoil area (London Mission) is representative of several churches in which elements of the parish and central fund plans are combined.

The Pasrur plan has worked so well that twenty-one pastors in a single mission district are being fully supported by their congregations, with average incomes almost twice as high as those of their people. The churches are gradually taking on other expenses besides the support of the pastor. They finance a missionary effort to give the gospel to people in another area, further north, where there are as yet few Christian converts. They contribute to a seminary fund from which are paid the salaries of two Indian professors in the theological seminary where candidates for the ministry are trained. These professors had been pastors of self-supporting congregations, and when they were invited to join the faculty of the seminary they objected to going on mission support. Representatives of the churches then came forward with proposals that salaries be provided through contributions from the churches. These congregations have as yet done little toward the building of churches or schools.

The Vidyanagar plan of payment to a central fund has provided the salaries of all the ordained ministers who work as pastors, considerable money for administrative expenses, and contributions toward the salaries of teachers and catechists. The congregations have all erected buildings used both for church and school purposes and houses for the teacher-preachers. The weaker congregations have been assisted somewhat in their building program by grants from the central treasury into which are paid appropriations from the Missionary Society and gifts from individuals outside the area.

The Nagercoil combination of the features of the two preceding plans shows a number of congregations supporting their pastors and a number to whom evangelists, who are supported from the central fund, are ministering. Inducements are offered to congregations to support their own pastor. They are allowed to extend a call, and if the chosen minister accepts and the arrangement is approved by the central administrative body, known as the Church Council he is installed and ordained. A minimum monthly salary of Rs. 25 must be assured or the appointment will not be approved. Congregations supporting their pastor are entitled to representation in the Church Council, and are invited to contribute to the central fund from which the evangelists are supported, and connectional expenses are met. A few congregations also maintain parish schools for which generous grants-in-aid are received from the government of Travancore State. Church building has been empahsized, and a number of rural congregations have erected commodious structures, of brick to replace the simple mud buildings of an earlier era. The Nagercoil plan differs from that in Pasrur only in the use it makes of the central fund and in the solicitation of contributions for it from congregations that are already supporting their own pastors. The men who work under the direction of the Church Council, and the district superintendents, who, as it happens, are practically all missionaries, are not mission employees, but Church-Council employees.

In favour of the parish-supported pastorate it is said that people contribute more generously to the support of their own local church and the pastor who minister to them. In areas where *jajmani* governs occupational relationships this type of pastorate fits into that system. The pastor establishes his *jajmani haq,* or occupational rights, and every family within the pastorate is encouraged by the influence of the system to make its fair payment. The pastor is likewise encouraged to give due attention to every family and thus establish his claim.

Against the parish-supported pastorate it is said: (1) that it results in harmful inequalities of pastoral income; (2) that it projects the personality of the pastor into a situation where it does not belong, thus obscuring the truth that offerings are made not to man but to God; (3) that it unfairly distributes the burden of maintaining a ministry throughout a given area, when prosperous congregations, that should help to support pastors for weaker congregations, rest content with supporting their own.

Concerning jajmani, it is said that it lays a wrong foundation for the support of the church and tends to reduce the ministry to the status of menial service, with which *jajmani* is most prominently associated. However, this objection has ignored the fact that in some areas the Brahman priest is supported by *jajmani.*

The missions of the so-called Free Churches apparently tend to the establishment of the parish-supported pastorate, those accustomed to state endowment to a central fund pastorate.

Several Correlations

A study of the relation of the debts of Christian families to their contributions to the church in all of the selected areas, except Etah, where the necessary information was not obtained, shows that debt has surprisingly little effect in preventing contributions. Of 2,208 families in debt, 91.7 per cent made contributions to the church in the twelve months preceding our visit to their villages. During the same period 93.9 per cent of the 954 who were not in debt also made contributions. As stated in another chapter, non-debtors include a group who are prosperous enough to have no need for credit, and a group who are so poor that no one will give them credit. Of prosperous non-debtors more than 99 per cent contribute to the church.

The average annual contribution of debtor families was Rs. 2-3-0; of nondebtor families, Rs. 2-6-11. Contributions of debtors amounted to an average of 1.88 per cent of their cash income; of non-debtors an average of 2.02 per cent.

The lay officials of the church in the village contributed an average of Rs. 4-13-9 against an average of Rs. 2-4-1 for all families. This equaled 3.34 per cent of their annual cash incomes. Ten village groups, which contain one or more lay officials of the church, show average annual contributions per family of Rs. 2-13-6, while ten village groups which contain no church officials show average annual contributions of Rs. 1-14-4. These groups were chosen at random from corresponding areas. The contrasting figures suggest that the organization of thc local groups and the selection and training of leaders result in raising the level of contributions. The lay official not only gives more to the church than he would as a private member, but he leads his Christian neighbors to give more generously.

The average annual contribution of 1,026 families whose head is literate is Rs. 3-14-7; of 2,397 families whose head is illiterate, Rs. 1-8-10. Families whose head is literate contribute amounts equal to 2.36 per cent of their cash income; those whose head is illiterate 1.6 per cent. The proportion of families contributing to the church is: (a) those with literate heads 95.8 per cent. It seems that mission money spent on schools re-enforces the support of the church by increasing both the capacity and the will to give.

6

Church Administration and Polity

Intorduction

The problem of administration with reference to any group begins before the first contact is made with its members by a representative of the church or the co-operating mission. Unless the agent of the church or mission, whether paid or honorary, has a wholesome comprehension of what the church is, of the relation of new converts to it and of what it means to be a Christian, he is likely to give a new groups conceptions that will add to the difficulties of administration and will retard their development as a unit in the Church of Christ. It will be impossible for us to account for the differences in levels of attainment between the several missions and churches unless we consider the contrasting conceptions and attitudes of their representatives in making contacts with new groups. One who presents Christianity as an expression of the desire of kind people to help, and invites his hearers to allow themselves to be helped, lays a poor foundation for a Christian Church. One who speaks of the soul's salvation from torment after death, but says nothing of God's kingdom of righteousness on earth, does no better.

Some of the groups encountered in our selected areas seem to have consented to join the church in the expectation that much would be done for them; others seem to have sought admission to the church to obtain inspiration and leadership in becoming the people they ought to be and in doing the things they ought to do. In one area a pastor told us of two village groups that were in striking contrast with each other. One group had made a bad start, and after more than half a century represented his most difficult administrative problem. The other had started well, represented his simplest problem, and provided his greatest encouragement. In the former village the senior elder, when asked how long his group had been Christians, said, "For fifty-two years, and we don't have a road to this village yet." Hearing this, an Indian lay member of our staff remarked, "And you haven't yet cleaned up the filthy lanes in front of your houses." In the other village, replying to the same question, its leader said: "We decided to follow Christ three years ago and tore down our idol shrine. Then we built out church. Two years ago we were baptized. But we are just beginning to understand how much more we ought to do and how much better we ought to be called Christians."

A district superintendent said, "In every group of professing Christians in this district there is a certain amount of Christian faith and godliness, but some groups are suffering from the mistakes of evangelists who talked to them over much of what the mission would do for them if they became Christians."

Preparation For Baptism

When a group have decided to become Christians, the question arises. What shall be required of them before they shall be baptized and brought into the church? It is not possible to determine what requirements have been enforced in the areas which we have studied. Conferences, assemblies, or councils may adopt resolutions fixing certain standard requirements for baptism, but ministers within the jurisdiction of those bodies may baptize candidates who have not met all those requirements or may withhold baptism until additional requirements have been met. From the records of a number of mission and church organizations it appears that no one would be baptized who had not learned the Lord's Prayer, the Apostles Creed, and the Ten Commandments, but inquiry in the area concerned shows that those requirements have been modified, either because of the inability of candidates to learn or of the inefficiency of the ministers and evangelists in teaching. We do not find resolutions saying that men will not be baptized unless their wives join them in professing Christianity, but we find this condition quite commonly enforced.

There have been two main schools of thought about baptismal requirements. One has advocated early baptism with a minimum of requirements; the other its postponement until formidable requirements have been met.

The late Bishop James M. Thoburn told of the baptism of several pioneers of a movement in the Bijnor district of the United Provinces. Having heard three or four open-air sermons and talked once or twice with the preachers, these men came to the missionary and said they had decided to become Christians. After finding their attitudes acceptable—that they believed on the Lord Jesus Christ, were desirous of being saved from their sins, and purposed in their hearts to do right—the missionary baptized them. The bishop expressed the opinion that to have refused to baptize them would have been to give enemies an opportunity to organize against them, and either by persuasion or by threats to keep them from confessing Christ. At that time, more than fifty years ago, baptism was regarded by Hindus as a kind of crossing of the Rubicon. A man's conversion to Christianity was a *fait accompli* if he had been baptized. He was then a subject for punishment, for vituperation, and out-casting. But if not baptized, there was a chance to keep him from becoming a Christian, no matter how much he had committed himself as to his faith or purpose.

Mr. Samuel Knowles, an advocate of immediate baptism when a convert has declared his acceptance of Christ, is said to have made it a custom to take water for use in baptizing with him to places where he was to preach in *melas,* bazaars, villages, or town *mohallas.* His theory was that baptism should be administered when confession is made and instruction given later.

The reports of Dr. John E. Clough and the Rev. A.V. Timpany, pioneer missionaries related to the mass movement of

Madigas in the American Baptist Telugu Mission, tell of groups of people who had heard of Christ from relatives, or neighbours, coming to camp meetings, confessing their faith and being baptized the same day or the next.

Ditt, the heroic pioneer of the Chuhra masses who have been converted in the United Presbyterian Church in the punjab, was baptized without instruction, if we except what he had received from a somewhat discredited lay convert in a neighboring village.

The work around Bijnor has not been considered to be very successful. Many converts have at one time or another denied the faith and successive pastors and superintendents have grown discouraged. Yet several thousand people who have followed those early converts into the Church now bear witness to Christ. And the present superintendent of the church in the district, the Rev. George B. Thomson, an Indian minister, draws his entire salary from the scattered community he serves, which also contributes toward the support of pastors and unordained assistants.

Out of the work of Messrs. Clough, Timpany, and their colleagues, and in the direct line of those converts baptized with little instruction, has come a Baptist community of approximately a quarter of a million with scores of congregations supporting their pastor.

The Tarus of Gonda District, hundreds of whom were baptized by Mr. Knowles and his associates, forsook Christianity en masse, returning to their primitive animism, or going over to Mohammedanism. A contributing cause, and perhaps, the only cause, of their apostasy was that successive preachers who went into the malaria-infested jungle of the Terai, in which the Tarus lived, contracted fever and died so that the converts did not after their baptism receive either the instruction or the pastoral care which the missionary had thought he would be able to provide for them.

In the Punjab, Ditt, and many of those who followed him, despite the seeming inadequacy of instruction and leadership in worship prior to and immediately after baptism, developed a strong christian loyalty and devotion, and a church of great strength and promise in that part of India has come into existence.

Turning to areas in which more instruction before baptism has been insisted upon, we select one in Gujerat. Bishop Cyrus J. Foss, speaking in Philadelphia in 1898, after a visit to India, thus described a service in which two hundred and twenty-five people were baptized:

Bishop Thoburn strictly questioned all the adults before we baptized them. They were arranged in rows sitting on the ground and were questioned somewhat as follows: "Do you believe in one God? "Do you believe in Jesus Christ?" "Have you put away every token of idolatry?" And when they had answered many such searching questions, I said to one of the missionaries: "Do these poor folk know anything of the Apostles Creed?" He took the question forward and then those adults repeated the Apostles' Creed. "Do they know the Ten Commandments?" I asked. And they recited them ... They had been thoroughly instructed.

These were among the forerunners of a church that has developed much strength.

In the Dornakal Diocese new candidates for baptism are placed under the care of teachers, pastors, or evangelists for a period of instruction and oversight. They are required to learn the Lord's Prayer, the Apostles' Creed, the Ten Commandments, and an outline statement of the life, ministry, death, resurrection, and ascension of Jesus. In addition they are expected to attend church regularly, to contribute to its support, and to bear witness in their communities as Christians. There is a well-established order of cate-chumens who are taught to regard themselves as Christians and are reported in the church statistics as Christians in preparation for baptism.

Pastors are disposed to relax these conditions somewhat in the case of converts from the higher Sudra castes. Doubtless this process is promoted by the ease with which educated men, rare among outcastes but common in the upper castes of Sudras, can learn what is required of them, and by the delight of the pastors to have people of social influence and economic strength join the church.

In the Nagercoil area, the well-established church that has arisen from the labors of the London Mission requires of candidates for baptism, besides their confession of faith in Jesus Christ as Lord and Saviour, a high standard of creedal knowledge, church contributions, and regularity in attendance at public worship.

It is not possible to base upon materials discovered in this study any pronouncement on the much-debated subject of the standards requisite for baptism. Successful churches have been established where the first converts were baptized with little training or testing and no less successful churches where, from the beginning prolonged training for baptism was required. We found instances of early baptism followed by wholesale apostasy, and instances of baptism after elaborate training and testing followed by the complete collapse of faith and denial of allegiance. In one area in Bihar, where several thousand Chamars have become christians since 1906, an earlier movement of Chamars collapsed and all converts apostatized after candidates for baptism had been given from three to six months' intensive training at the mission headquarters.

No course of instruction and no process of organization by church or mission can insure any group or any individual against temptation. A poorly instructed person or group may be more genuinely Christian than one that has been thoroughly instructed. And poorly instructed person or group may be more genuinely Christian than one that has been throughly instructed. And it is even possible to mislead seekers after God by overemphasizing the values of knowledge, forms of worship, and professions of faith and devotion. No survey can reveal the number and strength of mass movements that might have developed, but were prevented by unwise requirements or by misplaced emphases in preparation for baptism.

Whether baptism should be administered immediately after the first confession of faith and purpose to follow Christ, or only after training and testing, is apparently less important than that, after baptism, adequate provision should be made for pastoral care involving instruction, fellowship, worship and the full ministry of the World and the sacraments. If baptism is to be administered after limited opportunities for cultivation, it should certainly be only in those areas where the adequacy of the ministerial staff and the accessibility of the converts provide reasonable assurance of regular instruction and pastoral care after baptism.

The Importance of Church Organization and Administration

This study leads to the conclusion that the organization and administration of the church are issues of major importance. Where converts have received little instruction prior to baptism, but have been successfully incorporated into churches providing regular and frequent opportunities for worship and oversight by faithful ministers, they have become established as Christians, and by their improved conduct and enriched personalities have commended the gospel of Christ. But even where they have been well instructed prior to baptism and have provided convincing evidence of spiritual regeneration, but for any reason have not been organized into churches and provided with the privileges of worship and fellowship under the care of a functioning ministry, they have not become established in Christian faith and purpose, nor have their conduct and personalities honored the religion they have professed.

We have referred elsewhere to Ringeltaube's grief over the apparent lack of spiritual life in the groups he had baptized during the first years of his ministry in and around Mailady. From his description we conclude that those converts were indeed a very unpromising lot. But Ringeltaube established a church and made provision for regular worship and for the full ministry of the Word and the sacraments. His successors stressed the development of that church and its ministry and gave themselves devotedly and assiduously to its administration. And, as a result, there has developed out of that unpromising material a body of Christians whose character and culture afford a striking contrast to Ringeltaube's description.

Some of the most glowing accounts of conversions, of steadfast witnessing to christ in the face of persecution, of spiritual rebirth and moral transformation in the entire literature of mass movements, are found in the reports of missionaries concerning the beginnings of movements in areas where, to-day, conditions are least encouraging. One inclines to the belief that in some of those areas missionaries found such satisfaction in spectacular instances of early response to their preaching that they neglected and, perhaps, disparaged the continuing aspects of their ministry, such as the building up of the church organization, the enforcement of discipline, instruction, the cultivation of habits of worship and the use of other recurring means of grace.

The Value of Memoriter Work

Many questions have been addressed to us since the study began as to the value of memoriter work in the instruction of candidates for baptism or for admission to the church.

Two values of the memorizing of creedal statements, prayers, selected passages of Scripture, hymns, liturgies, etc., were outstanding in out observations in the several sample areas. These are:

1. The memorizing produces a sense of achievment in the converts' mind, strengthening his self-respect, and in the case of new converts marking their coming to Christ. We often met illiterate villagers who took great pride in their ability to recite passages which to them symbolized, if they did not express, their faith. Sometimes we were told that those same villagers had

at first insisted that they could not learn, and that they had been surprised and delighted to discover that they could learn and recite those passages. Several pastors remarked that in a new group it is nearly Several pastors remarked that in a new group it is nearly always more difficult to get the first man to learn than it is to get the second or any other person of normal intelligence, because the first man is sure he cannot learn and does not want to try. It needs only an example from among them to inspire the others to achievement.

One recent convert in Vidyanagar dramatically exhibited this feeling of pride in achievement when, being asked if he knew the Lord's Prayer, the Apostles' Creed and the Ten Commandments, he knelt and devoutly repeated the prayer, then arose and recited and elaborated the creed and the Commandments. He then told proudly how he was accustomed to expound the creed, the Commandments, the life of Christ, parables, Old Testament stories, and hymns to groups of his neighbours, including the higher castes, who were astonished that he, an illiterate, whom they had considered hopelessly ignorant, could learn so much.

2. The passages help to fix in the minds of those who have learned them a conception or picture of themselves as Christians. The minds of Indian villagers, including the outcastes, are stored with Hindu lore, stories from the Vedas, and couplets from the *Ramayan* of Tulsi Das, or from the works of other poets. The outcastes also carry a burden of memories that recall their status as oppressed, exploited, and despised members of society. They need a lot of assistance if they are to think of themselves as Christians.

A discerning Indian graduate pastor remarked that his most difficult task with new converts was to get Christianity into their subconscious minds, and that he was greatly assisted in this by teaching them to learn many passages and many hymns and to use them constantly in worship.

A trained teacher, who had become interested in psychology

during his two years in college, attempted an analysis of his own reactions. He said that, when in his school, he seldom thought of himself as a Madiga. There were high-caste Hindu students in the classes he taught and they honored him as their teacher. He taught a Bible class and eagerly sought to turn his students toward Jesus Christ as Lord and Saviour. But whenever he returned to his village where his parents, older brothers, uncles and cousins were living, his education, his position as a teacher and a respected man seemed unreal. He began to fear that he would wake up and find that he had been dreaming, that some illiterate high-caste neighbour would kick him, or, with words of abuse, the Bible or prays or goes to some higher-caste Hindu to talk to him of Jesus, and these acts restore his confidence and composure.

In the United Presbyterian Church, in the Pasrur area, lady members of the inquiry staff found that many humble village women knew as many as eight or ten of the Psalms. In talking of their religious experience these women frequently used the language of the Psalms. It was clear that their knowledge of his classic devotional literature was enriching their minds, helping to erase the conception of themselves as despised Chuhras and to substitute one of themselves as Christians.

The Lutherans in Guntur and Chota Nagpur and the Church of India in Vidyanagar make large use of liturgies, and many illiterate members have learned them so well that they are able to make the required responses without hesitation. In several other areas also we found a definite tendency toward a liturgical form of service. Pastors who have had years of experience of services consisting only of the singing of hymns, extemporaneous prayer by the pastor or by members of the congregation, a sermon and the benediction are now including the repetition of the Lord's Prayer and the Apostles' Greed by the congregation. Pastors who have previously included the Lord's prayer and the Apostles Greed are adding the Beatitudes, the twenty-third Psalm, or other selected Scripture passages, collects or pastoral prayers with responses by the congregation.

We nowhere found an encouraging situation where the process of storing the minds of converts with distinctive Christian material had not gone at least as far as the teaching of the Lord's prayer and a number of Christian hymns. And we nowhere found a very discouraging situation where congregations were accustomed to frequent worship. The best records of church attendance are in the areas where the congregations participate most actively in the services, and the poorest attendance records are in the areas where the congregations are given the least part in the services.

A great deal of energy has apparently been wasted in some areas by teaching the Lord's Prayer and the Apostles' Creed to candidates for baptism and church membership and then allowing them to forget both. During the filling of the household schedules a good many men and women told us that they had learned both, but did not remember them. In one village of thirty-six families the only men or women who knew the Lord's Prayer were the headman, two women, four recently baptized men, and three youths who had attended a Christian school. Every other adult in those families had learned both the Prayer and the Creed and had forgotten them because they were not used as instruments of worship.

Memoriter Instruction Insufficient

Much that needs to be taught to every group of professing Christians cannot be accomplished through memoriter work. The phraseology of the creeds is not always understood. In the examination of women in the Pasrur area it was discovered that a number who were able to recite the Apostles' Creed could not answer elementary questions about the birth, life, ministry, teaching, death, or resurrection of Jesus. Two women who knew the Lord's Prayer, the Apostles' Creed, the Ten Commandments and several psalms answered "Yes" to a question as to whether a Christian man, already married, ought to contract a bigamous marriage with the widow of a deceased brother.

Where group decision brings a number of families to confess faith in Christ the obligation is heavy upon the administrators of the church to emphasize the personal as well as the group aspects of religion. Group action is not a substitute for personal acceptance of Jesus Christ, but may prepare the way for it and support it. Yet an administration, not alert to the danger of neglecting the essence of religion in its enthusiasm for its forms, may allow groups to enter the church without knowledge of the necessity for an individual appropriation of the benefits of Christ's suffering and death. On the whole, our study was reassuring about personal religion in the mass movement.

We were often reminded, however, of the need for the constant heralding of the call of christ to the individual, especially for its clear presentation to men and women about to embrace Christianity after having lived under a regime of caste control. One of the most successful ministers in the Vidyanagar area said that in the mass movements caste solidarity brings many people to the church for instruction, but that if the preacher does his work faithfully, every man and woman will be led to such a personal experience of God in Jesus Christ that his caste associates cannot take him back to Hinduism or to animism. This is an overstatement of the preacher's powers, for no preacher, however faithful, can insulate a member of his church against temptation or insure that he will not yield to it; but it express a commendable aspiration of which there is happily much evidence in the ministry in each of the selected areas.

Post-Baptism Responsibility Greater Than Pre-Baptism

The chief responsibility of an ecclesiastical administration for any group of converts is encountered not before their baptism but after. The pre-baptism responsibility lasts for a short time only: no church or mission, so far as we discovered, ordinarily withholds baptism from active candidates longer than a year. In the Vidyanagar area we found that enrolled inquirers who do not show sufficient interest to learn, or who do not meet the requirements for attendance at public worship and for contributing according to their means, or whose conduct is considered objectionable, are formally dropped from the rolls.

Something of the same sort happens in other areas, but we mention Vidyanagar because it is the best example of a unified and centrally controlled procedure. But the post-baptism responsibility ordinarily continues through the convert's life and passes on to the lives of his children and his children's children.

The mission or church that encourages a group of people to embrace Christianity accepts a definite and heavy responsibility. It is not in the position of the professional evangelist in Western countries who conducts a "revival" or "mission" and at its conclusion departs, feeling that his work is done. To some readers this fact may seem so obvious as to make its statement unnecessary, but examination of the record makes us feel that many ministers have very inadequately realized its truth. Not many have taken the attitude of an independent "Pentecostal" missionary who said his responsibility was to get people converted and baptized with the Holy Ghost and that he could then leave them without concern and give his time to others. But many have failed to comprehend that the amount and quality of care given to a group of converts after their baptism is a major element in determining not only what they are to become, but whether others are to be won to Christ by the demonstration of his power in them or are to be kept away from Christ by their failure.

Newly converted groups have been left without the close attention they have needed while their ministers were pushing into new territory and and urging other groups to accept Christ. For example, we find a district superintendent, with a staff which he confesses to be inadequate to care for those already on the rolls, placing a third of that staff in new territory because of calls from new groups for instruction. And we learn of a pastor, with more than three hundred recent converts under his care in seventeen villages, doubling the areas of his pastorate by baptizing six new groups in villages from eight to twelve miles distant. During that year, in which he reported contributions for the church from his baptized community that averaged less than two annas perfamily, he received no one into full membership in the church, and all marriages of Christians within his pastorate were performed by non-Christian rites. Yet he and his missionary district superintendent wrote enthusisastic reports on the year's work, based on the number of converts baptized and the expectation of a further large increase in the near future.

When mass movements develop, baptizing new converts is easier and more attractive work than ministering to a group already baptized, helping them through their difficulties, administering discipline, and cultivating within them the characteristics of godly people. Unless the responsible administrators of the church persistently emphasize the more difficult and less spectacular work, it will be neglected. The most disturbing thought suggested by the data in several areas is that the present ministerial personnel have been so generally engaged in trying to win new converts, and has so long neglected the more exacting task of training and developing their baptized community, that they are poorly equipped for a work that is imperatively needed and has become extremely difficult.

The Immediate Task After Baptism

Probably the most critical month with most mass-movement groups is that immediately following baptism. Successful pastors and superintendents told us that they can do more to establish Christian worship and standards of conduct in that month than in any subsequent year, and that if the opportunity is not seized then, the task becomes increasingly difficult the longer it is neglected.

The immediate task after baptism includes the organization of the church, the inauguration or regular services of worship, the choice of leaders and the beginning of their training, and at least the first steps toward determining the relation of the converts to their caste associates, their other neighbours, and to many institutions and customs of the village. Critical situations develop frequently and rapidly in the days immediately following the baptism of a new group, especially in a village where there have previously been no Christians. Some form of persecution is almost invariably experienced. The group need the help that comes from fellowship in worship and from the presence and ministry of a pastor. If, when persecution comes, they gather for worship, a good start is made toward the establishment of worship as a force in their lives. A pastor can do more to teach his people to meet persecution with courage and patience and abstain from the desire for vengeance if he is with them then, than by many efforts at other times. When the first marriage is to be celebrated in the group after their baptism the pastor, by helping them to resist the demand of unconverted relatives and caste-fellows that the old idolatrous rites and coarse revelries be used, can do more to insure the establishment of Christian marriage customs than he can later by much more effort. The first in all of these and many more cases is a very critical one.

Early in their new life as Christians most converts face demands that they participate in idolatrous rites of one kind or another. In the Telugu country the outcastes have had a distinctive part in idoltrous community rites employed in times of epidemic to appease evil spirits and keep disease away from the village. Serious disturbances have arisen when the outcastes, having been converted, have refused to perform their allotted functions in these rites. Prior to conversion these sacrificial functions carried the mark of privilege or distinction for outcastes in their village communities. Says Bishop Whitehead:

> It is something to be proud of that, when the terrible calamity of cholera or smallpox threatens the life of the village, the calamity cannot be averted without their help. If they cannot feel that they are respected, the next best thing is to feel that in times of trouble they are needed.

Occasionally groups have decided that all except one family should become Christians, leaving that family to placate their Hindu neighbours when these issues shall arise. A Baptist pastor told us of one such family in a village he served. They attended church, sent their children to school, contributed to the pastors' support, and even wished to have their children married by Christian rites, but refused to be baptized because they had agreed to meet the demand of the Hindus that a Madiga play his traditional role in their occasional idolatrous community rites. The agreement of the group that this family should pursue that course compromised their position as Christians. To avert that situation, and yet prevent an outbreak of ill feeling against the converts, is a task requiring great resources of tact and firmness. Many pastors have dealt with its successfully.

The test comes to many groups or to separate families within groups in connection with sorcery. In case of illness in the convert's home it will be suggested that the sorcerer be called. Non-Christian neighbours often intervene at such times to urge compliance with this suggestion. The pressure becomes terrific. If thc pastor is not present to strengthen resistance, the family, even the whole group, is likely to yield. If the group does not acutally sanction the action, its members may at least be afraid to take the responsibility for advising noncompliance. The presence of a capable pastor or pastor's assistant is almost essential if sorcery is to be overcome in this situation.

Yet another kind of testing comes in the visit of the *bhagat*, the *pir*, the *sadhu*, or other non-Christian religious advisers of the group of some one or more families in the group. One of the chief obstacles to the development of a distinctive christian character in many of these mass-movement groups is the continued influence of these men. In one backward group of professing Christians in the Ghaziabad area we were given an estimate that these non-Christian religious professionals collect from the people in a year twice as much as is given for the support of the church. In another village in the same area one of these men came while we were conducting our survey, and succeeded in holding the heads of two families so that we could not get their attention long enough to fill out their schedules. The Christian *Chowdhri* of that village gold us that the pastor visits the village about once in three months, but that some one of these non-Christian advisers comes every month. This results in a divided allegiance, a kind of dual religious life, which inhibits spiritual growth. Rarely was this situation discovered where pastors reside, and it was most common in villages distant from the pastor's residence.

Christian Marriage Rites and Problems

The subject of marriage presents a complicated and challenging problem to church administration. While Christian marriage customs have been established in all areas studied, except Vikarabad and the three areas in the United Provinces, no church administration has reason to feel entirely satisfied with the existing situation. The marriage services in use do not appeal to rural Christians.

The Bishop of Dornakal tells of a group of Sudra inquirers who came to Dornakal to be baptized. They were very eager to learn. They broke caste and ate food prepared by outcastes. They were prepared to abandon customs regarded as inimical to Christian life or character, but they were uneasy about the marriage service. The bishop explains their reason:

> It is so cold and much too short. Their own marriage ceremonies last about a week and are full of significant symbolism. A twenty-minute service with strange, meaningless ritual was a real stumbling-block. However, it was explained to them that this could easily be altered. A form of marriage service was hastily sketched out which would last at least two hours, and which fairly satisfied them.

Despite the law of the Government of India prohibiting child marriage this evil custom is still prevalent and many Christian children are being married by non-Christian rites. Pastors in the United Provinces and three missionaries in the Nizam's dominions assured us that this was the chief obstacle to establishing Christian marriage. They should be encouraged by the success achieved in other areas. They were afraid that marriages of children below the legal age were being performed by Christian rites in the areas reporting general acceptance of Christian marriage. We have no reason to believe that their fears are well founded. The law fixes the minimum ages as fourteen for girls and sixteen for boys. Our household schedules, in the areas where Christian marriages are generally used, show many Christian boys and girls about those ages in village homes unmarried, and none below those ages married. On the other hand, in the United Provinces some girls as young as ten years, in homes that have been nominally Christian for a generation are shown as married.

Where success has been achieved it has required the close and unremitting effort of administrative officers. The resident pastor and the central officers of the church and mission have united in giving attention to the problem. Loose administration of the sort prevailing in those areas where the Christian community has exceeded the strength of the ministerial staff has nowhere succeeded in solving this problem.

The Christian Rite of Burial

The disposal of the dead has always been recognized as a legitimate concern of religion. Hindus and animists have performed religious rites in connection with it. One of the continuing tasks of the pastorate is to provide a Christian service at the grave or the cremation ground and a comforting and instructional ministry to bereaved relatives and friends. Where the church has been well established a Christian service in connection with the disposal of the dead is almost invariably held. In the scattered Christian communities of the United Provinces the pastors often do not hear of deaths among their people until weeks have passed. Obviously, this service cannot be rendered, except in isolated cases, where one pastor is trying to care for groups of Christians in fifty-two villages, as in Etah, or in seventy or more villages, as in many Methodist Episcopal parishes in the United Provinces.

In the autonomous Lutheran Church in Chota Nagpur (Govindpur area) a very popular memorial service is held in the cemeteries at sunrise on easter morning. The mounds over the graves are repaired and whitewashed a few days before Easter. To see lights approaching the cemetery in the darkness preceding daybreak, as groups come across the fields from surrounding villages, and to join in the richly symbolistic service of the Lutherans as they rejoice in the Christian hope of resurrection and immortality, is a memorable experience. The service means a great deal to the Lutherans who have come out of the great mass movement of aboriginal tribesmen in that area. The Anglicans in Ranchi have been so much impressed by the good influence of that service that they have adopted it. Pastors and laymen were unanimous in telling us that the service has helped both in fixing the custom of holding a Christian burial service and in strengthening the will to live worthily as Christians.

The Pastor's Relation to Children of Christian Families

The pastor's relation to the children of Christians presents one of his greatest privileges and a major responsibility. An analysis of Christian attainments shows that those heads of families who were born in Christian homes have, on the whole, reached higher levels than those who have been converted from Hinduism or animism. But in most areas the superiority is not so marked as one might reasonably expect. In the discharge of this responsibility also pastors in the United Provinces are severely handicapped by the wide territorial distribution of Christian families. A large majority of the children are deprived of all school privileges, including the Sunday school, and receive no definite religious instruction except as they share with the adults or some other Christian worker in the service of the pastor on his infrequent visits to their village.

Where Christian schools are maintained the situation is radically different, as the teacher gives much of his time to the children.

The Sacrament of the Lord's Supper

We were much impressed by the testimony of pastors and superintendents in the Vidyanagar and Govindpur areas as to the helpfulness of the frequent celebration of the sacrament of the lord's Supper, and also by the appreciation of that sacrament shown by many humble village men and women. The apparent dearth of spiritual life in areas where Christians have never participated in the Holy Communion, and the richness of that life in areas where the Communion service is a prominent part of the church program, present a contrast which compels recognition. In the Vidyanagar Deanery the pastor celebrates the sacrament of the Lord's Supper in every village at least once a month, and we were told both by him and by simple village laymen that it often leads to penitence, confession, reconciliation, and other good results.

The Administration of Discipline

The several areas provide weighty evidence of the value of church discipline firmly and sympathetically administered. This value is proved positively by the good results that have followed the administration of discipline, and negatively by the bad results from its neglect. We found that the pastor's influence is strong only where he has regularly admonished casual offenders against the law of the church and has brought persistent offenders before church courts, that it is weak where he has condoned defiance of church laws by ignoring it. Church membership is little esteemed where it is conferred easily, is not withdrawn from evildoers, and signifies nothing as to either character or reputation; but it is highly prized where conditions of admission are enforced, where it is withdrawn from violators of church law and signifies good standing as a Christian.

Under a regime that enforces discipline we find all Christian marriages solemnized by Christian rites. Under a regime in which discipline has been allowed to decay we find an elder of the church inviting pastors and even missionaries to a double wedding in which one of his children is married by Christian rites in the church and another is married by Hindu rites at the home. The pastor and the missionaries are hurt and humiliated, but the elder is not excommunicated, no expelled, nor even removed from his office in the church. Where discipline is enforced we find men who have been excommunicated coming in penitence to ask forgiveness and read mission to fellowship; but where it is ignored we find pastors convinced that they are powerless to act effectively against even such offenses as a polygamous marriage by a full member of the church. In the Dornakal diocese, in a Christian community of approximately 175,000 people, about 500 offenders are annually brought under discipline.

The importance of the first test requires emphasis. Rural India pays generous tribute to precedent. A first offense unchallenged sets a standard; a second unpunished establishes a custom. A Lutheran pastor told us that he prepared a group for baptism and impressed upon them the wrong of drunkenness. Unknown to him the professing Christian brother of one of his teachers twice got drunk in the village during the period when he was training the new converts. A few days after the baptismal service the entire group got drunk. He lectured them and urged them not to repeat the offense. Hardly a week passed before many of them got drunk again. When he threatened disciplinary action, they appeared to be surprised, and said frankly they understood that the rule would not be enforced, and that the wrong of drunkenness was not serious since he had taken no action against the brother of the teacher.

But we are told that discipline cannot be effectively enforced within a group unless it is made to appear reasonable to the group. They must not regard it as unfair. Though the pastor may initiate it the support of the group must be won or it will have little value. For this reason it has been found advisable to establish courts of discipline on the model of the *Panchayat,* an historic Indian institution composed of the recognized leaders of the group, which from ancient times has unofficially governed each village. In Hinduism there are caste and village panchayats. It is thus in the Indian tradition to have a Christian panchayat whose members will generally respond to the advice of a pastor or a superintending minister if it regards him as their leader. Some of the most experienced pastors, district superintendents, supervising missionaries, etc., told us that they had never known a panchayat to make a perverse decision.

The panchayats do not always correspond to the officiary of

the church. It has been found advisable sometimes to elect young men as church officials, because they are better qualified to discharge such duties as keeping records, collecting money and attending conferences.

The young missionary suffers peculiar disadvantages when he undertakes to administer discipline. So does the young Indian minister, especially when recruited from another area and not established in the confidence of the people he serves. Frequent changes in pastors, district superintendents, or other supervising ministers interfere with the administration of discipline.

The community sometimes desires to enforce rules which cannot be incorporated in the laws of the church. Experience shows that interference with such desires should be reduced to the minimum consistent with the well-being of the church.

Discipline is seriously complicated by interchurch competition. A Roman Catholic priest told the writer that discipline is made virtually impossible in his church by the readiness of Protestant clergymen to receive any of his people who are placed under discipline. The same charge was made against the Roman Church by Protestant ministers in five of the ten sample areas.

Supervision

Mass movements present a crystal-clear case for a strong supervising ministerial staff and a unified program. Pastors working under the conditions prevailing in the villages where their people life suffer serious loss of morale and disintegration of purpose if left to their own resources for planning their program and managing their work. Except in rare cases, the clergy recruited from the people and closely associted with them are not sufficiently educated or gifted to devise adequate programs and carry them through effectively. The Dornakal Diocese and the British Methodist Mission in the Nizam's dominions present imposing illustrations of the value of centrally planned and controlled programs in which the entire rural ministerial and teaching staffs are enlisted and ably led. While rugged individualism is not encouraged by this system of regimentation, scope is provided for initiative, and personality is not impaired. These church units have been fortunate in their leadership. Perhaps under other leaders these systems might not have worked so well.

The Autonomous Lutheran Church in Chota Nagpur presents another illustration of a unified program operated by a ministerial and teaching staff integrated in a common purpose, though there are indications that this unity of purpose and program, built up by the German missionaries in pre-war days, may be threatened by divisive forces now operating. Competition with the Church of India (Anglican), and a struggle over the position of the missionaries who have returned after an interval of a number of years, have weakened the integration of the staff.

In striking contrast to the effective ministry of pastors who are co-operating happily in a centrally planned, well-co-ordinated and supervised program are the many discouraged and inefficient pastors who have been left to develop their own programs locally, and have been unable to do so successfully.

Every church with which we came into touch in our ten areas has evolved some type of centralized administration with a supervising and directing ministry. In all nonepiscopal churches there is a strong trend toward episcopacy. While objection is made in some quarters to the use of the term, it is clear that an episcopacy, admitted or disguised, has been established in every church that came under investigation in this study. The British Methodist and london Mission groups, both nominally nonepiscopal, are represented in the well-advanced negotiations for a United Church in South India, that will be frankly episcopal, while seeking to incorporate elements of the congregational and presbyterian polities. The London Mission, while interdenominational, has, in the main, represented the Congregational Churches of Great Britain. Presbyterian bodies, already joined with other bodies in the South India United Church, are sharing in the proposed larger union that will openly accept the episcopacy. The Baptists, studied in the Cumbum area, have divided episcopal powers between the mission superintendent of the district and the pastor of a central church. Reporting to the Andhra Christian Council on the Cumbum area study, the Rev. A.R. Fishman, mission superintendent for the district, says:

> The organized church in the station (Cumbum town) supports a pastor who comes about as near to being a superintendent of district work as Baptist traditions and personal jealousies of the community will permit. The whole area is administered as one church, the churches listed as organized not having functioned as such for some time...For any of the virtues of the situation (throughout the district) credit is due to the late Dr. Newcomb and Mrs. Newcomb. During their forty years of service they developed the fine-spirit of personal loyalty and family-like solidarity which is one of the best fruits of the paternalistic system.

Under the paternalistic system, thus acknowledged, it is observed that very large episcopal powers have accrued to the missionary superintendent.

The types of superintendency evolved in the several areas are endowed with different powers and are operating under different restrictions, arising from regulations, traditions, and personal characteristics.

In the Methodist Episcopal Church the episcopal areas are so large and include such a variety of situations that unified programs have not been found practicable, and the bishops are unable to give close personal supervision in local situations. Episcopal powers are deputed to district superintendents, not all of whom possess the qualities of training, personality, and experience necessary to unify their associates in the construction and successful operation of an adequate ministerial and ecclesiastical program.

One of the great advantages enjoyed by the churches of the Dornakal Diocese has been that the compactness of the diocese, the similarity of the fundamental issues dealt with in all its component parts, the employment of a single vernacular, and the location of the bishop's residence have enabled him to keep in close touch with the situation at all times. So well are these advantages recognized that the Church of India has recently established a new diocese centering in Amritsar to render a comparable service to its Punjab mass-movement areas, and efforts are being made to establish a diocese in the western districts of the United Provinces. It has been found that bishops residing in Lahore and Allahabad, burdened with a vast variety of interests, could not provide the close supervision necessary for effective administration in the complicated conditions that prevail in mass-movement churches emerging in distant parts of their dioceses.

Not least among the needs of the pastors and their assistants for supervision is attention to their own spiritual needs. The bishop or the superintending minister, by whatever title he is known, has no more necessary function than to be the preacher's pastor. A number of pastors spoke to us in very appreciative terms of the spiritual help they have received from association with their superintendents; and two pastors, while declaring their loyalty to their superintendents, did not disguise their disappointment that on tours, and in conferences with the clergy, those leaders did not devote more time to the ministry of the Word and the sacraments and less time to methods and reports. One of the pastors said: "I wish my superintendent would be less my officer and more my priest. I need a *guru* and a confessor even more than I need a superintendent and a paymaster". Thus expressed, the sentiment is at least in the Hindu tradition.

A notable development of the ministry to the clergy in several areas in recent years has been the holding of Retreats, devoted entirely to the deepening of the spiritual life through study and worship. Another development has been Refresher Courses, combining the purpose of the Retreat with that of the training school.

Several experienced superintendents have spoken of the difficulties occasioned by the practice of combining in one office the supervision of the churches and of the clergy, the ministry to the clergy and the management of finance. The ministry of the bishops has been relieved of the handling of funds, but many superintendents who discharge certain functions of the episcopacy are laboring under the handicap of personally administering financial affairs. The Kistna Church Council, of the Church Missionary Society field in the Dornakal Diocese, administers finances through a treasurer, who receives and disburses funds under orders from the Council and its committees.

The Religious Education of the Church

Under this head we shall mention some of the methods found in use in the selected areas, or reported in other areas, some of which were visited but less thoroughly studied. It should not be supposed that only these methods are being used, or that any of them are in use only in the areas mentioned.

In the Dornakal Diocese lessons are prescribed for each Sunday and week-day service. Suggestions for sermons are made. Pastors and teachers, who, as previously mentioned, are doing much pastoral work, read the prescribed lessons and base their sermons upon them. All adults and children above eight or ten years of age are expected to attend these services and from eighty to eighty-five pér cent of them do so every evening. This results in one of the most effective programs of religious education for an entire area that we have found during the study.

The church calendar is used in the Lutheran and Church of India areas to insure the annual presentation to all congregations of such great themes as the birth of Christ, the crucifixion, the resurrection, the ascension and pentecost.

A syllabus of lessons to be taught during the year, one for each week, has been used with good results in the British Methodist Mission in the Nizam's Dominions and in the Ceylon and India General Mission in the Telugu field. The syllabus of the latter mission has included a Scripture verse each week and a new lyric each month.

Singing bands have proved valuable in the Methodist Episcopal Church in Gujerat. Young men have been organized and trained to sing many Christian lyrics and to accompany them on indigenous musical instruments. They have traveled to other villages and given programs attended by Christians and non-Christians. In the American Baptist and American Lutheran areas in the Telugu country short-term schools of Indian music have been conducted in which preachers and teachers have been trained for leadership of similar singing bands. *Kalakshepams,* in which the gospel has been presented in song and story, have been extensively used in South India. The effect of these singing bands upon those who participate is described as even more valuable than their excellent influence upon Christian and non-Christian audiences.

In view of what has been said about the lack of traditional color and drama in the life of Indian converts from a religion which is rich in such things, it is encouraging to know that efforts are being made to invest the lives of these converts with their indigenous folk atmosphere. A happy example is found in the songs for special occasions, as for use by women in transplanting rice, by men and women in the harvest, by households at sunrise and at sunset, reported from several areas. They are prepared for use with tunes used by Hindus at these times and are said to be popular.

Action songs on parables and miracles of Jesus are extensively used in the British Methodist Church in the Nizam's Dominions. many have been composed by Bible women and taught to the Christian women of their villages, who sing and act them at gatherings of Christians and non-Christians, especially at weekly gatherings of women. Some of these action songs have been expanded into dramas in which a dozen or more women participate.

In the Dornakal Diocese a number of dramas prepared by

order of the diocesan Council have been extensively used. Christian congregations have taken great interest in preparing them for presentation in their villages. Non-Christians have attended and been deeply moved. One of these dramas deals with the prophet Amos. The bishop found that many simple villagers in his congregations, after participating in this drama, could pass an examination on the book of Amos more creditably than most students in the ministerial training school. Another drama, *The Queen of Sheba,* has a powerful evangelistic influence, and is so popular that non-Christian landowners have paid to have it performed for their friends. One of them is quoted as saying that it made every Hindu in his village want to be a Christian. Dr. Mott Kieslar, Methodist Episcopal district superintendent at Lahore, has used a drama on the life of Christ with impressive results. Thousands have attended its presentation. Thorough preparation, attitudes of reverence in all participants, and avoidance of the direct representation of the Christ, are mentioned by Doctor Kieslar as essential to success, and he warns us that hasty preparation, or the participation of men and women who have not entered into the enterprise in a reverent spirit, may turn the sacred venture into a burlesque.

The Sunday school is used in every area. The pastor in a well-organized and graded United Presbyterian Sunday school in the small town of Pasrur has taught a Bible class for *mohalla* men for more than ten years. Thirty-one men were in attendance when we visited the class. Most Sunday schools in the areas studied are attended by children only, and despite the availability of a number of books of lessons and the publication of notes on the British and American International Lessons, many follow no regular course and can be called schools only by courtesy. A Telugu Lutheran pastor assigns the school-teachers and their wives to teach classes of children, while he teaches a class for confirmation.

Women's societies are used effectively in a number of areas. Village women are organized into missionary societies in the United Presbyterian Mission in the Punjab. They raise thousands of rupees annually for supporting a home mission district. Activity in the society has developed the religious experience and character of many members and has led to increased interest in the local church. Through Mothers' Unions, in the Telugu Mission of the Society for the Propagation of the Gospel, it is said women have been taught to pray and to teach their children to pray, and to appreciate the sanctity of Christian marriage, and the necessity of purity in life, thought, and speech. The responsibility of Christian women for presenting the call of Christ to their unconverted neighbors has been effectively combined with instruction in the care of children, sanitation, home economics, and kindred issues. Promotion of these Mothers' Unions is the chief occupation of several lady missionaries.

Boy Scouts in the British Methodist boarding school at Medak have been led into the cleaning up of villages. With the slogan: "A clean heart, a clean home, and a clean villages", these scouts have gone to villages to co-operate with pastors, evangelists, and teachers in community service. The Rev. F. Whittaker describes a visit to a village where an influential landowner had organized and long maintained a severe persecution of Christians:

> The Tiger (the landowner) gave out that we were scavengers in the pay of Government....The outstanding features of the main street of the village were a series of great yawning pits between the houses and the side of the road. Into these pits was thrown all the farm-yard manure, refuse and general rubbish of the neighboring houses. At the center of each was usually a pool of stagnant slime covered with thick, green scum—the breeding place of millions of mosquitoes, not to mention other more deadly carriers of infection. The village had suffered badly in a recent epidemic of cholera.
>
> We saw one standing cesspool, banked up on one side by the kitchen wall and on the other by the masonry of the well which supplied the drinking water for a whole row of

houses. There was the noisome stuff oozing its way into the well.

We set to work on the main street. Every morning we dug channels on the side of the road, filled in a quagmires of mud and filth, leveled up the ruts and cleaned up the village square. Then we hammered at the idea that there is a proper place for everything, even for the most offensive refuse. We pointed out that the right place for manure was not at their front doors but outside the village, beside their cattle sheds. Imagine our sense of triumph when three farmers volunteered with our help to fill in one of the most objectionable pits and move their manure.

This spirit of service is like a breath of new life which blesses him that gives far more than him that takes....Despite all obstruction the leading villagers backed us splendidly in all that we did. Night after night some three hundred or more gathered to witness our entertainments.

On the same tour this group participated in evangelistic and Christian worship services in various villages and helped to welcome into the church several groups of new converts. They visited one village of less than five hundred inhabitants where the entire population, high caste and low, declared their faith in Jesus Christ.

Church building has been found a most serviceable project in religious education in a number of areas. The Dornakal diocese requires of new groups asking to be baptized and received into the Church that they provide a building to be used as a church and a school, with either an adjoining room or a separate house for a school-teacher. This starts the group in their Christian life with a decided advantage over groups that have no fixed place for worship, and also over groups for whom a church is provided from funds contributed by others. It is sometimes found necessary to contribute from Diocesan or Church Council funds an amount sufficient to buy beams for the roof or wood for the windows and doors, while the people erect the building and meet the remaining expenses. Co-operation in the work and in contributing the whole or a share of the financial expenditures proves an excellent preparation for their new life as Christians.

The Christian Endeavor Society, the Epworth League, the Baptist Young People's Union, the Wesley Guild, and kindred societies of young people have proved helpful in some places; but, according to testimony received, have failed in others. A pastor in Travancore said that all of his best official members had been trained in the Christian Endeavor Society, and that members of that society were doing the best evangelistic work in his pastorate.

In the Bidar District of the Methodist Episcopal Church in the Nizam's Dominions *jatros* have been held annually for a number of years with results that are highly appraised. These jatros are a kind of adaptation of the Hindu *mela,* or fair, and the combination therewith of features of the camp meeting prominent in America a generation ago. They are held in out-of-the-way places which provide freedom from the distractions of cities, towns, and villages. Private prayer and meditation, preaching and Bible study are emphasized.

Summer schools for seekers and for the inspiration of recent converts are prominent in the Sudra movements in the British Methodist Church around Medak in the Nizam's Dominions.

Christian pictures to replace those of Hindu gods and goddesses represent a need more than an achievement. Roman Catholics have made pictures available, and they are found on the walls of the poorest Roman Catholic homes. Although objectionable from the standpoint of all churches represented in this study, we found these pictures in some of the homes in every one of the selected areas. They costs from two annas to eight annas each, whereas the Hindu pictures can be brought in the bazaars of almost every town for two pice each or less.

Ten or twelve years ago a series of tracts was issued by the Christian Literature Societies containing Bible stories illustrated with a picture in colors. We found these tracts on the walls of Christian homes in four areas.

7

The Power of Christianity

Introduction

Much has been written about the influence of social patterns upon religious conceptions. The evolution of religion among an isolated people certainly tends to conform to the accepted social pattern. The India of our times provides many examples of that fact; also of its corollary that the penetration of a community, previously isolated, by new social forces powerful enough to modify old social patterns, produces corresponding changes in religious conceptions.

The religion of a large proportion of the present generation of Hindus has conformed to the acceptance of a new social pattern in which *sati* and female infanticide have no part. The writer listened recently to a boy of high-school are read a paper on Hinduism based upon materials that wee two or three generations old. For the times when that lad's grandfather was young, what he read was in its broad outlines substantially true. But the religion he described bore so little resemblance to the religion of the present generation of Hindus that the writer, as he listened, found himself resentful at what was in effect a libel upon a great people whom he has learned to love and respect.

To-day the social pattern of the Hindu masses is being further modified, and corresponding changes in the Hindu religious outlook are evident. The depressed classes are acquiring a higher social and political status, their children are being admitted to government schools, they sit beside the higher castes on the trains and in the motor busses, and the religion of their former oppressors is adjusting itself to the new situation, with the result that they are now being admitted to some Hindu temples which formerly were rigorously closed against them. Women are taking part in public affairs, the result being that Hindu theology and religious practice are being modified. Women are seen as having a religious life and religious needs quite independent of those of their husbands; to take a single example of the reconstruction of religious practice, the time-honored *devadasi* institution, which made prostitution a religious rite linked with the temple is being abandoned.

Some may think that the above statements should be reversed, and that the social changes mentioned should be attributed to the influence of new conceptions in religion. It is true that new religious conceptions have been propagated and have attained a wide currency contemporaneously with new social patterns: in many minds and perhaps in some groups acceptance of the new conceptions in religion has preceded the new social patterns. The two forces have certainly acted and reacted on each other. But it is, we think, clear that changes in accepted social patterns are forcing a reconstruction of Hindu religious thought, even of the assumptions that underlie that thought.

Studious observers of the expansions of religion have also noted changes in social standards and patterns which have followed the acceptance of a new religion. There seems to be a power in Mohammedan religious conceptions that brings to pass radical social changes. This power is abandantly exhibited in India. One notes the changes that are rapidly consummated in the relations of husband and wife and of parents and children when a family of Hindus embraces Mohammedanism, and the wider social changes that ensue when a caste group goes over to Mohammedanism. Of course here, again, religious conceptions and social patterns act and react on each other, and it is not possible to chart the rate of growth or measure the strength of either at any given time. The new convert to Islam associates with people whose social pattern is different from that which has been his; and one cannot say with certainty how much his social pattern would be modified if he were subjected only to the Moslem religious conceptions, and not brought under the influence of the living example of his new confreres in religion.

The Hindu caste system has offered stubborn resistance to some of the teaching of Islam, with the result that Indian Mohammedanism is very different from that of other lands. The doctrine of the brotherhood of all Moslems has not prevented the maintenance of caste by many Indian Moslems. Until 1931 the census of India listed Mohammedan castes exactly as it did Hindu castes, and one discovers with surprise that there are followers of the Prophet who in the census proclaim themselves as Brahmans, and others who boast of their Kshatriya caste. Likewise, there are Mohammedans of the depressed classes against whom even their fellow Mohammedans enforce untouchability. Doubtless the Mohammedans in these matters adjust their religious thinking, by a process or rationalization, to social patterns which they are unwilling to abandon. But this successful resistance to a central teaching of Islam does not dispose of the fact that religious conceptions propagated by Mohammedanism have induced significant changes in social standards and patterns.

There is a like social power in Hinduism. The expansion of Hinduism to animistic tribes has continued for centuries and has been greatly accelerated in recent years. As these tribes have accepted Hindu conceptions they have modified their social patterns. The centrality of the doctrine of *karma* in Hinduism has given it an exceedingly strong power over the mind of its adherents, both new and old. Hindu converts from animistic tribes have been induced by the conception of *karma* to acquiesce in a degraded and oppressive social status. It seems extremely unlikely that social conformity preceded the acceptance of the religious conceptions of Hinduism, since the social position these tribes have been accorded is so low and carries with it so much of economic disadvantage.

Some, at least, of the social changes that follow adherence to these religions seem to be related to worship concepts and programs.

In Mohammedanism the exclusion of women from public worship promotes the withdrawal of women from public appearance. The worship program of Hinduism, with the concentration of priestly functions in the Brahman, alters, if it does not shatter, the traditional tribal organization.

Social Changes with Christian Conversion

Changes in social characteristics and standards and in the whole social pattern are taking place among groups that have embraced Christianity in mass movements. They take place much more rapidly with converts whose old social integration is destroyed by individual conversion. But we are concerned now with the social power of religion in the group. Some of these social changes in mass-movement groups seem to be very closely related to Christian worship. The conception that this is so came independently to various members of our staff as they examined social changes in the several areas of the study.

Beneficial social changes appear to have taken place most generally where Christian worship has been most firmly established, as in Nagercoil, Vidyanagar, Ranchi, and Guntur, and least generally where Christian worship has been least successfully inaugurated, as in Barhan, Etah, Ghaziabad, and Vikarabad. Where these converts have learned to worship God as revealed in Christ and have established habits of worship, they have acquired concepts of God and of themselves in relation to him that have powerfully affected their social standards, their conduct, and, in the course of time, their status in their villages. Worship of the God of Christ by these victims of the Hindu caste system is apparently destructive of the estimate of themselves that Hinduism had given to Malas and Madigas, Chamars and Chuhras. Belief in the love of God for them, enlivened and empowered by their worship, helps to create or to strengthen a sense of their value. Instruction, unless followed by worship, seems to achieve little in that direction. We found in the areas of the United Provinces many members of the Christian groups who had been taught that God is love and loves them, and who could recite John 3.16, but still thought of themselves, as their fathers and ancestors had been taught, as a degraded, worthless people. Many times we heard from them the excuse that they were only Sweepers of Chamars. But in the areas where regular worship has become a feature of group life, we heard extremely little of that sort of thing.

We have referred elsewhere to the psychological reactions of inferiority that have handicapped and afflicted the depressed classes. Centuries of acquiescence in the Hindu assignment to them of menial work, and of degraded social status, have produced in them numerous inhibitions. The *karma* doctrine that their degradation is due to their misconduct in previous lives has strengthened these inhibitions. Thus they have not responded normally to the stimulation of nature and environment. But Christian teaching, followed by active Christian worship, has introduced a new force into their lives strong enough to loosen and in many cases to destroy, those inhibitions and to restore the possibility of normal response to stimulations. As they prey to God with the conviction that he is no respecter of persons, as they praise him for his infinite mercy to them, and as they consider his call to render service in his name to other communities, they find release from the old inhibitions. As these old inhibitions are broken, unsuspected powers are released. They see opportunities and take hold of them with a confidence they had never known before. To members of the survey staff one of the greatest surprises the village inquiry produced was the discovery of the occupational variation that had been achieved by the older groups of Christians, and especially by those that had developed a strong worship program.

In the Nagercoil area the Nadars, who when the Christian movement began among them were confined almost entirely to drawing the juice of the toddy palm, fermenting and selling it, are now entering every kind of work in their villages, and have, indeed, been pioneers in the introduction of new occupations. In the Guntur area Malas and Madigas, formerly restricted respectively to weaving and leather-work, joined with coolie labour, are now engaged in a wide variety of occupations. It would be encouraging if enterance to these new occupations had been made possible by training in mission industrial or vocational schools, but it is even more encouraging to discover that this is not generally the case, for in the main the people have discovered the opportunities and taken advantage of them on their own initiative. The same thing is true in other areas, notably in Govindpur and in Pasrur.

Some of the most significant examples of this new power to recognize and respond to opportunity come from Pasrur, where Christians are found working as tailors, carpenters, masons, gardeners, watch-repairers, gut-makers, and even as potters. Here we discover that while an industrial school, that had been maintained on a level of efficiency reached by few of such institutions, had been trying to prepare Christian boys from the villages to work as tailors and as carpenters, relatively little success had been achieved, but village boy who had never attended the industrial school had begun to do those types of work in their villages, and were making a success of it. Prominent factor in the situation seems to be that boys who have never left the village have been freed from the old inhibitions common to their caste and have not in the process lost their adjustment to any phase of village life, whereas the boys who have gone to the industrial school, while obtaining more thorough training with better equipment than the village affords, have lost their adjustment to village conditions, and were not succeeding in establishing themselves in the villages to practise the trades they had learned:

A Sharing of Privilege

Worship in terms of Christian teaching has given many of these mass-movement converts a desire to share their blessings with their Hindu neighbors. Thus they have acquired a sense of mission, which is having revolutionary effects upon them. This is especially true in the Telugu areas, where we found abundant evidence that the sense of mission is prevailing over the sense of grievance, and results in establishing happy relations between Christians and higher-caste Hindus, and in bringing the latter to the Christian faith.

A typical instance came to our attention in a certain village of the Vidyanagar area. The Malas had been Christians several years, and had discontinued much of their quarreling with their traditional enemies, the Madigas. Under the leadership of the ordained pastor of their circuit and their local teacher and lay pastor they began to hold daily worship services with a program prepared by the bishop of the diocese and his helpers. The Christian Malas came to feel a sense of responsibility for the conversion of the Madigas and began to show a special interest in them, with the result that the Madigas were converted. Then the two groups, worshiping together, began to consider how they could win various groups of Sudras. Their relations with all castes improved, the Yanadis were converted en masse, and members of two other Sudra castes enrolled in classes for instruction and worship preparatory to baptism and admission to the Church. We consulted a representative of yet another Sudra caste and he declared that half of the Sudras of the village were inclined to become Christians and that all had been influenced in a large way by Christianity.

The worship program of various mass-movement groups seems to have contributed to improved relations with their neighbours in another way also. Before their conversion to Christianity the religion of these groups was regarded by both Hindus and Moslems as of an extremely low order. The community judgment is usually rather cynical when the depressed classes are seen becoming Christians. But if, following the change of allegiance, they see the development of a new religious life, characterized by a high order of worship and by marked faithfulness in worship, they are greatly impressed and begin to respect the worshipers. Respect for religious people has always been high in India, and has never been kept within community bounds. Moslem "saints" command the respect, even the veneration of Hindus, and Hindu mendicants believed to be particularly pious and unworldly win the resepct and support of Moslems.

Among the effects upon the worshipers themselves we note that cleanliness and an appreciation of beauty appear to be promoted by the development of Christian worship. We have reported elsewhere the overwhelming testimony of non-Christians that cleanliness has increased in these mass-movement groups following conversion. Such cleanliness is most in evidence—and non-Christian opinion is most united in declaring it—in those areas where Christian worship has been most firmly established. We and our non Christian informers observed it least in the districts of the United Provinces, where the geographical distribution of converts and other factors have prevented the formulation of a successful worship program. The growth of self-respect, the acquirement of belief in a personal God who takes an interest in them, and to whom they offer prayer and praise, and the assembling in church, all seem to contribute to the raising of standards of cleanliness.

The writer vividly recalls a group of Christian Malas in a village of the Vidyanagar area. Forty years ago the Christian movement reached the village and the entire Mola caste joined it. A small building was erected to serve as school and church. The people were desperately poor. Educational progress was slow. But now the majority of men under forty are literate. The standard of the school has been raised to the sixth class. Three teachers are employed and a large proportion of the children are making encouraging progress in their studies. Bricks have been collected for a new church building, much larger and in every way superior to the old.

But the most moving aspect of the picture is of the people assembling for worship. A bell was rung and they came hurrying from the fields and the village. Ten or fifteen minutes later they began emerging from their houses and gathering at the church. Almost without exception they had washed and changed their clothes. The women had oiled and combed their hair in the simple but beautiful style of the Telugus, and a large proportion wore a flower in the hair. Men, women, and children approached the church quietly, but with apparent joy and eagerness. Entering they each knelt for private prayer, then sat on the mat-covered floor in rows; the men and boys on one side and the women and girls on the other. They sang heartily, joined in the responses of the liturgy and seemed, almost with one accord, to be absorbed in the worship of God. It was hard to realize that these attractively clad, clean and neat-looking, orderly worshipers could have developed in forty years from a group of dirty, shiftless, Mala outcastes.

Here and there in nearly all of the areas we found Christian families growing flowers around their homes. We saw no flowers about the homes of non-Christians of the castes from which these mass-movement converts have come. Twenty of the twenty-two first-generation Christian families ho were questioned about their flowers said they had become interested in them after their conversion. One of these men said that when he first planted a few flowers in front of his house prominent Hindus of the village objected, saying that flowers were not for low-caste men like him. He added, however, that no one now objects, and occasionally high-caste Hindus of the village objected, saying that flowers were not for low-caste men like him. He added, however, that no one now objects, and occasionally high caste Hindus ask him for flowers. Many Hindus of the higher castes are lovers of flowers, but the depressed classes have generally been almost completely indifferent to them.

In the older areas some beautiful churches are being built. Their construction speaks eloquently of the rising appreciation of worship and of beauty and the increase of economic strength. One of the noblest of these structures is being erected at Martandam, for off the railway in South Travancore. Much of its cost is being provided from profits on lace made by women in the surrounding villages. The great cathedral of the Wesleyan Methodist Church at Medak, although erected with funds contributed in the main from Great Britain, is having a remarkable influence in stimulating the desire for better places of worship.

In a number of villages in the Nagercoil area the third in a succession of churches has been erected, or is being planned. The early churches have been outgrown both in a physical and in an aesthetic sense. In one of those villages we worshiped with a Sunday-morning congregation of more than four hundred in a commodious, chaste, and worshipful structure, built by the gifts of members of the church without missionary help from abroad. For nineteen years that congregation had contributed for the new church, which took the place of a smaller and cruder building erected forty of fifty years before with the aid of the mission. When the Christian movement began in the neighbourhood one hundred and twenty-five years ago, the humble Nadars and Sambavars had neither the capacity to appreciate, the religious understanding to use, nor the resources to make possible such a structure as their descendants have built, and to which they now so faithfully and joyously resort at every call to worship.

There are many villages in every area where the church building is small, crude, and ugly, and in several areas many of the buildings used for worship are neglected. Moreover, in the areas of the United Provinces very few of the village Christian groups have a church building of any sort, and without a building extremely few have a program of regular congregational worship. In the Ghaziabad area, after a very bad beginning, some success has been achieved in quite recent years in arranging regular services, and this has resulted in awakening a desire for a suitable place for these services. Raised platforms have been constructed in a few villages and set apart for worship. Already the practice of worship is causing attention to be given to the place of worship and some of these raised platforms are being decorated and otherwise improved. When the visit of the pastor to the village is primarily an occasion for discussion, whether the subject be the people's grievances and needs, the pastor's claims for support, or even the teachings of the church, the social effects seem small as compared with those that attend his arrival for a service of united worship. The lofe of beauty, which seems to be so clearly linked with worship in several areas, is not strongly apparent in those areas where worship has been neglected.

Women's Share in The Church

It is impressive also to not that the participation of women in the activities of the church seems to be promoted by the development of regular congregational worship. In the Nagercoil and Govindpur areas, and in the older Christian groups in the Telugu areas, women take part in the church activities no nearly equal terms with men. But in the areas where the worship program has remained weak, women hold back as if afraid. The contrast is revealed in these highly typical incidents:

(1) In a village in the Negercoil area, after the Sunday-evening service, the writer accompanied the pastor to the adjacent school building to attend a meeting of the Christian Endeavour Society. The leader was a young woman, nineteen years of age. She had never been out of the village for school, but conducted that public meeting without a trace of embarrassment. Thirty-six people were present—seventeen young men and nineteen young women; and four young men and five young women discussed the topic of the evening.

(2) In a village of the Ghaziabad area, although notice of our coming had been sent in advance, and the pastor and his unordained assistant had preceded us to the village to make arrangements, we were able to get only four women from the sixteen Christian families to attend the service with which we were to introduce our inquiry. The men were practically all there, but, although the group had been nominal Christians for twenty years, the women kept up the old pre-Christian attitude of aloofness.

Where regular worship has become established the women are as faithful in attendance and take part almost as freely as the men. But where that has not taken place the women gain little from the service of the pastor; they hold back from the visiting and discussion, unless, as is not often the case in most villages, he is accompanied by his wife or a lady missionary. In the Ghaziabad area, which we take as an example of small success in establishing regular worship, we found that only twenty-three women in a total of 328 families had ever taken the holy communion, and only eight of them had communed within a year, whereas in the Guntur area, where regular worship has been firmly established, in a total of 627 families 535 women had communed, 327 of them within a year. In Ghaziabad five times as many men had communed as women, but in Guntur the figures were practically even.

Parents with regular and prolonged worship experience more regularly send their children to school. It seems that having accepted one Christian institution, and having by experience learned of its values, they are more ready to try another. Perhaps also the experience of worship strengthens their hope for a better, richer life for their children. Whatever the explanation, the figures show that where Christian worship has become an established force in a village group the Christian school is attended by the children from Christian homes; it is not so in those villages where worship has not been well-established.

Closely linked with the above is the issue of child-marriage. In the areas where a strong worship program has been established we learned of few instances of children being married under the legal age. In the other areas we found that the parents are still in large numbers getting their children married below the age set by the law of the land and of the Church, and by non-Christian rites.

Where the membership of a local congregation has been converted in a mass movement the development of a rounded church program, including congregational worship, is much easier than where it is composed of converts that have not been socially integrated, and, accordingly, possess no experience of working together. So far as we have been able to learn, only in mass-movement areas are congregations holding services every evening of the year. Nowhere else in India do we find such a high proportion of Christian families contributing to the support of the Church as in the best of the mass-movement areas, and nowhere else is the level of contributions so high in proportion to income. We are, of course; not including in these comparisons congregations composed almost entirely, as some are, of mission employees, who by deductions made from their pay, or by tithing in response to urging by their paymasters, maintain high average contributions.

The Evils of Westernization

Social changes that are promoted by Christian worship are more prominent in the mass-movement groups than are other changes often associated in India with Christianity. The charge is commonly made that Christian converts are subject to forces that denationalize and Westernize. Westernization has made little progress among mass-movement converts except as they have left the villages and mingled with others in the cites. How seriously Westernization can be mistaken for Christianity, and is being so mistaken, is illustrated by the following incident: A young Rajput and his wife came to a missionary in Bihar saying they had decided to become Christians and would like to be baptized. Asked what had led them to desire to become Christians, the young woman with naive frankness replied that they had three reasons: (1) That they might eat together at a table rather than separately as their relatives insisted; (2) That they might eat chicken, of which he had become found while on war service over-seas; (3) That they might drink whisky. To them, whatever else Christianity might stand for, it meant freedom from three restrictions that they had found irksome in Hinduism.

There is no doubt that the identification of Christianity with certain "Western" indulgences and social standards has been made by many tens of thousands of India's people, nor is there any doubt that while commending itself to many as it did to the young Rajput couple, it has caused very large numbers to repel the appeals of Christianity. A prominent Hindu political leader told the writer that he three times set the date for his baptism, and each time changed his mind because of the thought of the influence that would likely be exercised upon his children by the nominal Christians of the city in which he lived, to whose conduct he objected. He recognized that what he complained about was not Christianity, but feared that it had become so intrenched in the Christian community that he could not take himself and his family into that community without danger to ideals that he wished to maintain for himself and his family.

In the most successful of the mass-movement areas there is evolving an Indian Christian culture that is throughly Indian and distinctively Christian, with a minimum of the kinds of Western influence that offend Indian standards of good taste, ethics, and pure religion.

8

The Influence of Christianity Upon Economic Conditions of Women

Introduction

The term "Christianity" is susceptible of an almost infinite number of interpretations. It probably does not convey exactly the same meaning at any time to two individuals, nor to the same individual on any two occasions. It is a term to which life is constantly giving new meanings and from which it often takes old meanings. Each person's understanding of it is compounded of many unstable elements.

In this chapter we are not concerned with a critical definition of what constitutes Christianity. We have to report observations upon groups of men and women who have been offered and have accepted widely divergent conceptions of the Person, the ministry, and the teachings of Jesus, who worship God in a variety of forms, who hold conflicting theories of the Church and its ministry, and who could not agree on what is the christian message for the world in these times.

It is not necessary for us to pass judgment on any of these conflicting conceptions or practices, for we shall, for the purpose of this chapter, endow the term "Christianity" with a meaning wide enough to comprehend them all. The term will represent the sum total of forces operating in, through, or in association with, the christian movement; although some of those forces are certainly not distinctively Christian, and some may even be in some particulars out of harmony with the life, character, and teachings of Jesus. It will include creedal instruction, the Church as an institution, its ministry and worship; the Bible and "Christian" literature; the Christian school, its teaching and supervising staff; organizations subsidiary to the Church, such as the Sunday school, young people's societies, and mothers' unions; and service of every kind performed, instigated or inspired by the Church or mission or the representatives of either.

We shall not attempt to apportion credit or blame for economic influences, traced to Christianity thus defined, between forces which are and forces which are not distinctively Christian, nor, indeed, to suggest what forces belong to each of those categories. The influence of a school or of a co-operative society maintained by a church or a mission, or by representatives of either, is, within the meaning of the term as used here, a part of the influence of Christianity.

However, practical considerations compel the placing of one limitation upon the comprehensiveness suggested. It is not possible to isolate Christian elements, either, real or nominal, in such agencies as Government or trade and to appraise their influence. Many Government officials, and some representatives of other agencies such as trade, for example, are members of Christian churches and supporters of missions. the service of some of these men and women has strongly influenced the economic conditions of mass-movement converts, as it has that of other groups, both Christian and non-Christian; but no effort has been made to trace such influence in our household and village inquiries and it will not be considered in our treatment of the subject.

Benefits to India as a Whole

Christian missions have added to the wealth of India by the large sums of money which they have imported from foreign lands. these amounts have been net additions to the national wealth, for they have not been paid for by exports of any kind. They have been used to support Indian ministers, school teachers, clerks, etc., as well as missionaries from the contributing countries; to erect buildings which have given temporary employment to thousands and to maintain schools, hospitals, and other social institutions. The sum of these gifts to India during the present century alone has been large enough to make a measurable difference in the average family income throughout the nation.

The monetary contribution of Christian missions to India's economic life has probably been exceeded by the monetary value of contributions made in service. Thousands of able men and women, Indian and foreign, have served India in the Christian movement at less than commercial rates of pay. Every aspect of national welfare has been promoted by this service and the economic life has largely benefited. To have paid for this service at Governmental rates out of the public treasury would have added largely to the tax burdens of the nation. The economic value of education received in mission schools, of life saved or health restored in mission hospitals, of spirits revived or minds refreshed by visits of catechists or Bible women, cannot be computed. Hundreds of thousands of men and women who do not profess the Christian religion bear grateful witness to help of the above types received from Christian institutions or individuals.

Christian Influence Upon Depressed Class Groups

The foregoing is but introductory to our primary purpose, which is to consider the influence of Christianity upon the economic condition of families that have participated in Christian mass movements.

Because critics of missions have often attributed the spread of Christianity among the depressed classes to the desire for material gain, missionaries seem to have been reluctant to discuss the economic consequences, or concomitants, of conversion. There seems to have been widespread fear that the declaration that converts or their descendants have derived material gain might give the critics a weapon with which to strengthen their attack, or might induce poor people to profess Christianity for the sake of economic improvement.

That economic benefits have come to many participants in

Christian mass movements as a result of conversion is, in the light of this study, indisputably clear. That is not a fact that need be hidden or discussed in whispers. Considering how Jesus tried to meet the needs of the poor, healing their diseases and other afflictions, and feeding the hungry, it would seem that the Church has no reason to apologize if its ministry to the poor reduces hunger and disease among them. Jesus let it be known that in some places he could do no mighty works because of the unbelief of the people, and if the mighty works of the Church have occurred among those who have believed in Jesus, this is not surprising.

Economic improvement is not an unnatural consequence of the application of the teachings of Jesus to the depressed classes and other poor groups in India. Moral improvement, education, increase of self-respect, elevation of the status of women and escape from social thralldom are recognized as legitimate aims and natural results of missionary endeavour. All of them contribute to the betterment of economic conditions.

Benefits Not Immediately Realized

The first observation about economic improvement following conversion is that it is not uniform in the communities studied, nor in the several families of any community. The mere profession of Christian faith, which is almost the only experience of Christianity common to *all* families included in the study, has not lifted anyone out of poverty. Improvement has nowhere, so far as we have learned, been immediate, and in quite a few cases the first difference registered in economic state has been the reverse of improvement. Conflicts have very often followed conversion, resulting in loss of work, destruction of property, withdrawal of credit, or in court cases.

Group solidarity may be achieved in renouncing a religion previously professed and adhering to Christianity, but not in the kind and degree of response to the many stimuli brought by Christianity. In no group do all members respond exactly alike to opportunities for instruction, for worship, for social release or for good works. As long as personalities differ, response to the impact of Christianity on individuals will be varied, no matter how strong group life may be.

The influence of Christianity has widened variations in economic conditions within mass-movement groups. The denial of opportunity tends to produce uniformity through general depression of the economic state; the bringing of opportunity tends to disrupt that uniformity. There are numbers of families within the Christian groups of each of our sample areas that are as poverty-stricken now as they were before they professed the Christian faith. In some areas such families form a distinct majority. In other areas they are a small minority. But these wider differences have not been effected at the expense of any members of the group. They have not made any families poorer, but represent the acquisition of new assets and the release of what may be called "frozen assets" within their personalities.

Improvements Effected Through Education

Let us look first at the small numbers of men and women from these mass-movement groups who have completed college or university courses. In nine of the ten sample areas, though not in families surveyed in all of them, we learned of college graduates whose fathers or grandfathers were poverty stricken illiterates when converted. Some of them hold responsible and highly remunerative positions. Some are serving the Church on sacrificial salaries. It is exceedingly unlikely that any of these men and women would have gone to college or even to high school but for the influence of Christianity. In one recent year at least seventeen young men and seven young women from Christian families converted in mass movements took degrees from the universities of a single province. While definite information is not available, it is doubtful if an equal number of men and women from the sixty millions or more of the depressed classes and aborigines, who have not become Christians, were graduated in the whole of India in the same year. Besides those who graduate, many Christians out of the mass movements attend colleges or technical and professional schools of collegiate grade for a time and drop out because of financial reasons or failure in examinations.

The increased incomes earned by men and women who have obtained the advantages of higher education are often widely distributed among their relatives and friends. the writer talked with one man earning Rs. 230 a month in a Government appointment who showed money-order receipts for monthly remittances, aggregating almost half of his income, sent to nine relatives, seven of whom were in school. These did not include his own children.

One mass-movement convert became a cook and never earned more than Rs. 12 a month, but before he died the monthly income of his sons educated in Christian schools aggregated Rs. 2,000. Another mass-movement convert, who did not learn to read until his late teens, lived to see one of his sons, likewise educated in a Christian school, serve as a Deputy President of the Legislative council of his province.

The professions of medicine, law, teaching, and the ministry are being adorned by men lifted out of the ranks of the depressed classes and from the homes of untutored aborigines. At least two men from such homes have been appointed to the judiciary. More than two score of ladies, who but for the conversion of their parents would have lived as women of the depressed classes, have become practising physicians, most of them as sub-assistant surgeons in Government employ.

Through high schools Christianity has brought opportunity for a smaller, but yet considerable, improvement in economic condition to may more families in the mass-movement groups. These men and women who had the abilities and the good sense to use the opportunities given to them are found working as clerks in Government departments, schools, professional offices, industrial establishments, and other institutions, as school-teachers and private tutors, as nurses, compounders, technicians, and health visitors, as tradesmen, railway employees, and insurance agents, as catechists, evangelists, and pastors and in many other vocations.

It is unfortunate that few of those who have obtained the benefits of a high-school education have remained in or returned to their villages, or have lived where they could assist in lifting the level of life in the groups to which they or their fathers belonged. In many cases, especially in North India, they have broken all contact with the villages of their forefathers.

When we come to primary and middle schools we find the benefits of the Christian movement more widely diffused and better conserved in the local population. Boys and girls who have passed only the primary and middle schools have not so generally left the villages.

Among the direct effects of primary and middle-school education upon economic conditions two are outstanding. These are :

1. Protection against fraud in the keeping of accounts, the signing of notes, etc. The amount of fraud practised against the illiterate by shopkeepe: , monkey-lenders, etc., is undoubtedly very great. One Hindu money-lenders, while protesting that his own record was clean, told the writer that 80 per cent of the money-lenders defraud their illiterate clients. Among practices which he said are common are (a) raising the amount of the note; for example, loaning Rs. 50 and preparing a note for Rs. 80, upon which the borrower places his thumb print in lieu of signature, under the belief that the note is for the amount he has received; (b) raising the interest rate; for example, promising a loan for 25 per cent but writing into the note a promise to pay 37½ per cent; (c) giving receipts for smaller amounts than had been paid, or giving as a receipt a document with a totally different content.

One literate person in a community may be able to protect the entire community against fraud. A resident school-teacher or preacher often renders such service. But a shrewd money-lender is often able to outwit an illiterate man and get him to sign a document under the pressure of a strong need or desire for money at once, without insisting that his literate relative or neighbour see and advise him first.

2. Opening doors to employment. Many men and women who

have completed a middle-school course and some who have lacked a year or two of completing it are employed as village school-teachers. Although salaries in primary schools are small they are a highly desirable asset to a poor family. In those areas where the Missions are maintaining a network of schools the employment of Christian teachers is sufficient to register quite a difference in the economic condition of Christian groups. In a group of villages in the Nagercoil area one out of every eighteen Christian families has an income from school-teaching.

Our thirty-eight hundred household surveys show more than five hundred persons employed in work that could not be done without at least a primary-school education.

Improvement Through Health Service

Without considering the indirect contributions of schools to economic betterment let us turn to improvements that are effected through hospitals and other health service, both curative and preventive.

Mission hospitals are not numerous in India, and most of them are located apart from the mass-movement groups. But in Etah, Govindpur Nagercoil, Pasrur, and Vikarabad the survey forms show Mission hospitals ministering to members of the households studied. Much health service is rendered by Christian agencies in every one of these ten areas. Pastors catechists, evangelists, school-teachers, superintendents, district missionaries, and Bible women agitate constantly for the improvement of health. Many of them render first-aid and dispense simple remedies. They often serve as unofficial agents for Government hospitals or dispensaries. A majority of pastors listed, among the chief demands upon their time, attention paid to the illnesses of their flock, visiting the sick, taking them medicines, and persuading them to go to hospitals or to call doctors. A Mohammedan physician in a Government hospital said that if Hindus and Mohammedans visited the hospital in the same proportion as Christians, his staff would have to be quadrupled. Asked why the Christians came more frequently, he replied that it was because the missionaries, pastors, and school-teachers brought or sent them until their prejudice was broken down, after which they came of their own accord when they needed treatment.

It is clear that much economic loss has been stopped by the contribution of Christianity to the prevention and cure of illness. The school-teacher and two members of the church committee in a village in the Vidyanagar area, in which malaria is endemic, estimated that in one year the loss of two hundred and twenty-one days of work had been prevented by the distribution of quinine by the teacher among the twenty-nine Christian families. McKee says that in the Punjab seizures and deaths from malaria normally outnumber those from all other causes put together. The economic loss from the scourge in every province in India is prodigious. Prophylatic doses of quinine are advocated by the medical profession. A large proportion of Christian ministers and teachers employed in mass movement areas distribute quinine at times. Much more could be done in that line.

Although one needs to be cautious in interpreting the figures, it will be profitable to examine the death rates for children in the homes surveyed in our ten sample areas. Our household schedules provide data for 14,663 sons and daughters of Christian parents. Some died in infancy, some in early childhood, some in their teens, and some in adult life. The lowest death rates reported are in families that have been longest under Christian influence, namely, those in Nagercoil and Govindpur. The rate in Nagercoil is 23.8 per cent; in Govindpur, 21.1 per cent. In both of these areas the Church has been firmly established, and intensive pastoral oversight of all Christian families has long been in operation. The highest death rates are in Etah, 45.3 per cent; and in Ghaziabad, 41.1 per cent. The Christian communities in Etah and Ghaziabad have nearly all been recruited within the present generation; they are scattered through many villages in small groups, and pastoral service, confronted by especially formidable difficulties, has been less constant and more restricted than in other areas. The rate in Etah is more than twice that in Govindpur. The rates in these ten areas correlate more closely with the length and intensity of Christian service to the groups concerned than with any other influence we have been able to test.

In the four Telugu areas the rates are as follows: Guntur, 30.3 per cent; Vikarabad. 32 per cent; Vidyanagar, 34.8 per cent; and Cumbum, 36.6 per cent. Vikarabad has had a smaller ministerial and teaching staff than the other Telugu areas, but a mission hospital has done considerable extension work in the villages covered by the study, and Vikarabad was the location, until a few years ago, of Dr. Hugh H. Linn's Mission Medical Tablet Industry. Doctor Linn has built up a large business in making and selling medical tablets for distribution by Christian workers to the sick, whom they are constantly meeting. Sales of quinine and cinchona tablets, or pills, have run into hundreds of thousands annually.

Improvement of Housing Conditions

Christian influences are also effecting improvement in economic standards by stimulating a desire for better living conditions.

In Nagercoil, where the Christian mass movement began one hundred and twenty-five years ago, and many families with several generations of Christian influence behind them were included in the study, 80 per cent of the houses are superior to the average prevailing in all other areas except Govindpur. Of the 20 per cent of Nagercoil houses that are inferior, approximately three fourths are occupied by first-generation Christians. Nowhere else is the evidence so extensive that a demand for better houses has been stimulated by the Christian movement, but there are a good many scattered families in other areas living in improved houses that indicate a standard of living associated with the Christian movement.

In the Vidyanagar area we found an illiterate man adding a second room to his house, because a daughter, attending a mission boarding school, insisted that he do it. The father, mother, grandmother, and four children had lived in one room until the daughter's experience and training in the school had made her want and demand another room. Again, at Pasrur, a pastor's advice and example were cited to explain an extraordinary number of recent improvements in one village, new rooms added to several houses, and windows put into a half dozen houses. In one village in Guntur, were the Christians houses are quite superior to those in most Telugu villages, a venerable church elder said that when the group accepted Christianity in his boyhood, their houses were worse than those of the outcastes in any neighbouring village. When asked to explain the difference, he replied, "The school, the church, and service." By "service" he meant employment on the railway, in the rock quarries, in offices and shops at Guntur and Bezwada, and as domestic servants.

The low standards of housing prevailing in all areas but Nagercoil and Govindpur indicate both poverty and indifference to better living conditions. By itself poverty cannot permanently keep an entire group from improving its housing. It is an obstacle to the building of new houses and the improvement of old ones, but is not insurmountable unless the desire for better houses is dormant. The unfavourable conditions of tenure of building sites and the limitation of house ownership seem to account to a considerable extent for the poor housing conditions. Legislation is needed to deal with this difficulty. Absolute ownership of the sites on which their houses stand should be substituted by law for the limited ownership that has operated so unfairly against the poor. For their protection the law should prevent the mortgaging of their houses. But, as achievements here and there show, even under present conditions of tenure much improvement is possible. The problem is to make people want better houses strongly enough to overcome poverty and get them. We found that such a desire is being stimulated, but the prevailing mood after every study of our data is one of disappointment that so many Christian families in these mass-movement areas are living in houses entirely inadequate for their needs, apparently without any active desire to improve them. About eighty per cent of the one room houses investigated are on sites that permit the addition of a room on the ground level.

Improvements Through Personality Reconstruction

Christianity has improved the economic condition of mass-movement converts by breaking down inhibitions and occupational restrictions. This has been done partly, but not exclusively through schools. Changes have been wrought in the attitudes of Christians toward work other than that to which they or their group had been accustomed and in the public attitudes toward the taking up of new work by these converts. Many Christians have acquired new concepts of themselves which have made it possible for them to undertake work that was inhibited by old concepts. Hindu and Moslem neighbours likewise have acquired new concepts of the Christians and have encouraged, or at least tolerated, work by them that would have been impossible had the old concepts not given way to the new.

This process has released powers of initiative so long inhibited that no one, least of all the converts themselves, suspected their existence. That a Sweeper should become a potter is unthinkable. Suggest to a typical Sweeper in any part of India that he make pottery and sell it to his Hindu and Moslem neighbours, and he will think you are either crazy or entirely ignorant of the conditions by which he is surrounded. Ask a typical Hindu if he or his neighbours would buy pottery from Sweepers or any other outcaste group in his village, and he will assure you that it is impossible. We tried this latter and the answers were without exception decisive denials. Yet in the Pasrur area we found Sweeper converts earning a comfortable living by making pottery and selling it to Hindus, Moslems, and Sikhs, as well as to their fellow Christians. The explanation is that the Christians have acquired a new concept of themselves, and that this or a like concept has been accepted by their neighbours.

Confirmation of this theory is provided by the decline of the use of the old term by which the Christians in this area were known before their conversion. The term "Chuhra" is falling into disuse. Hindu, Moslem, and Sikh informants told us that among themselves they seldom or never refer to the Christians of their villages by the old caste name.

The Madras *Census* of 1911 says, "One of the immediate effects of conversion (of an untouchable to christianity) is the commencement of deliverance from his bondage. ... In Nellore several of the erstwhile serfs appeared at a recent show in the role of successful exhibitors of prize cattle."

In many villages where the conversion of groups of untouchables led to severe persecution, because it was foreseen that they would no longer be content with their bondage, public sentiment has become reconciled to their deliverance, and has accepted as masons, carpenters, tailors, farmers, even as teachers and ministers of religion, men who were previously condemned to work only as sweepers, leather-workers, or coolies.

Reduction of Interest Charges

In several areas interest charges have been lowered through the influence of Christianity. This has been achieved by two means chiefly: (1) Through the organization by the missions of co-operative societies. The societies have made credit available to their members at a rate below that commonly charged by money-lenders and merchants. The latter have reduced their rates to many others who would otherwise have joined the societies. (2) By making the converts better risks. A Hindu money-lender in Nagercoil said that he considers a Sambavar who attends church a twenty-five percent better risk than one who does not attend, and the average second-generation Nadar Christian a fifty per cent better risk than the average non-Christian Nadar. We did not interview a sufficient number of money-lenders to be able to say whether they would generally assent to the above statement. But in the areas where the Church has been most securely established and a Christian character most clearly stamped upon the groups, prevailing interest rates are much lower than where the Church remains weak and a distinctive Christian character is lacking.

Reduction of Wasteful Expenditures

We discuss elsewhere the evidence that Christianity has effected a reduction in drink and drug consumption and in gambling. Where, and to the extent that, reduction in these vices has taken place, economic conditions have gained. The testimony of many neighbours of these Christians regards the cessation or the decrease of drinking and gambling as a cause of increased prosperity. One covert in Ghaziabad area estimated that he and seven other Christian men of his village had saved an average of Rs. 15 each annually by giving up drink. The others agreed. Hindus in the village said the estimate was not excessive. In Pasrur we got from two Christian men, who admitted that they still used intoxicants, estimates of their annual expenditures on liquor. They averaged Rs. 7 each. The economic effects of decreased drinking are not confined to the money saved, for in many cases drinking results in the loss of time from work, in dismissal from employment, in decreased effectiveness while at work, in the destruction of property and in expenditures for medical relief.

Some gain has been made in several areas through campaign against extravagant weddings. The chief cause of preventable indebtedness is extravagant expenditures on marriage ceremonies. Where the Christian service is substituted for the old rites, the minister, assisted by the elders of the church, is sometimes able to prevent unreasonable expenditures. A number of groups of Christians testified that much less is spent at their weddings now than in pre-Christian days. A group of inquirers in the Vidyanagar area mentioned the reduced expenditures at weddings as one of the minor benefits they expected to gain from being Christians.

However, this means of effecting improvement is more notable for the opportunities it offers than for the use hitherto made of it. We are not sure that in some areas extravagant expenditure at weddings has not increased in keeping with new assets derived from improvements produced by other processes.

Influences That Make Economic Conditions More Difficult

But the influences of Christianity, as defined in this chapter, have not all been on the side of improvement in economic conditions. The missionary, and very frequently his Indian ministerial colleague, coming to the Christian groups as intimate advisers on a wide range of affairs, often unconsciously, and sometimes consciously but with little understanding of what may follow, bring new social patterns, new standards of expenditure and new scales of value that exercise, for a time, at least, a disconcerting and deleterious effect upon economic conditions.

The village schoolboy sees the missionary, the pastor, and the school-teacher wear a collar and a necktie. He concludes that as a Christian he should wear a collar and a necktie, and teases his father to buy them and a shirt with which a collar and tie can be worn, instead of being content with the simple and less expensive *kamis* common in the village.

A girl sees the lady missionary, the pastor's wife, or the woman teacher wearing Western-style shoes and stockings, and decides that she wants shoes and stockings, and that, as a Christian girl who has gone to school, she needs them to mark her difference from the ignorant girls and women about her.

This is not to say that it is always economically injurious in the long run for the boy to want the collar and tie or for the girl to want the shoes and stockings. In some cases the desires release energies or arouse a will to earn money with which they may be met. But one finds a good many families in some areas whose economic position has been made more difficult because the ambitions of the rising generation to be properly outfitted have developed more rapidly than the new resources necessary to provide for their realization.

Some years ago a report on tuberculosis, submitted to the Calcutta Corporation, found that Indian Christians were suffering from tuberculosis more than Hindus. One of the explanations offered was that Christians were accustomed to expand a larger proportion of their income on clothes and consequently had less to spend on food. The life of most village groups can be enriched by the creation of certain new needs, or, rather, an appreciation of certain needs and a desire to provide for them; but when a desire is created for things that meet no genuine need, the community is not enriched but improverished.

Boys and girls who leave their village homes to attend boarding schools sometimes return with exaggerated ideas of their importance and rights as "educated" people. Boys do not find work they consider proper for them and refuse to do what is available, with the result that sacrifices made to keep them in school result only in the necessity of supporting them in idleness. Girls refuse to do their share of the work of the home or the fields and become a burden to their families or to the unfortunate men who marry them. But these cases form a minority in what is yet a small body, for the mission boarding schools have provided opportunities for relatively few village boys and girls.

There is evidence of the growth within several mass-movement groups of sentiment that threatens considerable economic loss through the boycott of certain occupations. The leather-workers have a virtual monopoly of the raw material of the leather industry. Handled wisely this position may be made to contribute to the economic uplift of Christian converts from these castes. But there is developing a disposition to turn away entirely from all work connected with raw skins. A number of Chamar converts around Ghaziabad boasted that they do not remove the skins of cows or buffaloes or collect bones for sale, although these are historic rights of their caste and yield considerable profit. They suggested that as Christians they ought not to do work of that kind, as they make higher-caste people despise them and their religion. Christians of the Sweeper caste, less concerned about the social penalties attached to removing skins and collecting bones, which are less severe than those they experience as Sweepers, are taking over these functions from their Chamar fellow converts.

In several places we found that pastors and educated laymen have refused to admit to full membership in the Church anyone who was working as a sweeper. As many Sweeper converts in these places were unable to get other regular work, they were compelled to choose between remaining out of church membership and sinking lower into poverty.

In many places poor Christians could make a reasonable living by working as washermen or barbers, but they are prejudiced against those occupations and persistently avoid them. In the large cities a few Roman Catholics run barber shops for the upper classes, but so far as we know Protestants have not attempted to enter that field.

A serious obstacle to economic improvement is the occasional development of a spirit of dependence upon the Mission. This is most common among boys who have been given free or nearly free education in boarding schools. Instead of looking for opportunities for earning a living and fitting themselves therefor, they assume that the responsibility for assuring them a job belongs to the institution or the people that made it possible for them to get an education. This spirit also occasionally infests village communities. Some preachers, having themselves received scholarships in middle schools, high schools, and theological schools, are unwise enough to instill in the minds of those to whom they minister a belief that if they make their condition appear distressing enough, the mission will help them financially. A few missionaries have been so lacking in understanding as to respond to appeals set up in that way. However, there has been, we gather, much less of that kind of thing where mass movements have taken place than in other areas of missionary work.

Some income has been sacrificed by Christians refusing to work on Sunday. Two Hindu creditors of Christians complained that their debtors could not meet the payments due to them because they earned no Sunday wages. But our schedules showed that three of the four men they named had each earned more money the previous twelve months than had any of the eight Christian men of their village who were accustomed to work on Sunday. The Sunday rest from ordinary work has not injured the economic conditions of any group, so far as we could tell. It is most common in those groups that are most prosperous, but whether that is a cause, an effect, a combination of both, or a mere coincidence, we do not know.

9

Status of Women During British Period

Introduction

"If a person who died a hundred years ago came of life to-day, the first and most important change that would strike him is the revolution in the position of women."

This observation made by Mr. Natarajan sums up the achievements with regard to the status of woman during the British period.

This changed status of woman during the British period was the cumulative effect, as observed before, of the interplay of forces, both objective and subjective, which emerged and operated during last hundred and fifty years.

The Impact of the Policies of the British Rulers

The British rulers, who introduced a new type of economy, state structure and educational system, created thereby the preconditions for the transformation of the position of the Indian women. However, as we have noticed, the new economy which Britain introduced in India was adapted to the needs of the subservient to the British economy. The new political set up was so devised that though it brought about the political unification of the Indian people on the basis of a single strong centralized state for the first time in their long history, it essentially functioned as an instrument of foreign domination. The new educational system was also evolved and adjusted to meet the requirement of the British rulers viz. to turn out an efficient personnel for this administrative and economic systems.

The social policies of the British government, as we have seen, were so devised that they hardly attacked in a positive manner the multitude of evils that ravaged the Indian society.

The attitude of the British to the social problems of the Indian society was best reflected in their declared policy of non-interference in the religious matters. It, however, happened that though the British government was indifferent and apathetic to the problems of the social advance of the Indian people, such advance did take place during the British period. This was due to the fact that the contact of India with Britain led to the growth of a new form of economic structure, though a distorted one, and also to the study of the English literature by a section of the Indians which helped them to assimilate the western democratic and liberal ideology, an ideology subsequently utilised by them to start social and religious reform movements in India.

The Role of New Intelligentsia

The new intelligentsia, which assimilated the basic ideas underlying the western liberal culture, played, as previously stated, a decisive role in bringing about the reform of the Indian society. They carried on a battle simultaneously on two fronts. On the one hand, they struggled against the British rulers who passively or actively supported the forces of social reaction. On the other hand, they engaged themselves in the herculean task of cleansing the augean stable of the ossified and decadent Indian society corroded by reactionary and undemocratic social customs and practices. They tried to locate the cause of the degeneration of the Indian society, evaluated its reactionary tradition, analysed the values behind this tradition and reactionary social institutions and formulated and strove to work out a programme of the reconstruction of the Indian society on a rational and democratic basis, suited to the conditions of India. With a view to achieve this, they carried on an extensive educational campaign among the people and increasingly pressed the government to use the legislative powers to initiate social and religious reforms. They often took pledges to practise those reforms personally also and suffered innumerable hardships such as social ocstracism and others as they strove to implement their reform programmes. They, further, founded various local or national, specific or general, social reform organizations.

Rise of Women Workers

Their efforts subsequently resulted in the emergence of women workers devoted to the cause of the elevation of the position of the Indian women, an event unprecedented in the history of India. These women participated in and led the liberation struggle of the Indian women, a struggle which often involved great suffering for them. The new womanhood which emerged during this period and built up as well as conducted various women's organizations for the uplift of women and which further took active part in the nationalist movement played an important role in the great social and political transformation which the Indian society experienced in recent times.

Role of Political and Class Struggles

The role of the political, trade union, kisan and youth movements, which sprang up in the country, in generating a new and heightened social sense among the Indian women as well as in making them actively participate in their thousands in outdoor social political, economic and cultural movements was tremendous. Its full significance is not properly realized in elevating the status of women. This was another unique feature of the new development, a feature which was observable only during the British period in marked contrast to the earlier phases of Indian history.

REVOLUTION IN THE OUTLOOK ABOUT WOMAN'S STATUS

Qualitative Change in Woman's Position

The cumulative effect of all the forces mentioned above has indeed brought about a remarkable revolution in the status of women in India. However, it should be noted that though a new and a qualitatively different development has taken place during the British rule, it has not still attained its democratic goal completely both in theory and practice. In fact, it signified only the first stride towards that goal. Nay, only the first round of the battle was fought. In this first round, woman secured equality of status, at least in principle, and as embodied in the Constitution of Free India.

The real advance which has been made during this period is actually in the revolution that has been brought about in the outlook with regard to the conception of the status of woman and her role in society. Now woman is no longer looked upon as a child-bearing machine and a helot in the home. She has acquired a new status and a new social stature.

Creation of New Womanhood

The political and class movements and the women's organizations have created a womanhood which has some broader social purpose in life. The purdahridden women came out of their age long seclusion when the nation was fighting for freedom. They defied lathi charge, faced bullets and courted Jails not for the sake of a young family member but for the liberation of the motherland. The new woman is slowly realizing the fact that the home is not the only centre of activity. Even the upper class woman thinks that she should associate herself with some social activity and should not while away her leisure. Ray Strachey has described the role of the women's movement in Britain which is applicable to India also. She observes: "The popularity and sources of these organisations was indeed so great that by the end of the seventies it had become fashionable almost to the point of necessity for wealthy women to engage in charitable work; and while the more thoughtful worked seriously and in an organized manner at lasting reforms, the more foolish took a mania for "slumming". A pet charity was at that date almost as much a part of the equipment of a smart lady as was a rope of pearls." Though the work done by these upper class ladies had a rather superficial character, still it "was always a widening of her experience beyond the drawing room of her own home."

Wider Social Consciousness

The growth of social consciousness stretching beyond the needs of the small family or caste people is the greatest achievement of the era. The fact, that there are women who devote their lives as Sevikas (servants) of humanity in the Nishkama Karma Matha, Wardha Ashram, the Bhoodan Movement, or as active workers in various outdoor public activities, reveals that a new womanhood is emerging in the arena of Indian social life. A number of women are devoting their life to educational, political, trade union, kisan, academic, social, cultural or general emancipation work. This signifies that they have got of the grooves of the narrow social life confined to a score or more of relatives. One writer describes this development thus: "Women are gradually realizing that they have personalities of their own as human beings and that their mission in life does not end with becoming good wives and wise mothers but also in realizing that they are all members of the civic community and of the body politic." The modern woman is not living a passive life. She is not only the wife or the daughter of some one. On the contrary, she possesses her own individuality. She is, therefore, slowly revising her attitude towards caste, joint family, marriage and such other social institutions. Recently a girl was married to a boy who was not only ugly but also morally low. The boy also was tricked by the elders into the marriage. He ill treated her to such an extent that she ran away from home and took shelter in her parents' place. She declared: "I am not going to tolerate any of these things. If the life for me becomes intolerable, I will prefer to commit suicide rather than succumb to this." The girl was determined to employ all methods for remaining away from her husband and in case she failed, she decided to commit suicide as the last resort, rather than accept her servile position.

Larger Participation in Social Life

Hundreds of women are now participating in serious outdoor work. The new woman, who has developed out of a new historical phase, should not be confounded with the superficial types who also have emerged during the British period. She should not be identified with the so-called "modern" women who dress themselves in ultra-modern ways, who contemptuously look at the other down-trodden people and who always interpret the concept of equality as absence of any responsibility and assertion of privileges. The new womanhood has been depicted in one of the resolution of a woman's organization thus: "We are neither etherial damsels nor dolls, nor bundles of passions and nerves. We are as much human beings as men are and we are filled with the same urge for freedom."

Uptil now the connotation of the word service, as far as woman was concerned, implied the service to her husband, relations in law and family guests. Due to the spread of the new liberal culture and the new goals that this culture unfolded before woman, the conception of the culture of the service has undergone a change. "Along with men, women of India have also begun to realize that the supreme goal of woman's life is not circumscribed to merely love making, dutifulness to husband, child-bearing and domestic work. They have begun to realise that woman's life has a higher and a more serious objective."

Participation in broad extra-domestic socially useful activity has also been made possible due to the development of mechanical devices, which assist to decrease the drudgery of domestic work and permit woman more leisure. It should, however, be remembered that in India, very few middle class families can afford to adopt costly labour-saving devices. Even then cheap and apparently insignificant mechanical means as water taps in place of wells as sources of eased the life of the urban women. Even the street lighting has increased the freedom of movement. As Viola Klein puts it: "The introduction of gas and electricity likewise affected women's life enormously. It greatly reduced household labour; while such apparently simple things as street lighting no doubt increased their liberty of movement."

Equal Status granted by the Constitution

Thus the new objective as well as subjective factors collaborated in creating a new conception of the functions of women. The crowning achievement of the modern Indian history is the recognition and granting of equal status to women through the Constitution of the Free Sovereign India. The Constitution has proclaimed the equality of man and woman in all domains of life. As declared in the Constitution: "The State shall not discriminate against any citizen, on ground only of religion, race, caste, sex, place or any of them." Further in the Sixteenth Article it is mentioned that, "There shall be equality of opportunity for all citizens in matters relating to employment or appointment to any office under the State."

Today woman is equal of man. This is no mean achievement for "Indeed, the establishment by legal prescription of the common humanity of the two halves of the human race and acceptance by the State of Mill's view that one girl ought to count for it exactly as much as one boy represent the most far reaching change of our epoch in as much as on it other major changes hinge."

FEMINISM IN INDIA AND BRITAIN COMPARED

Herculean Task

Though the theoretical and juridical basis for women's equality has been laid down, the building up of the entire structure on this foundation remains to be done. It is a task of herculean dimension. The women's movement shall have to strike out a new path, march along a different road. It will require a new vision, new methods of struggles, a new type of leadership.

Before we portray the conditions which still prevail in India and which have to be faced, combated and changed by women, let us try to understand the type of feminist movement which has developed in India. It will help us to assess how far the leadership of the present feminist movement would be able to shoulder the responsibilities of the new tasks which confront women.

Feminist Movement in Great Britain

The feminist movement in India, upto now, exhibited features which were in marked contrast to that in Great Britain. The women of England, in the early 19th century, for the first time in history, raised their voice against the basic unequal treatment accorded to woman. This movement had to face formidable difficulties. The mind of the males also had not yet been permeated by democratic principles and, therefore, they were bitter opponents of the demand of equal rights to women. When the first meeting for the agitation of the demand was held in London in 1869, with a woman as the president, "One gentleman, a member of the Parliament, took occasion to darg into one of his own speeches the fact that two ladies, wives of Members of this house' had recently disgraced themselves by speaking in public and he kindly added that he would not `further disgrace them by mentioning their names." The first woman medicos had to enter the surgeon's hall in 1870 in the midst of shout, jostle and throwing of mud hurled at them by the male students. The attitude of the society of the time has been pithily described by Mr. James Stuart thus: "I agree" he said," that the arguments for women are the same as the arguments for men. The only difference is that in the case of working men these arguments apply, and in the case of women they do not apply." In the later stages, women like Mrs. Pankherst and her daughter had to serve terms of imprisonment for their struggle for franchise for women.

Emily Davidson, in the process of the struggle, threw herself under the feet of the horse of the mounted police and was killed. This incident is poignantly described by Ray Strachey. She remarks, "All over the world, people read of it and all over the world it was known that there were women in England who courted death for the conviction that women should be free." Thus for English women, the vote and its subsequent advantages were the results of a strenuous and bitter fight for getting it.

Story of Indian Feminism

The story of the Indian Feminist movement is quite different. In India, the cause for women's freedom was first espoused by enlightened males who had imbibed liberal ideas. Upto the twenties of the present century the struggle was carried on by men. It was only after Gandhiji's entry into politics—when the nationalist movement under his leadership was transformed from a middle class movement into a mass movement—that women themselves for the first time raised their voice against the disabilities from which they suffered. Further due to the general atmosphere of democracy and respect for human personality which was engendered, women secured many democratic rights and social freedom even without struggle. In fact they realized many of their rights as grants.

Limitations of Indian Women's Movement

The securing of dejure equality by the Indian women as a by-product of a general nationalist political movement and their actual subject status as a result of the general persistence of old economic, social, institutional and ideological legacy of an under-developed country has generated a peculiar contradictory situation in the country. As these de jure rights have been secured as gifts and not extorted as by-product of a gigantic, organized and well fought out struggle by women themselves, they still persist as liberties whose real implication is not even grasped by vast bulk of womanhood.

Indian woman has participated in some political movements. But a conscious movement to reconstruct the social and institutional framework of Indian society to eradicate the oppressive aspects of social heritage and those particularly oppressive to women has never been launched on a very serious scale. The Indian feminist movement has upto now lacked vigour and momentum.

Very rarely women's organizations have launched mass women's oppositional movements as a protest against the non-enactment of a progressive bill for women's rights into law. The ineffectiveness of the feminist movement was clearly revealed when the Hindu Code Bill was watered down and passed as the present Act with all its limitations. Nor do we find women's collective struggle to eradicate an oppressive social custom or a reactionary ritual. Absence of organized women's collective struggle is the basic weakness of their emancipation movement in India.

Puff, Powder and Poshak Parishads

Individual women leaders have suffered tremendously for the

women's freedom cause. A Pandita Ramabai might have chosen self-exile from her native village for exercising her right to receive education and suffer thereby. A Dhankorbai might have chosen a life of great hardships for committing the crime of widow remarriage. A Kamaladevi might have undergone lot of hardships for woman's freedom. A Vidyagauri Nilkant might have continued to receive education in face of bitter opposition of reactionary forces. But the mass of women have rarely been drawn in active struggle for securing woman's rights and freedoms. The movement has still been circumscribed to individual women or at best to small groups. Hence the criticism has been levelled by some that the movement has halted at periodically convened conferences where only upper class women assembled, many of them considering them as occasions to display their fine apparels, treating them as new variety of social function rather than rallies for making great decision for militant mass women's struggles for achieving emancipatilon. These conferences hence have been branded as "puff, powder and poshak Parishads."

UNRESOLVED TASKS

De jure and De facto Status—Contrast

This weakness of the present feminist movement is all the more alarming and startling when we try to visualize the enormous tasks with which it is confronted after Independence. Though woman has acquired juridical equality with man, her actual position is still very unstisfactory. The forces of reaction have continued to remain strong in Indian society even after a decade of freedom. 92 lakhs of marriages performed in contravention to the law against child marriage revealed the state of affairs in social life. The social oppression of married woman which still persists on a large scale was revealed by studies of Rescue Homes.

The horrible oppression of widows still persists almost with the same unabated fury.

The authoritarian patriarchial and caste mores still smother the lives of millions of women. Nay, as a number of studies reveal caste, traditional authoritarian family mores and male-oriented religious practices are gaining new vitality. Only a short time back a court gave judgment in favour of the husband who asserted his right to beat his wife.

Though educated women are increasingly taking to occupation, still, as we said in our survey of the position of women employed in various occupations, they do not get equal pay for equal work, nor have women opportunities for the right type of occupation. Marriage still is the only life for an average woman.

The mass of the Indian people live in horrible conditions, hence the problem of women's economic improvement becomes a part of the total social reconstruction. The general position of the woman who is earning a livelihood is the same in India as elsewhere in the world. As described by Viola Klein, "A woman worker, doctor or soldier still keeps her household, brings up her children (at least to some extent) and mends not only her own but her family's stockings. A girl coming home from the office is as a matter of course expected to help her mother wash up while her brother is excused from domestic work."

Not only in the social field but also in the sphere of education, woman's backwardness is striking. Though an increasing number of girls is taking higher education, the total number of literate women is still insignificant.

Further, though the number of women's organisations has increased, the work done by them is not extensive and sufficient. They merely try to impart training in some crafts and provide opportunity for some general and craft education. They have not become effective mouthpieces voicing women's demands nor have they functioned as a powerful bulwark against the onslaught of social reaction.

Further, whatever advance in the position of woman is revealed, is to be found in the urban areas. The rural woman is still suffering from poverty, ignorance, disease and superstition. Even the programmes like Community Development Projects or National Extension Schemes have not significantly touched the village women."

Even in the sphere of legislation also the absence of a uniform civil code applicable to all communities indicates the slow march of the movement of women's emancipation. Further, a greater problem before the Indian womanhood is the implementation of even the few progressive enactments that have been passed.

Recent Reports on Suicides

The recent reports of innumerable cases of suicides reveal the harrowing state of the conditions of women. The Saurashtra government appointed a committee to inquire into the number, nature and causes of suicides in that state. It was revealed that during the period of 1951 to 1955, 1129 cases of suicides had occurred, i.e., per year nearly 226 suicides took place. The separate figures of women are not available for the whole phase but in 1955, 256 women committed suicide. Recently Shri Morarji Desai also disclosed in the Bombay Legislative Assembly that 3824 suicides were committed in the state in 1954 and 1955 of which 1983 were by women. The causes in both the reports were found to be unemployment, poverty, domestic quarrels, joint family life, ill-treatment, disappointment in love and others. As it could be seen from these, the causes are more sociological than psychological. These instances prove that women's problems are not yet solved, her status is not high and she has not developed any other means to break away from the shackles excepting that of committing suicide.

PROBLEMS CONFRONTING INDIAN WOMEN

This sad spectacle of the condition of woman reveals how the women's movement is confronted with the following tasks:

1. It has to organise a vast movement to destroy the deadweight of the old institutional and ideological legacy which specially proves oppressive and discriminatory against them.

2. It has to organize ceaseless struggles to establish a social

and economic order which would really provide employment to all, security of work and pay. Here it shall have to join hands with the movements of all those forces which are underprivileged, who suffer from the extant economic and social arrangements and who are trying to change the arrangements. The problem of woman's real emancipation is bound up with the problem of general economic emancipation.

3. The problem of general economic emancipation is bound up with the fundamental problem of establishing a social order, wherein unemployment, and scarcity of jobs would disappear. The women's movement has to confront the fundamental issue viz. how far the present economic order as being visualized and worked out by the Indian Union will really solve this economic problem.

4. All over the world, those social orders which are torn by contradictions and are planning for competitive economic and political wars are again evolving new ideologies which while recognizing juridical equality of man and woman attempt also to drive woman to a life of child-bearing and kitchen work. The dangerous trend which has been developing in a number of advanced countries is also trying to raise its head in backward countries. It is slowly evolving in India also. Will women's movement withhold its onslaught?

The Indian womanhood is at the cross-roads of history. It has secured juridical equality, a great epochal landmark in her long history. But will this juridical equality materialize into real emancipation? or will she become a victim of a new type of subjection?

THE BRITISH PERIOD

There had been, from very early times, a steady deterioration in the position of Indian women down the centuries, which neither enlightened public opinion nor well meaning rulers could check. The disruption of the Moghul empire in the eighteenth century and the consequent political confusion throughout the country only added to the miseries of Indian women, and as a result, when the British period started, the position of women in India was the worst in the history of the country. Child-marriage was the general rule for all respectable castes of Hindus, and had even spread to some sections of the Muslim population. Sati was widely prevalent and even the Sikhs, as we have seen, practised it though forbidden by their Gurus. Purdah was strictly enforced on Muslim, and to some extent, Hindu women. Feminine literacy was regarded "as a source of moral danger since only dancing girls could normally read and write", and "ladies of orthodox families would have been shocked if a report had spread that they were acquainted with singing and dancing". Polygyny was practised by all those who could afford it. Prostitution was rampant, and every city and town teemed with singing and dancing girls, and no social function was complete without a `Nautch' as the performance by professional dancers was called. Almost all Hindu temples openly or surreptitiously harboured Devadasis.

This was roughly the position when the British took over the rulership of the country, but by the time they left in 1947, all this had changed. Child-marriage and widow-burning had been effectively stopped throughout the country, and widow remarriage legally permitted. Female education was introduced and encouraged to such an extent that literacy, far from being reckoned a moral lapse, came to be considered a desirable accomplishment for girls. Polygyny, though not abolished, was looked upon as old-fashioned, and not in keeping with the dignity and restraint expected of an educated, cultured gentleman. Prostitution was recognised as a social evil and association with prostitutes, a mark of depravity. Political equality of the sexes was accepted in principle, and many women held responsible positions under the Government, while some were elected or nominated to the legislatures. The advance made towards women's emancipation in India after the country gained independence, as we shall see in the next chapter, was even more rapid, but this was made possible by the sound foundations laid during the British period.

Several factors contributed towards the uplift of Indian women during the British period. First and foremost was the direct influence of the British, a people noted for their chivalry towards women; the general awakening of Asians in the twentieth century was another important factor, while the political struggle for Indian independence gave a tremendous impetus to the feminist movement in India.

Early European

In spite of the achievements of the British period, it must be mentioned that the early contacts of Indians with European society in India were disappointing and foreboded evil rather than good to the women of India. The first of these contacts was with the Portuguese. Vasco da Gama, it may be recalled, landed in Calicut in the year 1498, about three decades before Babar won the battle of Panipat and founded the Moghul empire. Compared with the Europeans of the Mediterranean region, the nations of the Atlantic seaboard were, at the time, culturally backward, and the Iberians, in particular, fresh from their victories against the Moors, were bursting with the crusading zeal when they came to India. Hence the Portuguese showed considerable iconoclastic spirit, and their treatment of Indians raised much antagonism against them in the country.

Further, early Europeans were not in a position to bring their women with them to the east, and Portuguese soldiers were often compelled to consort with the scum of Indian society; when the morally scrupulous, who dreaded to live in sin, wished to marry, it was not the respectable class of Indian women that they could get, but rather the women of lower castes of dubious morality; as such, the first impression Indians got of European society in India was not very high.

The Portuguese, however, did, in their own way, what they could, to elevate Indians. They converted to Christianity many Hindus and Muslims, by preaching when they had to, and by force when they could, Albuquerque, it may be recalled, abolished Sati by law in the Portuguese territories in India three centuries before William Bentinck stopped it in British India.

The Portuguese influence was generally confined to the coastal regions of India. They had no territorial ambitions but were mainly interested in the monopoly of the lucrative trade with the east; as such their policy was to dominate the Eastern Seas and hold sufficient number of strategic ports on the lifeline of their commerce to ensure the safety of their shipping. The success of the Portuguese, however, brought in their wake the Dutch, the Danes, the French and the British, and in the struggle for empire among these powers, the British eventually emerged as the dominant power in India. From the historic Battle of Plassey (1757), in which Clive defeated Suraj Dowla, till 1947 when they left India, the British were the undisputed masters of the Indian political scene. And most of the great reforms that led to the emancipation of Indian women were effected during this eventful period in Indian history.

The start of the British, it may be stated, was even more disappointing than that of the Portuguese. The Portuguese ruled their Indian possessions in the name of the Crown and had a Viceroy in Goa and Governors elsewhere in India who were answerable to the Crown for their actions. But the Indian empire of the British was something of an exotic growth which had no planning behind it; it was an empire thrust upon a few adventurers and merchants who were compelled to arm themselves in self-defence against the lawless conditions of the time and found themselves in possession of kingdoms they did not know what to do with.

Unlike the Portuguese, who ardent Christians and believed that they had a mission to convert the heathen, the British were merchants who were interested only in their dividends. The early Britishers in India were merely paid servants of the East India Company which had obtained some trading settlements in the more important of the Indian ports. During the chaotic times that followed the collapse of the Moghul empire, the factors in these settlements found that they could not get protection from local rulers, and hence raised their own armies of mercenaries, mostly Indians, to defend their possessions. In course of time the number of soldiers and the size of these possessions increased to such an extent that the factors were able to dictate terms to Indian potentates in the matter of trade concessions and monopolies. The commercial prosperity of the British eventually led to political ambition, and what with the never-ending quarrels among Indian rulers and effective interference by the British, the Directors of the East India Company found themselves rulers of an Indian empire larger than any known to history. It is doubtful if, in the whole history of colonialism, a private agency had held sway over the destinies of so vast a multitude of human beings. The Sepoy Mutiny of 1857, however, led to the transfer of political power from the Board of Directors of the East India Company to the Crown.

The same problem that vitiated the life of early Portuguese settlements in India confronted the British too-shortage of women of their own race. The soldiers, who were not particularly noted for self-restraint, and even officers, were often obliged to consort with the women of the city, and drunken brawls were a familiar feature of Indian brothels frequented by Europeans. Such was the odium attached to the way of life of early European settlements in India that the word Ferangi, the name by which Europeans were generally known in India, became a byword for loose living. The Ferangis also brought a new disease to India, and syphilis is even now called after them in many parts of India.

While Europeans of the lower income group freely resorted to the brothels, the higher classes found polygyny and concubinage, rampant in India, worthy of emulation, and many kept harems in grand Indian style. Nor did the life of men like Warren Hastings, who held the highest position in the land, do much to elevate the moral tone of the British settlements.

Under these conditions, good Christians who tried to hold up to Indians the superiority of Christianity over Islam and Hinduism, had a rough time. While dwelling upon the handicaps of the Gospel-worker in India, the missionary Schwartz said:

> It is extremely difficult, when describing our situation here, to give any one a just conception of it without adverting to

> the profligacy of Europeans. The great among them aim at nothing but to live in pleasure and become rich. It not readily successful in their latter attempt, they resort to unjust means the employment of which hardens the mind to so alarming a degree that they will hear nothing of the word of God and too frequently plunge into the most frightful infidelity.

Another good Christian, Terry, happened to hear the opinion expressed by Indians concerning the Europeans of the time.

> It is a most sad and horrible thing to consider what scandal there is brought upon the Christian religion by the looseness and remissness, by the exorbitances of many which come amongst them, who profess themselves Christians of whom I have often heard the natives, who live near the ports where our ships arrive, say thus, in the broken English they have gotten:'Christian religion, devil religion; Christians much drink, Christians much do wrong, much beat, much abuse others'.

Well, the Directors of the East India Company were concerned with their profits and not with the morals of their staff, and as a rule no questions were asked about the way of life of Britishers in India as long as the annual balance sheets showed substantial margins of profit. Yet it must be said to their credit that they made a sincere attempt to raise the moral standard of their servants in India. The crux of the problem, they correctly diagnosed, was the disparity of sexes in the European population of the settlements, and to remedy this,

> ... the Company took upon the task of supplying women to their servants in India. Accordingly, a shipload of European women were landed in Calcutta to the delight of the settlers. But the demand proved so far in excess of the supply, that the gay ladies, following strict economic laws, took to prostitution as more profitable and pleasant than marriage. They were so prodigal of their charms and easily-got money

that most of them lost their attractions and had to petition the Company for maintenance or repatriation. After this bitter experience, the Company left their servants to find women for themselves.

As a matter of fact, most of the Europeans who came to the east were society's hard bargains, and the early stages of British colonial expansion were marked by a preponderance of such elements in their settlements in India. It was admitted by all that the atmosphere of the British settlements in India was not congenial for the growth of morals, and there was a clause in the Charter granted to the Company in 1793 which empowered the authorities in India to refuse entry into the country to any one they considered undesirable; and for the purposes of this Clause, missionaries and other gentlemen with delicate consciences who could not withstand the moral climate of the settlements were generally considered undesirables. A strict check was maintained in Indian ports for such delinquents, and any person who, in the opinion of the authorities, was not likely to fit in with the social pattern of the settlements was forbidden to land, and had to either go back to Europe or escape to the Danish or Dutch settlements where vigilance was less strict.

Anyway, this state of affairs did not last long. With the expansion of the territorial possessions of the East India Company, Englishmen at home began to take an increasing interest in India. The license of the Restoration period also brought its inevitable reaction in England, and with the rise of the moral standard at home, the affairs of the British settlements in India and the way of life of the 'Nabob' as the Englishman in India was nicknamed in England, came in for a good measure of public criticism.

The worst attack against the 'Nabob' came from the missionaries. Protestant England was rather late in entering the mission field, but once missionary activities started, the movement gained considerable momentum, and the English missionary was not a little surprised to find that there was a ban on the entry of missionaries into British India. They thought it preposterous that, while many non-Christian rulers of Asia not only allowed but even patronised missionary work in their dominions, the British, who were supposed to be Christians, did not even permit the presence of missionaries in their territories in India. Hence from the pulpit, platform and the press the missionaries canvassed public opinion in their favour, the 'Nabobs' fighting back against what they considered missionary interference with their private affairs in the east. The issue was clinched when the question of the renewal of the Company's Charter came up before the Parliament in 1813, and after a wordy warfare, the objectionable 'missionary clause' was deleted from the Charter. The Indian episcopal question was also taken up, and a Bishop was appointed for India with his See at Calcutta.

Form now on, things improved. Missionaries and clergymen regularly came to India, together with civil servants and army and navy officers of a type different from that of the bad old days. The British settlements became safe for ladies, and wives of many Englishmen came with their husbands to India. These pioneers laid the foundation of a sound European society in India, and the British settlements not only ceased to be the moral plague-spots of India, but came to be looked upon as examples to be followed by cultured Indians.

Calcutta, the then capital of British India, was, naturally, the centre of this new Anglo-Indian society. Its high moral tone, almost amounting to snobbishness, was reflected in many incidents of the time which would also show the watchful eye stern British moralists kept on the 'Nabob' and his activities. As an instance may be cited the casual mention, in a court of law, by a lawayer that Bishop Middleton attended a 'Nautch' in the Government House at Calcutta, which created a sensation in England. The worthy Bishop emphatically denied the allegation but vaguely referred to an invitation he had received from the Governor-General to a party in the Government House; he himself did not attend the function, he clarified, but some ladies of his household did. It was then up to the Governor-General to say what happened next. Lord Hastings, accordingly, sent an explanatory letter to the Lord Chancellor in which he admitted that there was a party in the Government House which was attended by the ladies of the Bishop's House. There was, however, no 'Nautch'; and Indian woman sang, His Lordship confessed, but she did not dance- "the mere movement of her feet, while she was singing, not deserving the name".

The incident shows the high standard of society at the time. The days of Warren Hastings and Clive were gone for good. The very fact that ladies of the Bishop's House attended the function would show that Government House parties had definitely become respectable and decorous. There was, no doubt, some Indian music which wagging tongues exaggerated into a 'Nautch'. A regular 'Nautch' of the old days meant many half-naked dancing girls and more drunkards.

The social theories and practices of the ruling classes began to impress Indians, and the possibilities of a new Indian society in which respectable ladies could socially mix with men, without moral lapse or scandal, came within the realm of practical politics in India, perhaps for the first time in the history of the country. The freedom enjoyed by European women, their appearance in public functions without embarrassment or outrage to modesty, the advantages of monogamy, the soundness of marital relations among Europeans in spite of the absence of Purdah, their family life, all impressed the better class of the Hindus and Muslims, who began to wonder if their notions of society with its seclusion of women were the best possible.

Abolition of Sati

Perhaps the boldest step the British took towards social reform in India was the abolition of Sati by law. The British had all along been following a cautious policy of non-intervention in the social and religious affairs of India, as they knew very well that it was practically impossible for them to rule their vast Indian empire without the co-operation and goodwill of their subjects. The ruin of the Moghul empire as a result of the anti-Hindu religious policy of Aurangazeb, and the difficulties the Portuguese had to face in India because of their proselytising zeal, were fresh in the memory of the early British in India and they did not wish to make the same mistakes and invite a threat to the safety of their empire. Yet all responsible Britishers felt that Sati was something they could not tolerate in their dominions because of the humanitarian issues involved; the institution stood, more or less, on a par with human sacrifice.

The selection of the right moment was, however, important; moreover, the people had to be made acquainted with the proposed legislation. In the initial stages, the District Collectors were instructed to use their personal influence, dissuade widows from immolating themselves, impress upon relatives the undesirability of killing their kith and kin, and generally make it difficult for society to burn widows. The efforts of the collectors and their subordinates met with partial success, and in some collectorates the number of Satis decreased appreciably.

Enquiries were also made to find out which regions were the worst affected, and statistics collected. In Bengal the British were in a favourable position to collect reliable data, and the statistics for the years 1815-28 showed the following figures for Bengal:

Year	*Number of Satis*	*Year*	*Number of Satis*
1815	378	1822	583
1816	442	1823	575
1817	707	1824	572
1818	839	1825	639
1819	650	1826	518
1820	598	1827	517
1821	654	1828	463

Rajputana was, by all accounts, the worst affected region, and here the percentage of widows burnt was as high as twenty-five. In the south, Tanjore was reckoned just as bad; when the Rajah of Tanjore died in 1801, the queens, we are told, quarrelled for precedence in self-immolation. There were, it may be mentioned, niceties of distinction to be observed in the matter of burning the women of the mighty; as a rule, it was the privilege of the seniormost queen to be burnt with the dead body of her husband on the same pyre, and the juniors had to be content with separate pyres of lesser magnificence. When a junior queen, for any reason claimed the privilege of joint burning with her husband, and the senior objected, the matter was generally decided by a panel of judges proficient in the law and lore of Sati; concubines and other low types were invariably burnt separately.

Correct statistics for places other than Bengal could not be collected, "but it is doubtful if, even during the period when the institution was widely prevalent, the percentage of widows who were burnt was more than thirty during peaceful times. Widows past child-bearing age, pregnant women and mothers with infants-in-arms were not permitted to die with their husbands. Further, there were also spirited women who refused to yield to a cruel public opinion and a false sense of conjugal fidelity, and decided to outlive their husbands". As we have already noticed, the Tantrics too rejected Sati, and they always found some excuse or pretext to save the life of widows under their control.

With all this, the number of widows who perished annually in flames was quite considerable, and Lord William Bentinck decided to abolish the institution by law. Apart from discussions with others, Bentinck had also to wrestle with himself before taking the final step. In a minute dated the 8th November 1829, the conscientious Englishman wrote:

To consent to the consignment, year after year, of hundreds of innocent victims to a cruel and untimely death, when the power exists of preventing it, is a predicament which no conscience can contemplate without horror.... With the firm undoubting conviction entertained upon this question, I should be guilty of little short of the crime of multiplied murder if I could hesitate in the performance of this solemn obligation. I have already been stung with this feeling. Every day's delay adds a victim to the dreadful list which might have been prevented by a more early submission of the present question.

Bentinck's convictions were shared not only by Englishmen but by a good number of enlightened Indians, of whom the most important were Dwarknath Tagore and that indefatigable pioneer of social and religious reforms in India, Rajah Ram Mohan Roy. Roy has been rightly called the Father of Modern India. In opposition to the large number of orthodox Hindus who made formidable representations to the Governor-General against his uncalled for interference with their time-honoured right to burn their women. Roy and his associates sent a petition supporting the proposed legislation, stating that Sati had no religious sanction but was an accretion of the middle ages, and physical force was often used in burning unwilling widows. Some portions of the petition may be cited, especially those that deal with the use of force. One passage runs:

> Your petitioners are fully aware from their own knowledge and from the authority of credible eye-witnesses that cases have frequently occurred where women have been induced by the persuasions of their next heirs interested in their destruction, to burn themselves on the funeral pyres of their husbands; that others, who were induced by fear to retract a resolution rashly expressed in the first moments of grief of burning with their husbands, have been forced upon the pile, and there bound with ropes and pressed with green bamboos until consumed by the flames; that some, after flying from the flames, have been carried back by their relations and burnt to death.

Roy had personally seen the use of force in Sati. When his brother Jaganmohan died in 1811, he tried to dissuade the widows from mounting the funeral pyre, but his relatives hurried her off to the cremation ground; she tried to escape from the flames, but sturdy men with long poles of green bamboo pressed her down to the burning pyre.

It would appear that a widow, as a rule, in the general atmosphere of sorrow and despair following her husband's death, announced her decision to burn herself with the body of her husband. The decision, once announced, was irrevocable, as already noticed. But with some widows at least there was difficulty in sustaining the determination till the grim tragedy was enacted in the cremation ground, and it did happen, at times, that a widow, unnerved by the thought of death or by the sight of the flames, made a bid to escape, at the last moment. The attempt, if successful, no doubt saved a life, but it brought upon the widow and her family eternal disgrace, and precautions were taken to prevent such an eventuality. Widows suspected of weakness of will were often drugged or plied with liquor and made virtually senseless before the cortege started from the house; in certain cases, the pyre was built in a deep pit so that once a widow either jumped or was pushed into it, escape became impossible; other methods of preventing flight and disgrace were tying the hands and legs of the widow when she mounted the pyre, and posting strong men with long, green bamboo poles to press down women who showed restiveness.

The main contention of the advocates of Sati, who opposed legislation, was that the institution was purely voluntary, and it was cruel on the part of the British to deprive a pious and devoted Hindu lady of the enjoyment of her marital rights in Paradise with her husband, if she was so inclined. The arguments of the opponents did not, however, avail, and on the 4th December 1829, was passed the famous resolution by which Sati was made "a crime of culpable homicide punishable with fine, imprisonment or both".

The orthodox did not keep quiet. They started an agitation and appealed to the Privy Council, alleging that the legislation was a piece of flagrant interference with the religious rights of the Hindus. Rajah Ram Moham Roy went to England to represent the opinion of enlightened India, and he pleaded for the confirmation of the Act. The appeal was, however, judged by the Council on its legal merit alone, and was dismissed.

The law, though enforced with vigour throughout the British dominions, did not immediately stop Sati all over India. The Punjab was still outside British India, and some of the Maharajahs of Indian States were reluctant to follow the lead of the British. In Rajputana, the practice lingered long, and cases were reported as late as 1861.

The custom of Sati had been so deep-rooted in Hindu society and the ideal so closely associated with the devotion of the good wife for her husband, that inexplicable cases of suicide by widows have been reported in many parts of India, even after Sati had passed into one of the evil institutions of the past. One case was reported in Gujarat in 1931, and Mahatma Gandhi denounced it, maintaining that real Sati was "the immolation of the spirit and not of the body". In the year 1950, two cases of Sati were reported from Jodhpur, and in November 1961, a case from Jaipur.

Wodow Remarriage

When Sati was abolished by law, the persecution of the widow became an avowed social policy among certain castes and communities. The death of her husband was taken as proof of the widow's sin, and in order to help her expiate it, in many regions of India, there developed a curious system of routine persecution of the widow by barber women who were paid to drag her, soon after the husband's death, to some water-front where she was given a ducking to the accompaniment of blows relieved by violent language. This torture was believed to elevate the soul of the widow and prepare her body and mind for the training in misery that was to be her lot till the end of her life.

The fact that the widow, as a rule, lived in the house of her husband, made her life all the more miserable, as the mother-in-law, never too soft towards her daughters-in-law, could only look upon the widow as the virtual destroyer of her son who would not have died, according to the then prevalent interpretations of the law of Karma, if his wife was virtuous. Hence the widow was never allowed to appear cheerful or wear bright clothes or ornaments, and any tendency on her part to look presentable was reckoned a sin against eternal verities; she had to drudge day and night and was the victim of all kinds of insolence by the other women of the household including servants; and the tragedy became all the more poignant when the widow was a child, as very often happened.

In certain regions, particularly in the south, the head of the widow was shaved in order to make her unattractive, and she was shunned as an ill omen by all. Many widows, under these conditions, ran away from their homes, and for a Hindu woman who left her home there was, at the time, no place except the street, as even low castes did not associate with her.

As such, the natural consequence of the abolition of Sati was the recognition of the right of the widow to remarriage. But in this, the British were reluctant to take the initiative. The suffering of the living was less spectacular than the agony of the burning widow, and the British Government were inclined to treat the question of widow-remarriage as a purely social matter to be decided by Hindus themselves. Fortunately, enlightened Hindu public opinion had made sufficient leeway to make legislation possible in this direction, by the sixth decade of the nineteenth century.

Of the many energetic Indians who championed the cause of the widow during this period, the most important was Iswarchandra Vidyasagar who hailed like Rajah Ram Mohan Roy, from Bengal. The main obstacle against widow-remarriage, according to the orthodox view point, was that it was not sanctioned by the Hindu law-givers. The question of the widow had been settled so well and so long ago by Hindu society, that the opinion of the ancient law-givers on the point was taken for granted and no possiblity of any important law-giver ever having permitted widow-remarriage was even suspected. So what was the surprise of the complacent Pundits when Vidyasagar published, in 1855, a pamphlet entitled *Remarriage of Hindu Widows* in which he quoted several passages from Hindu scriptures sanctioning widow-remarriage, and vehemently pleaded for legislation in its favour! The Pundits condemned the pamphlet and its author, maintained that the alleged permission for widow-remarriage was meant for the bygone golden age in which men were good and women virtuous, and not for the degenerate Kali Yuga of our own days with its evil men and impious women, and Vidyasagar was asked to shut up. But Vidyasagar refused to shut up. He pointed out that even Parasara whose code was considered the most authoritative for Kali Yuga permitted widow-remarriage. The heated controversy raged throughout India.

The British, however, were inclined to think that the injunctions of the golden age of Hinduism were also applicable to their benign period, and decided to legislate in favour of widow-remarriage. There were, acording to the Hon'ble J.P. Grant, the author of the Bill, forty petitions signed by sixty thousand people against the proposed legislation, whereas, in its favour, there were but twenty-five bearing five thousand signatures. In spite of this overwhelming opposition, the measure was adopted and passed into law on the 25th July, 1856. The preamble to the Act thus explained its need:

> Whereas it is known that by the law as administered in the Civil Courts established in the territories in the possession and under the Government of the East India Company, Hindu widows with certain exceptions are held to be, by reason of their having been once married, incapable of contracting a valid second marriage, and the offspring of such widows by any second marriage are held to be illegitimate and incapable of inheriting property, and whereas many Hindus believe that this imputed legal incapacity, although it is in accordance with established custom, is not in accordance with the dictates of their own conscience, and whereas it is just to relieve all such Hindus from this legal incapacity of which they complain, and the removal of all legal obstacles to the marriage of Hindu widows, will tend to the promotion of good morals and to the public welfare ....

For obvious reasons, while legislation for the prevention of Sati was effective, the Hindu Widow-Remarriage Act remained, for all practical purpose, a dead letter for a long time. Sati could be stopped by the police, but policemen could not arrange the remarriage of the widowed daughters, sisters and wives of the sixty thousand signatories to the petition opposing the Bill and their more numerous followers. Though some organisations like the Brahmo Samaj and Arya Samaj actively supported widows-remarriage, and even a Widow-Remarriage Society was formed to work as a marriage bureau for widows, so deep-rooted was the prejudice against widow-remarriage at the time that even the most vociferous advocates of the reform often evaded the issue when it came to be a question of their own sons, brothers or themselves marrying widows. A notable exception was the son of Iswarchandra Vidyasagar, who married a widow.

On the whole, with the best efforts of the reformers, in the earlier stages only some child-widows whose marriage had not been consummated could be remarried; anyway, the Act gave encouragement to those bold Hindus who wished to flout antiquated conventions, and some cases of widow-remarriage did occur among reformers and revolutionaries. In Madras, for instance, G. Subramania Aiyar, the founder-editor of *The Hindu*, got his widowed daughter remarried, which created a sensation in the south and led to the ostracism of the veteran reformer-journalist.

In the Census of 1881 the number of Hindu widows stood at the formidable figure of 2.1 million, and reformers like Ranada, Telang, Dadabhoi Naoroji and Beramji Malabari of Bombay began to despair. The futility of mere legislation to promote widow-remarriage was now plain to every reformer, and in August 1884, Mr. Malabari addressed a note to the Government explaining the ineffectiveness of the Widow-Remarriage Act because of the opposition of the orthodox and the general disabilities of women, which prevented widows from taking advantage of the law, and stressing the need for doing something positive in the matter. The note pointed out several cases of widows who had gone astray because of the refusal of their male relatives to get them married even when they wanted marriage, of infanticide, and of excommunication of widows who married. He put up a number of suggestions for encouraging widow-remarriage, of which the following were the more important:

1. No Hindu girl who has lost her husband or her betrothed, if she is a minor, shall be condemned to life-long widowhood against her will.
2. Arrangements may be made in suspected cases to ascertain whether a widow has accepted perpetual widowhood voluntarily or whether it has been forced upon her.
3. Every widow, of whatever age, shall have the right to complain to the authorities of social ill-usage (over and above excommunication) and that proper facilities shall be afforded to her for the purpose, such as gratuitous service of counsel, exemption from stamp duty, attendance at court, and so on.
4. The priest has no right to excommunicate the relations and connections of parties contracting second marriage, besides excommunicating the principals.

Mr. Malabari had devoted his life for the uplift of Indian women but he happened to follow the Zoroastrian religion and as such, was not considered competent to recommend legislation for the Hindus. The British Government sent his note to the Governors for their report, and the response was not satisfactory; so they decide to defer action "until sufficient proof is forthcoming that legislation has been asked for by a section, important in influence or number, of the Hindu community itself".

As for the opinion of some of the orthodox Hindus on the subject, the view of Mr. S.H. Chiplonkar, C.S.I., may be cited as an example. He said:

I know that neither Mr. Malabari nor the Government who undertook to circulate his note among Hindu gentlemen for the responsible expression of their opinion had the remotest idea of insulting the feelings of the community. But the result has, nonetheless, been the same. In short, those insinuations are a gratuitous and unmitigated libel upon the whole Hindu community, and as a gentleman, Mr. Malabari must withdraw them unreservedly and express his regret for having circulated such a libel and that too under the auspices of the Government. I am sure if the Government had been fully aware of the circumstances, they would never have consented to become the medium of giving wider publicity to such a libel.

So much for Malabari's efforts to get Hindu widows married. How little legislation had been able to achieve in the matter of widow-remarriage can best be seen from the following figures for widow under twenty-five years of age, in the Census of 1931, the first taken after the promulgation of the Prohibition of Child-Marriage Act of 1929:

Age Group	*Numbers of Widows*	*Age Group*	*Number of Widows*
0-1	1,515	5-10	105,449
1-2	1,785	10-15	183,998
2-3	3,485	15-20	514,394
3-4	9,076	20-25	846,959
4-5	15,018		

The census report particularly mentioned that the increase in the number of child-widows under the age of five was due to the rush of marriage of children anticipatory to the Prohibition of Child-Marriage Act. Anyway, the number and age of Hindu widows shown in a census taken seventy-five years after the passing of the Hindu Widow-Remarriage Act, are a sad reflection on the power of legislation to alter established conventions.

Well, it is now over a century since the Hindu Widow-Remarriage Act has been passed, but widow-remarriages are still extremely rare among orthodox Hindus. Though routine persecutions and the crueller forms of humiliations have now been given up, widow-remarriage is still associated, among the Hindus, with sullying the memory of a dead man. Further, the feeling that the widow is second-hand goods is so strong in India that even old widowers are reluctant to marry widows, when virgins are readily available.

Parsis and Monogamy

The distinctive feature of Christian society, as is well known, is monogamy. Of all the religions in the world, whether Aryan or Semitic, Christianity alone has maintained an uncompromising attitude against polygamy, and its practical-success has now brought all enlightened peoples of the world to its way of thinking. The obstinacy of the church on this point had, no doubt, considerably inconvenienced kings like Henry VIII, but on the whole, all Christian persuasions with negligible exceptions have conformed to the conception of "one spouse at a time", whatever may have been the extra-marital lapses of some of their followers.

In India Hindus, Muslims, Buddhists and Jains had all permitted polygyny, and kings and nobles had specialised in harems. The large majority of the general population had, no doubt, all along been monogamous but monogamy was reckoned a misfortune of the economically backward, and every poor man with ambitions had dreamt of a harem. As such the monogamic society was something foreign to Indian conceptions, at best an abstemious ideal to be realised in Rama Rajya, but seeing its smooth working among the British, many enlightened Indians felt that they could adopt it with advantage. As in other reforms, Rajah Ram Mohan Roy championed the cause of monogamy too, and disinherited, in his will, any of his sons who might indulge in polygyny. The time was not, however, ripe for legislation in favour of monogamy, and hence reformers were content to practise it as an individual virtue, and never agitated for its enforcement by law.

As a community, the Parsis were the first to accept monogamy in India, barring, of course, the Christians.

The Parsis, as the reader is probably aware, are immigrants from Persia who follow the Zoroastrian religion. During the Muslim conquest of Persia and the wholesale conversion of the population to Islam, some Zoroastrians, refusing conversion, fled to India. Here, under Hindu kings, noted for their traditional hospitality to refugess, they were allowed to practise their religion, and most of the immigrants settled down in Gujarat. With the spread of Islam in the Middle East, Zoroastrianism became practically extinct in Persia, and the immigrant Parsis, shorn of their ancient glory and with no co-religionists anywhere else in the world, dwindled into an insignificant island community among the Hindu and Muslim population of Gujarat. In course of time, they forgot their language and most of their scriptures, borrowed many customs from their Hindu neighbours and adopted Gujarati as their mother-tongue. They had, however, retained sufficient individuality to be known as a seprate community.

It was then that the British became the masters of India. The dormant vitality of the Parsi community burst forth, and they took advantage of the splendid opportunities they found. With the development of Bombay as the main port of Western India, most of the Parsis migrated to the rapidly rising port, and within a short time they emerged as an important community of the new city. They forged close commercial ties with the British, and the shipping and stevedoring work of the port became more or less the monopoly of the community. Their industry and enterprise won the admiration of the British, while their freedom from the many social restrictions that made contact between the British and the major Indian communities difficult, enabled them to mix freely with European society.

The Parsis thus came in closer contact with British society than the Hindus and Muslims, and were the first to adopt the monogamic laws of the ruling classes. Ancient Zoroastrian law, no doubt, permitted polygyny, but few Parsis were actually polygamous as a plurality of wives was the luxury of kings and nobles, and the Parsis had neither among them in India. Anyway, few Parsis knew exactly where their religious law stood in the matter of marriage, as most of the scriptures of Zoroastrianism were not brought to India, and what books had been actually brought either perished or became unintelligible through neglect of study; in this too, there was an added need for legislation.

Accordingly, at the instance of the Parsi community itself, the Parsi Marriage and Divorce Act was passed in 1865. By this Act, the existing form of marriage, known as Asirvad (Sanskrit word for blessing), performed by a Parsi priest, was recognised as valid in law; both polygyny and polyandry were forbidden, and divorce was permitted under certain conditions.

The Parsis adapted themselves to modern conditions with remarkable avidity and formed, along with Indian Christians, the spearhead of attack against feminine illiteracy and Purdah in many parts of India.

Indian Christians

Christianity was not introduced into India by the Europeans. The traditions of Christians in Kerala would indicate that Apostle Thomas came to India and founded their Church. Mylapore, near Madras, is even now venerated as the site of the Apostle's martyrdom, and the existing shrine here is believed to contain the relics of the Apostle. Though some historians are inclined to doubt the validity of this tradition, all, acquainted with the history of Christianity in India, are agreed that from very early times travellers have reported the existence of large Christian communities in South India. When the Portuguese came to India towards the close of the fifteenth century, they found a flourishing community of Christians in Kerala ruled by a semi-independent Bishop from Western Asia. The accounts of the Portuguese show that the community had a martial tradition, and could put in the field, at short notice, twenty thousand fighting men. The portuguese wished to bring this community (Known as Syrian Christians because of the Syrian Liturgy they followed) under them, for political and religious reasons, and there was continued animosity between Kerala Christians and the Portuguese throughout the period of the latter's domination of the West Coast. We need not go into the details of these quarrels here, but it must be mentioned that the Portuguese were zealous Christian who never missed an opportunity to convert the heathen, and in the coastal regions under their control Christian communities became a prominent feature of the population.

Besides, throughout the Muslim period and even before, Nestorian missionary enterprise from Western Asia had established several Christian centres in India. Because of their knowledge of Persian, a good number of Armenian Christians obtained service under Muslim rulers in India, and the Moghuls had several Armenian bobles under them. Further, there were Christian mercantile communities from Syria and elsewhere, who had trading interests in India, and many of them had settled down in the improtant cities of India.

The Jesuits, again, had established themselves in several parts of Moghul India under Akbar and Jehangir, who were well disposed towards Christianty, and had sizable congregations in several places; their activities, however, received a setback during the reign of Aurangazeb, but after his death the Jesuits again flourished.

The age that followed the disruption of the Moghul empire may be termed the era of European adventurers in India, some of whom became rulers of independent principalities. Of these adventurers mention may be made of the Irishman George Thomas, who played an important role in the ever-shifting political scene in and about Delhi towards the close of the eighteenth century, and of the fierce German, Walter Reinhardt; the latter founded the principality of Sardhana and bequeathed it to his wife, a Muslim lady who later accepted Christianity and is known to history as Begum Samru. The Begum ruled Sardhana from 1778 till 1836, an unusually long lease of reign in those troublous days of short-lived kingdoms and rulers; most of her army-officers were European adventurers, and her military strength was well respected by Indian rulers and the East India Company alike.

The British, as rulers, did not interest themselves in Gospel-work or proselytisation, but after the removal of the obnoxious missionary clause from the Charter of the East India Company in 1813, regular missions came to India from America, Great Britain and other Western countries, and a period of intense missionary activity started throughout India.

As a result of these various efforts, the number of Christian communities in India increased considerably, and by the end of the

British period, Christians became the third important community in India, numerically stronger than the Sikhs or Parsis. Taking the population of India as a whole, they are lesser in number than the Muslims, but in the state of Kerala, they are more numerous than they.

As already stated, the distinctive social feature of Christian communities, whatever their denominational differences, have all along been monogamy. Even the Syrian Christians of Kerala who, after the rise of Islam, had been practically isolated from the main centres of Christianity, preserved the institution of monogamy unimpaired, though they adopted some of the customs and manners of the Hindus among whom they lived.

The Purdah too failed to attract Indian Christians. In South India with its dominant Hindu population, middle class women have all along been free from the tyranny of veil, and here Christians had not experienced any difficulty in letting their women go out without covering their faces. But in North India, especially in regions under strict Muslim conventions, women of the Christians too had to move about in closed litters, as ladies who went out without veiling their faces were not considered quite respectable and often invited trouble; in their own houses no Christian ladies anywhere in India observed the Purdah, but all were free to appear before friends and guests, though in deference to the general conventions of the east, they took care to assume a subordinate role in the public life of the community. With the spread of the British influence no invitation was necessary to the Indian Christians to throw off the Purdah, wherever they had to observe it reluctantly, and grant social equality to their women.

The Christian communities, distributed throughout the country, often worked as the nucleus for the spread of female education in India. When enlightened Indians and foreign missionaries started schools for girls, orthodox Hindus and Muslims were reluctant to send their girls to these schools, but Christians and Parsis were generally eager to take advantage of the educational facilities offered by them. Similarly, Indian Christians were the first among the communities of India to encourage educated women to take to public service. The community was economically backward, but with them no odium was attached to paid work for respectable women; as such Indian Christian women gladly took up service under the Government, in private institutions and in commercial concerns when opportunities offered. In fact, for a long time Christians were the only community that could be persuaded to send their girls for training and and employment in the nursing service, and even now this branch of the medical profession is dominated by Christians in India. It is also worthy of note that the Travancore-Cochin area in Kerala, which has a high percentage of Christian population, has consistently held the first place for literacy in India, both male and female, for several decades.

In marital matters, Indian Christians are governed by the Indian Christian Marriage Act of 1872. This Act, like the Parsi Marriage Act of 1865, is mainly based on English Marriage Laws, and its provisions are in the nature of confirmation of practices already in force in the community.

Female Education

Before we deal with female education, a word may be said about the education of males in India; for women, down the ages, have been generally under the tutelage of men in India, and no education of girls was possible unless men were prepared to educate them.

At the beginning of the British period, primary education in India was considered a purely private affair with which the state had nothing to do. In villages each community or caste (only higher castes enjoyed the privilege of literacy; very low castes were forbidden the knowledge of letters) ran its own schools. While Muslim schools were usually attached to the local mosque, a Hindu village school, especially in South India, was the spacious Verandah of some convenient house. As education was reckoned the prerogative of the favoured few, the number of pupils who studied under a teacher in one of the Verandah schools was few; the young scholars ranged in age from five to fifteen or so, each getting individual attention and learning what he was able to grasp. The beginners traced the alphabet in sand with their index fingers, while senior scholars sat cross-legged near them reading the palm-leaf text-books prepared for each by the teacher. All were to read aloud so that the teacher could correct mistakes, usually to the accompaniment of severe blows, and the whole village resounded with the discordant notes of youthful scholars attempting to master the mystery of letters. The teacher was paid by subscription collected from parents of the boys who attended the class. There was neither state aid towards education nor a common fund. Only those who wanted their children to be educated had to pay, Girls were not considered good enough to receive instruction in the complicated art of reading and writing. This was, generally, the position of education with the middle classes whether in the villages, towns or cities in India, at the beginning of the British period.

The rich, however, appointed their own teachers and, thanks to the size of the joint family, there was enough work for a teacher in one of the bigger, better classes of households. At times, a lady teacher was engaged to instruct girls when the head of the family was progressive enough to consider literacy a desirable accomplishment to women.

The missionaries may be said to be the pioneers of modern education in India. They started their own private schools for the education of the children of their congregations, and for the benefit of those others who wished to send their children to these new institutions. The missionaries, with their experience of the educational system of Europe, introduced graded classes in their schools with a set curriculum for each class. At first the instruction was conducted in the local language by Indian teachers or by foreigners who had learnt it for the purpose, but wherever they considered it desirable, English was introduced as a second language or as the medium of instruction. Non-Christians in the initial stages of missionary educational enterprise, were reluctant to send their children to these schools because of the proselytising zeal of the teachers and the Bible classes which were then inseparable from missionary institutions. But the rising power of the East India Company and the demand for English-knowing Indians for service in the Company's Government led to a good many Indians learning the language of the rulers, for which the best institutions then existing were the mission schools. The Hindus in particular, who had studied Persian under Muslim rulers without losing their religion, took advantage of the new educational facilities, and their children attended the compulsory Bible classes as the price of learning English which opened up for them possibities of securing lucrative posts in public service. These English-educated Indians eventually bloomed forth into pioneers in social reform.

As the power of the East India Company spread in India, the British felt that education could not be left entirely to private agencies and the Government had a responsibility to promote literacy in the country. As early as 1826, Sir Thomas Munroe drew up a programme of public instruction for the Madras Presidency. In conformity with the spirit of the age, the programme was mainly concerned with the education of the upper classes; the theory was that if the upper classes were educated to saturation point, culture would either overflow or filter down to the lower orders by some sort of a law of gravity and permeate the whole society.

Such theories, however, did not last long. Not only democratic ideals were fast growing in Europe, but the British were finding that the spread of education was bringing them more allies in India; for the new, English-educated Indians were all friendly towards the British, while the old indigenous schools of thought remained antagonistic. Hence in Sir Charles' famous despatch of 1854, the question of primary education was actively pursued, "in order to combat the ignorance of the toiling millions which is the greatest curse of the country". The proposal embodied the creation of a new department of education, a system of training for teachers, the adoption of the principle of giving grants for private-managed educational institutions and "the encouragement of female education".

But before coming to the encouragement of female education

The very important decision of the Government to introduce English as the medium of instruction in India may be mentioned. When the question of public education was taken up, there was considerable difference of opinion, not only among Indians but among British educationists themselves, about the desirability of forcing a foreign language on India. While the majority of Indians thought that their children should be taught in their own languages, the more advanced section of the reformist element was all in favour of English a study of the literature of which, they maintained, would open up new visions for India. This point of view was stressed in a letter written by that zealous pioneer, Rajah Ram Mohan Roy, to Lord Amherst. Roy wrote:

> If it had been intended to keep the British in ignorance of real knowledge, the Baconian philosophy would not have been allowed to displace the system of schoolmen which was best calculated to perpetuate ignorance. In the same manner, the Sanskrit system of education would be the best calculated to perpetuate ignorance if such had been the policy of the British legislatures. But as the improvement of the native population is the object of the Government, it will consequently promote a more liberal and enlightened policy of instruction.

Anyway, Lord Macaulay, to whom the work of going into the details of the question and reporting to the Government was entrusted, was so contemptuous of oriental learning that His Lordship had no difficulty in pouring ridicule on all those who were in favour of Indian languages, and strongly recommended English as the medium of instruction in India. The Government accepted his recommendation and introduced a curriculum of studies for Indian schools on the model then obtaining in England, with English as the medium of instruction. The far-reaching consequences of this decision are thus described by a modern authority on Indian affairs.

> A no less important contribution to the development of Indian life which Macaulay made was his famous minute on education. Divested of the narrow prejudices against Hindu

> civilisation and of the shelf of books for which he was prepared to exchange the entire treasures of oriental literature and the cheap rhetoric about 'seas of treacles and seas of butter' which marred the famous document, its main thesis of an education based on the 'New Learning' and through the medium of English was, in the circumstances of the time, the most beneficently revolutionary decision taken by the British Government in India.

Beneficent, no doubt, as far as India was concerned; but there are people who doubt if it was equally beneficial to the political and commercial interests of the British. For the new education brought, in its wake, new theories of nationalism and democracy to India but for which British rule in India would have possibly prolonged after 1947.

English education broadened the outlook of Indians considerably, and they began to feel that their institutions were not the best in the world. In the light of this knowledge of their ignorance, an ardent zeal for reforms seized newly-educated Indians and a vigorous era of religious and social uplift ensued. Caste and untouchability, polytheism and idolatry, Purdah, child-marriage, illiteracy, taboo against sea-voyages, were all vehemently attacked, and education and emancipation of women actively pursued.

The first modern schools for girls in India were, again, started by Christian missions. Because of the age-old Indian prejudice against mixed classes even for children, convents and Protestant missions started 'Zenana' schools staffed by lady teachers to which girls alone were adimitted. There were, however, the ever-present danger of 'conversion' in these schools, apart from the fear of pollution by promiscuous mixing with beef and pork eaters. As such only the bolder type of Indians who were prepared to face social ostracism would send their children to these schools.

Followers of the Brahmo Samaj (a sect founded by Rajah Ram Mohan Roy, in 1828) and the Arya Samaj (founded by swami Dayanand, a Kathiawar Brahmin, shortly after) who had, more or less hived off from orthodox Hinduism, actively supported female education; they either sent their children to mission schools or started their own schools for girls.

The Muslims, as a community, were slow to appreciate the benefits of the new educational system for girls. While there were individual reformers (like Badrudin Tyabji, who sent his daughters to England for higher education) in the fast rising ports of Bombay, Calcutta and Madras where Indians were developing a cosmopolitan outlook, farther north in the main centres of Islam there was considerable antagonism to English education for girls. Even Sir Syed Ahmed Khan, who claimed to be an ardent social reformer and founded, in 1871, the journal *Social Reformer*, pronounced his weighty opinion against Muslims sending their girls to public schools to study English, though he was generally in favour of English education for boys and founded the Aligarh School on British lines. The stranglehold Purdah had obtained on Indian Muslim community was mainly responsible for this; few Muslims could get over its insidious influence even when they attacked its more grotesque forms.

The initial stages of the female education movement in India were marked by youthful or individual enthusiasm rather than by organised efforts. In 1849, for instance, the boys of the Elphinstone College, Bombay, on their own initiative started a school for girls and volunteered to teach in it themselves; their zeal for women's education was so great that they even started a woman's journal for the benefit of those illiterate women who were willing to have the contents read out to them.

Apart from missionary institutions, the Bethune School of Calcutta, may be said to be the first regular, secular school for girls in India. It was started in 1847 by Iswharchandra Vidyasagar and Drinkwater Bethune who noticed the reluctance of the Hindus and Muslims to send their daughters to mission schools because of the Bible classes and the conversion complex. Vidyasagar himself took over the management of the school in 1851. The school proved a great sucess, and Bethune was struck by the intelligence and bearing of Indian lady scholars whose talents for study "surpassed those of European girls of the same age". The Bethune experiment was soon copied all over India, and girls' schools became a regular feature of the educational system of every Indian city and town.

In Bombay that celebrated trio Francina Sorabji, Ramabal Ranade and Pundita Ramabai were the three lady pioneers who dedicated themselves to the education and uplift of their sisters.

> Francina Sorabji's chief interest was education, her chief influence a unifyingness which compelled love and obliterated all differences. She had the vision to realise that Oneness was among our chief needs in India; and she set herself to solve this problem by bringing together children of all communities, including the Hindu (majority) community in the schools she founded. The Hunter Commission paid a tribute to the service she was rendering to the cause of education, and many were the delegates from all over India who, from time to time, came to study her methods and principles.... Her activities were not confined to education. In an age when welfare organisation had not even been conceived, she did practical social service work in Poona and the adjoining villages.

Ramabai Ranade was her junior in age, but she worked in close collaboration with Francina Sorabji. While she actively worked for female education, Mrs. Ranade selected for her special field the economic advancement of widows and destitute women.

> The Industrial Home of Service which she founded at Poona is a self-supporting and expanding organisation conducted by capable Maratha women upon the business lines of its foundation, and branching out to fulfil the growing needs of the day. It was her own idea to visit Hindu women in prison, to make human contact with them and to read to them in the Vernacular. This was long before unofficial Visitors were appointed by Government. In Bengal such bodies did not materialize till 1910.

Pundita Ramabai, the third in the trio, was a rare genius whose concern for her sisters was accentuated by her own sufferings, and her biography reads like a page from a medieval romance. Her father, Ananta Sastri, was a wandering Hindu pilgrim, and Ramabai herself was born in the forest of Gangamula during the pilgrim's progress through the jungle. Her parents and a sister died of starvation in the famine of 1877, when she was twenty-four, and she lost her husband in 1882. The lot of Indian women in general and of widows in particular thoroughly roused her, and she embarked upon a career of social service for the uplift of her sisters which ended only with her death in 1922. In 1889 she founded the Sarda Sadan (Home of Wisdom) in Bombay for the education of women in general and of widows in particular. In 1890 the Sadan was transferred to Poona because of the rising cost of living in Bombay, and by the year 1900 the inmates of the various 'Homes' she was running reached the phenomenal figure of two thousand, most of whom employed in educational and humanitarian work. In the initial stages of her social service career there was much opposition from the orthodox, but her force of character, charming personality and capacity for work overcame all opposition and she had the good fortune to see, before her death, most of her dreams come true.

The efforts of these tireless pioneers began to bear fruit, and the old prejudice against feminine literacy was definitely overcome in India, and the upper classes were feeling that literacy was an accomplishment to girls. Girls' schools were opened in every city and town, but the overall impact of female education on the population as a whole was not very impressive in the initial stages. The Indian Education Commission of 1882-83, reviewing the situation noticed:

> Female education is still in an extremely backward condition and needs to be fostered in every legitimate way. In some provinces, the sympathies of the people do not yet run sufficiently in this direction to induce local bodies to devote to female education any of the funds at their disposal. Hence we think it expedient that public funds of all kinds-local,

> municipal and provincial—should be chargeable in an equitable proportion for the support of girls' schools as well as boys' schools; and the former, being in an earlier stage of development should receive even something more than that might appear to be a strictly impartial share of encouragement.

Another difficulty that stood in the way of female education was the shortage of women teachers. Parents always preferred lady teachers in girls' schools, and sufficient number of women were not coming forward for employment as teachers, especially as girls' schools were steadily increasing in number throughout the country. The Commission took account of this, and stated that "In order to induce girls to look forward to teaching as a profession, it seems desirable to encourage pupil-teachers wherever the system is practicable". There was also paucity of lady-inspectors, "since the male inspectors both revolted against the seclusion complex and terrified even the smallest children".

With all this, the popularity of female education was on the upward trend, and year by year the number of girls attending schools increased. In 1826, the percentage of literate women in the Madras Presidency was half, or one per two hundred; Madras, it must be remembered, was the most progressive region in india at the time. In many other places hardly one woman in a thousand could read and write. By 1881, the position had so far improved that the census showed one woman out of 180 as able to read and write for the whole country. By 1886, the figure for Hindus alone had risen to one per cent.

Apart from this general rise in feminine literacy, there were encouraging signs that Indian girls were prepared to go for higher education and even for careers. The Bethune School added a collegiate wing to its buildings, and claimed the honour of being the first arts college for women in India, and produced the first Indian lady graduate in the year 1883. In 1886, arts colleges, throughout India, showed a roll of forty-five lady students, half of whom belonged to Bengal. Medical Colleges also began to attract women students, and in the same year, "six girls were studying in the Madras Medical College, eighteen in the Grant Medical College, Bombay, and three in the Medical College at Calcutta".

As long as child-marriage was the general rule, it was difficult to make any appreciable progress towards the spread of female education, as among the better classes of Hindus girls were married before they were old enough to learn the three Rs, and the lower classes were not interested in female education. But in 1929, the Prohibition of Child-Marriage Act was passed which raised the minimum age for marriage of girls to fourteen. Once the old convention, that a girl had to be married before menstruation, was overcome, marriage did not always take place at the age of fourteen; in fact, girls grew into young ladies of seventeen or eighteen before marriage proposals started coming in, and all that the parents could do, in the meantime, was to let their daughters continue their studies till marriage. And it even became fashionable for parents, whose daughters were remaining unmarried for want of desirable proposals coming or for want of cash to provide dowry, to give out the plausible explanation that the girls were so passionately fond of their studies that it was impossible to put ideas of marriage into their heads.

There also developed an economic incentive to higher education for girls among the middle classes. The old antagonism to paid work for educated women was slowly dying, and girls who were able to get through the matriculation examination found respectable jobs waiting for them as teachers, clerks, typists, etc. and in many impecunious middle class families with no adult or able males, working girls fulfilled the role of breadwinners.

Once this advantage of female education came to be appreciated by the middle classes, the difficulty was not to find girls for schools and colleges, but rather to find schools and colleges for girls. But by now the sanctions of Purdah had been sufficiently undermined to make co-education possible in practically all schools and colleges in India. Except in regions where the Purdah sat heavily on women's neck, there was no need to run girls' schools in villages or towns, where there were not enough girls to fill the classes, just to promote female education; parents were quite prepared to send their daughters to existing institutions attended by boys.

As female education progressed, women began to take to careers too. In medicine they found a profession particularly suited to their genius, and a regular Women's Medical Service was organised, and in many places in India women's hospitals were exclusively run by lady doctors. Women took to law too, and some of the more energetic of them, even to engineering. Physical culture and sports also claimed their attention, and a good many young ladies took active part in inter-collegiate and high school sports and tournaments, all over India.

The spread of modern education was showing up its defects too. The old emphasis on the 'eligibility for public service', as the main function of modern education, continued even after its need had ceased, and every year schools and colleges all over India turned out matriculates and graduates in their thousands for whom no jobs could be found. The new education, instead of qualifying, disabled young men and women for taking up the traditional occupations of agriculture and crafts-manship, and the country was flooded with educated but frustrated youths who did not know what to do with themselves. A complete re-appraisal of values, in education in general and in women's education in particular, became the imperative need of the country, and the All-India Women's Conference was insistent in its demand for specialised education for women to enable them to fulfil their peculiar role in society. An important institution that came out of this demand was the Lady Irwin College, founded in 1932 in Delhi, in order to make women "utilise the advantages of science in their homes and to add to them the loveliness of art". The need for special courses of studies for girls in high schools and colleges was also felt, and many educational institutions introduced domestic science in their curriculum of studies; the Madras University instituted post-graduate courses in dietics, cookery, house-keeping, hygiene and sanitation, and many other universities followed the example of Madras.

A word may also be said about that interesting experiment in female education, the Women's University of Poona. It was founded in 1917, at a time when Indian nationalism had burst forth with particular vigour under the leadership of Tilak, in order to correct the erroneous tendencies in, modern education, and put female education on a new footing in keeping with the ancient traditions of India. But its media of instruction were Indian languages, and during the British period its degrees were not recognised by the Government. Only in 1949, after the British left, did the University obtain recognition.

Laudable as these efforts were, the main problem, illiteracy remained unsolved. In the Census of 1951, the first taken after the British left (in 1947), feminine literacy stood at 7.87 per cent. In Travancore-Cochin the percentage was as high in 46.1 in Delhi 29.9 and Coorg 24.1. In other regions the percentage was much lower, the lowest, Vindhya Pradesh, showing 1.4. These figures are not impressive when compared with similar statistics in Europe and America, but comparisons between India and the West in these matters cannot possibly give us a true picture of the tremendous efforts that had gone to obtain 7.87 percentage of feminine literacy in an economically backward country of about 200,000,000 women, of whom hardly one in a thousand was literate.

Women and the Fine Arts in India

A direct result of the spread of education in general and female education in particular was the rise of literary women in India and the liberation of dancing from the brothers. So inseparably was dancing associated with loose morals in medieval India that the term 'dancing-girl' in many parts of the country was reckoned a synonym for a prostitute or shameless woman, though oddly enough, some of the great gods and goddesses of the Hindu pantheon were conceived as vigorous dancers.

The folk of India and the aborigines, who were happily free from many of the restrictions imposed on the higher classes had, no doubt, their communal dances in which both men and women took part. Among the respectable, however, mixed dances were looked down upon as bordering on promiscuity, and even now ball-room dancing of the Western type has not found favour with Indian society. A sharp distinction had always been maintained between entertainers and spectators in India; as a rule, only men were permitted to watch and appreciate dancing by professional women in respectable social functions. In temples, however, where music and gestures were of a devotional type, women were not debarred from watching dancing even when performed by the profane.

The convention had to be kept up in stage-shows too. It is not known if actresses took part in the public performance of the plays of Kalidasa, Bhavabhuti, Sudraka and other ancient dramatists of India, but during the medieval period, down to the early decades of the twentieth century, the role of women on the stage was generally played by effeminate men dressed in feminine clothes. On certain occasions women performed on the stage, and when they did, the performers were not always of the respectable type.

Though public appearance on the stage was thus forbidden to women of good breeding, in the houses of nobles, girls were at times taught music and dancing for the entertainment of the members of the household and their relatives; while the study of music was often continued even after marriage, dancing was considered undesirable for young ladies growing into mature womanhood, as it involved physical movements that offended notions of modesty founded on statics.

With the spread of education and the general decline of the Purdah, music and dancing began to be cultivated among the upper and middle classes, and these fine arts came to be considered, along with literacy, accomplishments to girls. In many girls' schools the curriculum included music and dancing. This new interest in fine arts grew rapidly among the middle classes, and by the third decade of the twentieth century it became fashionable among the upper middle classes to make sure, before a marriage proposal was finally accepted, that the girl had learnt music and had a working knowledge of the Mudras (gestures in classical dancing). At times the bride-to-be was even asked to give musical recitals for the satisfaction, if not the entertainment, of the wooing party, and the bolder even asked for a dance performance in the classical style. The Vina, a stringed instrument, has been the favourite of Indian musicians from very early times, and proficiency in playing it came to be considered an asset for girls in the Indian marriage market, especially in the south.

Once music came to be recognised as an accomplishment to respectable girls, women of the better classes with the necessary talents and training took to music as a profession, and the proficient no more fought shy of giving public performances. There was no further need to keep lights under bushels, and modern India produced some famous lady musicians, of whom the best known is perhaps the South Indian singer M.S.Subbalakshmi, who has specialised in the classical music of India. Other exponents of the classical tradition are Patamall of Madras, and Kesarbai Kerkar and Hirabai Barodkar, both of Bombay. A great number of Indian women have also obtained distinction in popular music, of whom mention may be made of Begum Akhtar of Lucknow, Rasoolan Bai of Banaras and Jutika Ray, Sandhya Mookerjee and Meera Chatterjee of Bengal.

One of the pioneers in liberating Indian dancing from its unholy associations was the late Mrs. Leila Sokhey, a close friend and associate of Anna Pavlova, better known in India and abroad by her adopted name Menaka. She popularised Indian dancing in the West as no lady before her had done. For the benefit of young Indians, she established a school in Khandala for teaching dancing and choreography. Of other well-known exponents of Indian dancing, mention may be made of Rukmini Devi of Madras, Balasaraswati, Gauri Devi (daughter of the painter Nandalal Bose) and Mrinalini Sarabhai who have contributed not a little to raise the status and prestige of Indian dancing. Besides these ladies, eminent dancers like Uday Shanker and Ram Gopal toured extensively, with their ballets, in the East and West, and brought international fame to Indian dancing.

With the patronage it thus enjoyed in India and abroad, dancing became a respectable, as well as profitable, profession for young Indian ladies. And among the younger generation of Indian women-dancers.

Shanta Rao, noted exponent of the ancient *Mohini Attam* of Malabar, and the *Bharata Natyam* and *Kathakali* schools, is considered one of the finest exponents of pure *Bharata Natyam,* Kumari Kamala is a charming young dancer and former infant prodigy from South India, an exponent of *Bharata Natyam*, who, with her special grace and wonderfully expressive interpretation, has brought a compelling popularity to the art. Kumudini and Shevanti have graced the stages of India and abroad in the Ram Gopal ballets. Indrani Rahman, the Travancore Sisters, Vijayantimala, Sarla Sehgal, Tara Chaudhury, Shirin and Roshan Vazifdar, Vinoo Indrani, Anjali Hora and Satiavati, have all established themselves as dancers of quality in *Bharata Natyam,* Roshan Kumari, Damayanti Joshi, and Rani Karna are fine exponents of *Kathak.* The Jhaveri Sisters, Nyana and Ranjan, who have depicted the lilting beauty of the dances of Manipur through several ballets produced by the Indian National Theatre, are among other enthusiasts who have brought to the Indian dance a fresh impetus and popularity.

Many of these young exponents of Indian dancing have travelled abroad and performed before discriminating audiences; and they have played as great a part in making India better known to the outside world as her philosophers, politicians, poets and diplomats.

The arrival of films into the entertainment world gave a further impetus to the cultivation of histrionics in India. The first Indian pictures were produced in the second decade of the twentieth century when acting and dancing had not yet come out of the shady by-lanes of the cities, and producers were compelled to draw their actresses from the existing classes, as the peculiarities of film production prevented the stage-convention of men playing feminine roles being adopted for the screen. With the rising popularity of films, the industry flourished but all its women employees still came from the same old source, and as a result films gained in clientele while the industry suffered in prestige though not in profits. Anyway, even after the study of dancing had become popular among the respectable classes, acting for the screen was still looked upon with disfavour. Such was the odium attached to film-acting that when, at a fairly advanced stage in the progress of the industry, some young ladies belonging to a respectable but impecunious family in Bombay appeared in minor roles in an Indian picture, the incident created a sensation in the city, and the whole family was threatened with ex-communication.

This atmosphere could not, for obvious reasons, be continued for long; the movies and later the talkies came to occupy a dominant position in the field of entertainment in India, their tremendous educative influence obtained universal recognition, and the film industry in India had to be made safe for respectable ladies, especially as some thirty per cent of the acting staff were women. Sabita Devi, Sulochana, Durgabai Khote and Nalini Tarkhad were the pioneers who built up the prestige of film-acting in India. With the debut of Devika Rani, a grandniece of poet Rabindranath Tagore, in the first Indian talkie, Kismet, produced in 1930, the tide against respectable young ladies acting in films definitely turned, and today, a galaxy of stars, too numerous to be named individually, adorns the firmament of Indian talkies which are produced in all the important languages of India.

In the realm of painting and the plastic arts, Indian women have not, it must be admitted, attained the distinction they have in acting and dancing. The death of Amrita Sher Gil at a comparatively young age deprived India of a promising woman-artist who was rising to eminence in the art world. Li Gotami, Sheila Auden, Sushila Yawalkar, Sheroo Sidwa, Mary Roop Krishna, Premoja Chaudhuri and Amina Ahmad may be mentioned as other Indian women artists of distinction.

The paucity of women artists in India is more than compensated by the large number of talented women writers the new education has produced. The spread of female education has not only revived the feminine genius of the ancient Vedic and Buddhist days, but has also enabled Indian women to play almost as important a part as men in building up the new literature of India.

As we have already seen, at no time in the history of India have women been completely shut out from literary pursuits, and even in the worst days of feminine illiteracy and Purdah, individual names of gifted writers and composers, both Hindu and Muslim, had cropped up on the Indian literary scene. The Bhakti movement in Hinduism produced a volume of devotional literature in India and women had their full share in enriching it. Andal, a Tamil lady, Kumari Molla, a Telegu, Muktibai, a Mahratha lady, and Madhbai Dasi, a disciple of the Vaishnava ecstatic Chaitanya, and the renowned singer Mira are names that stand out in the realm of Bhakti literature of India, and their songs and writings have come down to us as the inspired outpourings of souls on fire. Molla, who wrote the Telegu *Ramayana* in the sixteenth century, was as scholarly as she was religious, and even now, "disputed points of prosody and syntax are settled by reference to her".

There were also Muslim women writers and composers in Moghul India. Gulbadan Begum, daughter of Babar, the founder of the Moghul empire, is reputed to have written the *Humayun Namah,* a record of considerable historical importance, and Jahanara, daughter of emperor Shah Jehan, a biography of the Muslim saint, Khwaja Mohinuddin Chisti. Zebunissa, daughter of Aurangazeb, was the leader of feminine fashion and culture in her age, and she is said to have written many poems. Even Nur Jehan seems to have found time to write poetry amidst her various pre-occupations. But the literary fame of imperial personages usually rests on their royal prestige, and we have few works of distinction by Muslim women of medieval India. As a rule the strictness of the Purdah prevented them from coming into direct contact with life outside the four walls of the Zenana, and what works have been attributed to them are marked by rigid conventionalism and a desire to imitate Persian masters rather than to give expression to their own personality.

But in the middle ages, it is good to remember, not only in India but throughout the world women were never very active on the literary scene. With the rise of the feminist movement and the spread of female education, women writers began to appear in every field of literary activity in India, from composing poems to the writing of text books in arithmetic. English education also brought in new styles and literary forms which enriched the literature of all the main languages of India, and women writers laboured equally with men for building up this new literature. Their number by the middle of the twentieth century had become so large that their mere names and works will fill a chapter of this book and as such, a list is not attempted here.

Indian women have also shown remarkable talents in writing in English, and some have even won international fame. Toru Datta, a Bengali lady who travelled widely in Europe, may be said to be the first Indian woman to attract attention in England by her literary compositions. But her death at the age of twenty-one, in 1876, robbed India of a poetess of great promise.

Sarojini Naidu burst upon the Indian literary scene as a gifted poetess, but after the tragedy of Jallianwala Bagh she gave up the Muse and took to politics, and what is Politics's gain is Literature's loss.

Of the prose writers among the younger generation mention may be made of Shanta Rao and Kamala Markandeya who are rising to literary fame.

Indian Freedom Movement and Women's Emancipation

The revolt of 1857 is often claimed by Indian writers, whose patriotism is stronger than their sense of judgment, as a national war against foreign rule, but the objective historian will find it difficult to conform to this view. The Mutiny was just one of those many rebellions of semi-independent rulers who wished to throw off the suzerainty of an imperial power when opportunities presented themselves, which had been a regular feature of Inidan history down the ages. It was essentially a rebellion of feudal chiefs who rose against the British, and not a popular national movement. If successful, would have put the hands of the clock a hundred years back; in the larger interests of India it is good that the Mutiny had failed.

After the Mutiny, the British lost faith in their feudal friends and turned to the middle classes in India for support. Fortunately the newly educated middle classes, to whom the leadership of India was slowly passing, were all great admirers of the British and their institutions. Many of them found employment under the Government, and some rose to eminence, winning kinghthoods and other highly coveted distinctions of the nineteenth century. Most of them were also ardent social and religious reformers who affected a contempt for polytheism and idolatry, caste and vegetarianism, child-marriage, polygyny and Purdah; in religious matters, the Hindus among them were either members of the Brahmo Samaj and its offshoot, the Prarthana Samaj, or rationalists who, like their brethren in Europe, said in their hearts that there was no God. Nationalism in India was still far off, and the discovery of India's past glory was yet to be made. The new Indians were inclined to look to the West for inspiration and if anything, wished to sever their connection with India's past.

The British felt highly complacent about this development for which they were responsible. So when the Indian National Congress was formed in Bombay on the 28th December 1885, it had all the blessings of the British Government. The founders and members were men of the new learning, lawyers, journalists, teachers and even administrators, all men of liberal views; all that they wanted was to voice the opinion of new India. If, at that time, any one had predicted that the Congress would turn out an organisation for driving the British out of India, its members, no less than the British administrators, would have been shocked. In fact, Telang, one of the founders of the Congress, hearing that in Bengal there was antagonism that the report was false and all was well with Bengal. In a meeting held in the Town Hall of Bombay to consider the Ilbert Bill, he said:

> It has been asserted that the Bengalis entertain feelings of hatred and hostility to the British nation. Well, gentlemen, having had the honour, as you are aware, of being appointed to serve on the Education Commission, I had recently to spend a few months in Calcutta. And during the period of my stay there I came into close, intimate and frequent contact with the leaders of thought and the leaders in public affirm, and to affirm very confidently, that this hatred and frank conversations with many of them, having thus seen them in a sort of mental undress, so to speak, I venture to affirm, and to affirm very confidently, that this hatred and hostility is a mere figment of some alarmist brain and has no existence in reality. (Loud Cheers). I think that, believing this, as I do believe it, to be the truth upon the subject, I am bound, if not by any other obligation, at least by gratitude for the kindness which I received from my Bengali brethren while I was among them, to make this statement to correct misapprehension.

Thus went on merrily, Congress-British friendship in the great days of nascent Indian nationalism.

In the meantime oriental scholarship was making new discoveries about ancient India. In the beginning of the nineteenth century, India was generally considered a culturally and religiously backward country which had not got out of the superstitions of the middle ages, and even the little culture the country possessed was reckoned the culmination of centuries of evolution, but by the beginning of the twentieth century it was admitted by all that India was the leading light of Asia in ancient days and her position in the nineteenth century, far from being her highest attainment, was the lowest point to which she had degenerated down the centuries from her dominant position in Asian civilisation. It was now discovered that from the time of Asoka right down to the Muslim period, India had been the torchbearer of Asian culture, and her priests, missionaries and merchants had carried her civilisation not only to the backward regions of South East Asia but also to Central Asia, China, Tibet and Mongolia, and that Indians were heirs to a heritage which the British, their masters, could not boast of. There was no more need for Indians to be ashamed of themselves or their ancestors.

One of the immediate effects of this new discovery was the rise of the Arya Samaj which revitalised Hinduism in the Punjab. Unlike the apologetic Bramo Samaj, the Arya Samaj marked the resurgence of militant Hinduism which was prepared to measure swords with the Christian and Muslim at once. From Bengal rose the powerful voice of Swami Vivekananda who proclaimed from house-tops the message of Advaita, and he travelled to the West to teach real Hinduism to the Europeans and Americans.

This renaissance could not be confined to religion but soon spread to the social and political field. A generation of younger politicians rose who were fired with a new zeal which looked to India's past for inspiration rather than to the West. Gokhale now founded the Servants of India Society; its members were to be dedicated men, Sanyasis more or less, who were to take to politics in the ancient spirit.

But under the fiery leadership of Tilak the ideal of the political Sanyasi did not find much favour. Tilak preferred the militant message of the *Gita*; he combined scholarship with politics, propounded new theories of the antiquity of the *Vedas* based on ingenious astronomical calculations, and organised resurgent Maharashtrian nationalism around a cult of Shivaji. He uncerenmoniously asked the British to pack up and leave India to Indians and fought for his ends with all the means he could command. The Plague Policy of the Bombay Government and the partition of Bengal hastened the end of Anglo Indian amity, and repression started its wandering career.

The first decade of the twentieth century was marked by outbursts of violent anti-British feelings in several parts of India, and the cult of the bomb found favour with frustrated revolutionaries. A serious rift threatened the very existence of the Congress; the nationalists advocated a vigorous anti-British policy while the moderates, who had not yet lost all faith in the British, stood for a more conciliatory, attitude, and in the Surat session of the Congress, held in 1907, there was even hurling of shoes against the presidential chair.

From then on the fortunes of the Congress swayed between the extremists and the moderates. The second decade of the twentieth century started with a lull in the Congress politics, mainly because of the senility of the leaders of the moderate group and the vigorous prosecution of Tilak which led to his exile and consequent absence from India. The outbreak of the First World War too had a paralysing effect on the Congress.

The end of the war saw a revival of Indian nationalism which closed the rift in the Congress ranks; most of the old moderates had died, and the dilatory tactics of the British Government in the matter of granting Dominion Status to India drove the remaining into the hands of the nationalists. The Congress support of the Khilaphat movement brought the Muslims too into the Congress fold. And at this important juncture in its history, the leadership of the Congress passed into the able hands of Mahatma Gandhi who, after spectacular campaigns in the cause of his countrymen in South Africa, had returned to his homeland and entered the field of Indian politics.

The fight for Indian independence is a subject for the political historian, and hence its detailed accounts can find no place in this book, but its effect on the emancipation of the women of the country rightly forms a fit subject.

Gandhiji was a peculiar individual in whom Indian mysticism and Western pragmatism were curiously blended. He had the benefit of an extensive English education and had stayed in England for several years, but essentially he remained an Indian sage of the classical tradition. His religion was based on the *Bhagavad Gita* tempered by the Sermon on the Mount. A great protagonist of the active principle in life, he was a confirmed pacifist of the type of the Buddha. Gandhiji had married and had children, but he gave up sex at the age of forty. He believed, like many ancient Indian moralists, that the need for procreation was the only justification for sex, but unlike them he was a firm modern advocate of sex equality. He preferred widows to remain unmarried, and widowers too, as he considered celibacy superior to sex life, but he fiercely attacked forced celibacy on widows and widowers alike. He carried on an unrelenting crusade against caste and the subjection of women. His loin-cloth and saintly life conveyed conviction, and Hindu India, always ready to honour a saint when it found one, accepted his leadership not only in politics but in morals too, and to many Hindus he exercised the authority of a modern Manu.

It may be mentioned, political reforms in India in the earlier stages went hand in hand with social reforms, and the founders of the Indian National Congress were zealous social reformers too. In fact the annual sessions of the Indian Social Conference (founded by Ranade) were held in the same Pandals as those of the Indian National Congress till 1895, when Tilak, who held that the political movement was to have over-riding effect on other questions, objected to it. But the more moderate elements in the Congress were for the progress of social uplift as part of the national programme for freedom.

Gandhiji was generally of the latter view. While he rejected violence in Indian politics as not only futile but also unethical, he accepted the principle of boycott of the British and their goods, when persuasion failed to achieve a desired political objective, a course of action pronounced valid in the annual session of the Congress in 1906. Unlike Tilak, who was a rash crusader, Gandhiji was a patient, tenacious tactician who was quite prepared to negotiate and bargain when such a policy could achieve his ends without an open rupture with the British. He was even willing to accept the 'substance of independence', as Dominion Status was then conceived by many Indians, if the real stuff was not immediately forthcoming.

To the credit of the British, it must be conceded that they themselves were prepared to grant India Dominion Status or Responsible Government (implying thereby that their Government was irresponsible), but the quarrel was mainly over the time factor. When, after the First World War, the Congress asked for immediate Dominion Status for India, the British considered the demand as premature. The issue was clinched, and in the third and fourth decades of the twentieth century there were country-wide agitation in India, civil disobedience, boycott of British goods, picketing of shops dealing in foreign cloth and liquor, large-scale arrests, breaking of the salt and forest laws, Lathi charges and shootings, and in the resultant bitterness, the Congress, mainly under the influence of Pandit Jawaharlal Nehru, declared, as Tilak's party did of old, in favour of complete independence for India. The struggle went on with unabated vigour till the outbreak of the Second World War after the end of which India became independent.

Under Gandhiji's able leadership the political struggle which had, till then, remained a movement of the educated upper middle classes, transformed itself into a national mass movement, vivifying the drowsy village life of India and attracting even the Muslim masses. Nor was it confined to men only. Gandhiji passionately pleaded for the participation of women in active politics. And it is a tribute to the extra-ordinary power of he man that not only those who had the benefit of English education, but even the most orthodox of the Hindus sent their women from their age-long seclusion in the home out into the open to wrest political power from the British. Gandhiji's appeal was always to he heroines of ancient India whose brave actions their modern daughters were exhorted to follow. Few had an adequate conception of the life of these ancient heroines, but that did not matter; the whole country vibrated with a new enthusiasm and women, encouraged by their men, came out in their thousands from the cities, towns and villages of India to fight for the freedom of their country. The non-violent nature of the struggle was eminently suited to the genius of women. The took out processions, picketed shops, quietly broke laws and courted arrest, and while not engaged in active out-door work spun yarn on the Charkha (spinning wheel) to paralyse the textile industry of Great Britain. And what is most important, when large-scale arrests deprived the struggle of male leadership, women led the battles, and the ability, energy and skill of many of these women leaders were an eye-opener not only to the British but to their own countrymen too.

Indian women showed themselves at their best in the Salt Satyagraha campaign initiated by Gandhiji on the 6th April 1930, by his breaking the salt law. At first Gandhiji was reluctant to permit women to join the salt raid, and asked them to confine their activities to picketing liquor and foreign cloth shops. But in the light of the new freedom they found and the equality they asked for, women felt it their duty to shoulder the responsibilities connected with the national struggle on an equal footing with men. In view of the non-violent nature of the proposed campaign, the physical weakness of women could not be advanced as an argument for their exclusion. The spirited letter sent to Gandhiji by Mrs. Margaret Cousins, on behalf of the Women's Indian Association, would show the reaction of women to Gandhiji's decision. The letter complained:

> Gandhiji has left the care of his Ashram entirely to women. This division of sexes in a non-violent campaign seems to us unnatural, and against all the awakened consciousness of modern womanhood. In these stirring critical days of India's destiny, there should be no water-tight compartments of service. Women ask that no conferences, congresses or commissions dealing with the welfare of India should be held without the presence on them of women. Similarly, women must ask that no marches, no imprisonments, no demonstrations organised for the welfare of India should prohibit women from a share in them.

Gandhiji reluctantly chose a few ladies to break the salt law, but thousands of women all over the country broke the law without being called upon to do so. When Gandhiji was arrested, Mrs. Sarojini Naidu took his place, and in her wake came Rukmini Lakshmipathi of Madras. The arrest of leaders, instead of curbing the movement led to its spread into the villages and consequent mass upheavals which turned half the population of India into lawbreakers. The Government tried to combat this upsurge of the people by arrests, ill-treatment of the arrested, and by making prison-life intolerable. And when practically all available male leadership in the country was locked up in jail, "women became dictators of war-councils set up to direct the day-to-day activities. Outstanding among them were Avantikabai Gokhale, Smt. Kamdar, Shantabai Vengsakar, Smt. Durgabai, Smt. Vedantam, Kamalamma Satyavati and Krishnabai Panjikar".

The struggle continued after a short respite occasioned by Gandhiji's departure from India to attend the Round Table Conference, but after his return in 1932, the Civil Disobedience campaign was again revived and continued till 1936, when the Congress decided to accept office in some Provinces. With the outbreak of the Second World War, the Congress Ministries resigned as a protest against the Central Government's decision to join the war without consulting the Provincial Governments. The struggle again started.

In 1942 when the Japanese raided India, Gandhiji declared that India had no quarrel with Japan, and it was the presence of the British that brought the war to Indian soil, and as such, he demanded, that the British, in decency, should quit India. But the British were neither in a position nor in a mood to quit India. So on the 8th August 1942, the Congress passed the famous 'Quit India Resolution', and the fight for Indian freedom entered its final and most desperate stage, Thousands of men and women were again arrested and a reign of repression converted the country into a prison camp. The British were fighting for their very existence, with all the resources at their command, and were not inclined to tolerate any activity that might have adversely affected their war efforts.

We need not go into the details of this tragic phase in India's freedom struggle. Suffice to say that the defeat of Nazism brought new values into international politics by which the age of imperialism and colonialism came to an end, as far as Asia was concerned, and India was one of the first subject Asian nations to gain independence.

The difficulty of doing justice to the part individual women played in the struggle for Indian independence can very well be appreciated from the fact that in the Salt Satyagraha alone over 80,000 people were arrested of whom more than 17,000 were women. Some of the women who led the movement have already been noticed; of the others who either led the struggle or lent support to it, mention may be made of Kamaladevi Chattopadhyay, Vijayalakshmi Pandit, Krishna Hutheesingh, Lilavati Munshi, Lakshmi Menon, Violet Alva, Sushila Nayyar, Jaishri Raiji, Hansa Mehta, Perin Captain, Joshiben Captain, Maniben Patel, and the Dave, Zutshi and Mhatre Sisters. Swaruprani, Jawaharlal's mother was badly beaten up in the Salt Satyagraha of 1930, and Kasturba, Gandhiji's devoted wife, died in prison during the 'Quit India' campaign.

The slow progress of the political struggle produced its discontents too, and these went underground and embarked upon direct action. Here too women played their part. The names of Aruna Asaf Ali, Sucheta Kripalani and Usha Mehta are of particular importance in this sphere, while in fields afar, Col. Lakshmi organised a women's corps under Subhas Chandra Bose.

When the partition of India released a spate of violence on both sides of the partition line, women of India rose to the occasion and did splendid relief work; as leaders in this more peaceful but no less important field, Rajkumari Amrit Kaur, Achamma Mathai and Dhanvanti Rama Rao deserve particular mention.

All told, in Gandhiji's own words, "the part the women of India played will be written in letters of gold"; they also proved, if proof was necessary, that there was hardly any field in which women could not shoulder responsibilities just as well as men.

Political upheavals are potent factors in effecting social revolutions and it is doubtful if a century of preaching and social work would have brought about the same change in the position of Indian women as two decades of political struggle did. Direct attack is often less effective in social reforms than such flank movements.

It must, however, be mentioned that Muslim women were not so enthusiastic as their Hindu sisters in responding to Gandhiji's call. For one thing, the authority of Gandhiji prevailed more with the Hindus than with the Muslims, and though in the initial stages of Gandhiji's leadership there was some Hindu-Muslim cohesion against the British, when the freedom struggle gained momentum the Muslims showed a tendency to hive off from the Congress under the banner of the Muslim League and the leadership of Jinnah; for another, Purdah sat more heavily on Muslim than Hindu women. As such Muslim women, with negligible exceptions, remained outside the active political field, and in consequence, the struggle for Indian independence had better effect in liberating Hindu women. As late as 1935 Sakinatul Fatima Wazir Hasan bemoaned, thus, the small part played by Muslim women in the political life of modern India:

> Just as in the field of education, so in the political and social sphere of our national life the part played by Muslim women has been very small. Among the upper and middle classes, Purdah is still the rule, and orthodoxy which seems to have found its last resort amongst the Muslims of India, is firmly entrenched. There is no other Muslim country in the world where, in social matters like the Purdah, marriage, and status of women generally so much dullwitted reaction prevails as in India.

Women's Suffrage in India

While the British were resisting the freedom struggle in India, they also introduced political reforms which, they considered, were good enough for the country. The old village Panchayat system was reorganised on democratic lines, and the elective principle was introduced in Municipal Councils. The Government of India also had Legislative Councils of nominated members, both in the Provinces and the Centre, to advise the viceroy and the Governors on legislative matters. After the First World War, the need for enlarging the existing Legislative Councils and reconstituting them on elective principle was felt, and the question of enfranchising women, along with men, for electing candidates for Legislatures was first mooted in India.

It may be recalled that adult franchise for women was granted only as late as 1928 in England, and as such the British were not in a hurry to enfranchise Indian women. Throughout the democratic world at the time there was a genuine fear that the enfranchisement of women on equal terms with men would lead to the formation of political parties based on sex, and women, who were larger in numbers in most of the democratic countries, would take over rulership and relegate men to the kitchen. And the treatment meted out to women by men all down the centuries was not such as to inspire confidence in a state dominated by women.

All told, when the Montagu-Chelmsford reforms were contemplated, there was considerable difference of opinion not only among the British but among Indians themselves about the advisability of enfranchising women. Educated Indian women, however, maintained that they had as much right to vote as men, and the more progressive sections of the male population concurred with them. So, when Mr. E. S. Montagu, the then Secretary of State for India, came to India in 1917 to study conditions in the country for framing a new constitution based on limited franchise, Indian women decided to present their case before him. Accordingly, a deputation of them waited upon him in Madras on the 1st December, 1917, and presented a memorandum detailing the various reforms Indian women wished to recommend for the new constitution. The memorandum demanded the enfranchisement of Indian women and pointed out, with considerable pride, that in the Indian National Congress, since its inception, "women have voted and been delegates and speakers, and which, this year, finds its climax in the election of a woman as its president". This president was Mrs. Annie Besant, the first woman to honour the presidential chair of the Congress.

Mr. Montagu has recorded, in his diary, his impressions of the women's deputation, for the benefit of posterity. The relevant entry reads:

> We had an interesting deputation from the women asking for education for girls, more medical colleges, etc., etc. One very nice looking doctor from Bombay, Dr. Joshi, was present, the deputation being led by Mrs. Naidu, the poetess, a very attractive and clever woman, but I believe a revolutionary at heart. She is connected by marriage with Chattopadhyay of India House fame. They asked also for women's votes. The woman who drafted the address, Mrs. Cousins, is a well-known suffragette from London. Cousins himself is a theosophist and one of Mrs. Besant's crowd. Mrs. Besant herself was there. They assured me that the Congress would willingly pass a unanimous request for women's suffrage.

The deputation received a patient hearing and a courteous reply but the women of India were considerably surprised to find that the Montagu-Chelmsford scheme, when published, had no provision for the enfranchisement of women. Nor did the Southborough Franchise Committee, which collected evidence on the franchise question, recommend the enfranchisement of Indian women, though there was considerable agitation by them for the right to vote. The Committee thought that "until the custom of seclusion of women, followed by many classes and communities is relaxed, female suffrage would hardly be a reality" and as proof thereof they pointed out that, in certain places where there were women in the list of voters for local bodies, hardly any cared to exercise the right.

Indian women were not quite satisfied with this argument and they continued their agitation for enfranchisement. Hence, soon after the introduction of the Government of India Bill in Parliament in 1919, evidence was collected by a Joint Committee of both the Houses of Parliament to examine the demand of Indian women for the right to vote. A Committee which consisted of Mrs. Annie Besant, Mrs. Sarojini Naidu and Miss Herabai gave evidence in favour of the demand for the enfranchisement of Indian women to the Joint Committee. After studying the recommendations submitted by this body, the Parliament left the question to be decided by the elected legislatures of India.

The first among Indian States and Provinces to grant votes to women was progressive Travancore where matriarchal traditions have, as we have seen, through the centuries, accorded a better status to women than elsewhere in India. Madras enfranchised its women soon after, in 1921, and Bombay followed close on Madras. The Bengal Legislature could not pass the resolution for enfranchisement of women in 1922 but had to wait till 1925 to change its mind. In the Punjab, women were enfranchised in 1926 and in the Central provinces, in 1927. Bihar was the most reluctant of the major Indian Provinces to recognise the political equality of women; an attempt was made to enfranchise women in 1922, but the resolution was defeated and could not be passed till 1929. By this date, however, practically all Indian States and Provinces had enfranchised their women.

The right to vote, however, should not be confused with the right to legislate. The Indian legislatures had no power to remove the existing restriction against women standing as candidates in elections, and this right was reserved by the Parliament. So, when the question of enfranchising women was left to the Indian legislatures, an agitation was started for removing the sex disqualification of women to enter legislatures, and as a result, the clause that barred their entry into the Councils was deleted from the Reforms Bill by the Parliament.

The Central Assembly too fell into line with the Provincial Councils, and granted women the right to vote and enter the Assembly, as far as those Provinces, which had enfranchised women, were concerned.

In the elections held in 1926, Madras was in a position to put up women candidates for the Legislative Council. Mrs. Kamaladevi Chattopadhyay and Mrs. Hannan Angelo were the first women candidates to contest the elections; neither could win, but the defeat of Kamaladevi was as good as a victory since she polled

4,461 votes against 4,976 secured by her successful rival; in recognition of the claim of women demonstrated by this election, the Madras Government nominated Muthulakshmi Reddi to its Legislative Council.

Though women were, no doubt, enfranchised on terms of equality with men, the number of women-voters on the electoral rolls was far below that of men, ranging from one woman to ten men in Madras to one to 114 in Assam. This disparity was mainly due to the minimum economic and educational qualifications required of the voter, to satisfy which there were fewer women than men. We need not here go into the weary details of the 'wife-hood qualification'. 'daughter-hood qualification', reservation of constituencies, distribution of seats based on communal ratio, and other tortuous expedients suggested by the Statutory Commission, the Lothian Committee, the Franchise Sub-Committee of he Round Table Conference and numerous other bodies, to remove the disparity in sex ratio of Indian voters, but suffice to say that Indian womanhood, now thoroughly roused to its political rights, would be content with nothing short of adult franchise for women as well as men. In September 1931, representatives of various women's organisations in India met in Bombay with Mrs. Sarojini Naidu as their president, and drafted a memorandum demanding "the immediate acceptance of adult franchise without any sex distinction". and the All-India Women's Conference, the Women's Indian Association and the National Council of Women in India, the three important organisations that could speak authoritatively for the women of India, adopted the memorandum and sent copies to all the authorities concerned.

The Indian National Congress endorsed this demand and embodied it in the Declaration of Fundamental Rights of Citizenship in India under the new constitution. While this remained the ultimate aim of the Congress, Indian leaders, as we have seen, were prepared to give the Government of India Act of 1935 a fair trial. The Act enfranchised some 14 per cent of the population of India, and the ratio of women to men in the new electoral rolls was roughly 1 to 7.

In 1937 when Congress Ministries were formed, in Bombay, Madras, Bihar, Orissa, Central Provinces and Assam, there were a number of women in the legislatures, and some held very high positions as Ministers and Deputy Speakers. Mrs. Vijayalakshmi Pandit held the portfolio of Local Self-Government and Public Health in the U.P. Government; Smt. Rukmini Lakshmipati and Smt. Jyoti Venkatachalam held Ministerial posts in the Madras Cabinet; and Smt. Anasuyabai Kale and Smt. Shiphai Malani were elected Deputy Speakers in the Central Provinces and Sind legislative councils, respectively.

The Congress Ministries as already stated, had a short life. The principle of responsibility in the Provinces with irresponsibility at the Centre was found unworkable, and in 1939 the Congress Ministries of the Provinces resigned. Apart from effecting certain prison reforms which happened to lessen the rigours of jail life of some of the ministers during the 'Quit India' campaign of 1942, little tangible good came but of this experiment in dual Government.

With independence, the Declaration of Fundamental Rights of Citizenship, was fully implemented by the Congress and women were granted complete political equality with men.

The Banda Act

A legislative measure of far-reaching importance in the matter of the emancipation of Indian women was the passing (in the year 1929) of the Prohibition of Child-Marriage Act, popularly called the Sarda Act after Rao Bahadur Harbilas Sarda, the sponsor of the Bill. Apart from removing the obvious evils of child-marriage, it promoted, as we have seen, female education. After the passing of the Act, love-marriages became a possibility among the higher castes of Hindus; at any rate, in the majority of cases, both boys and girls, at the time of their marriage, were old enough to understand the significance of marriage and express their opinions about their partners in life.

As early as 1873 social reformers in India had obtained Government approval for a Bill fixing a minimum age for marriage, but there were strong protests from Hindus and even Muslims against the measure. The plausible argument of the opponents was that consummation of marriage took place only after the girl reached maturity, and there could be no possible harm if the mere formalities of a ceremony were gone through earlier. The question of love-marriage was entirely ruled out as an undesirable Western practice unsuited to Indian ideals of modesty. Anyway, the reformers could not win their point for a long time.

While the mere formality of a marriage ceremony could not be objected to by a Government forsworn to non-interference in the religious observances of their subjects, the killing of childwives by sadists could reasonably come within the purview of criminal law, and in 1860 when the Indian Penal Code was enacted, sexual intercourse with a girl, whether one's wife or not, of less than ten years of age was brought within the definition of rape.

> About 1891, again, the attention of the Government and the public was drawn to several cases in Bengal which were brought to light in which girls of tender years either died or were multilated, and it was proposed to raise the age of consent within marriage, from ten to twelve. This proposal was widely opposed throughout India, but both the Government and advanced public opinion took a firm stand and the Bill was passed. Sir Andrew Scoble, the sponsor of the Bill, met the objections raised on the basis of religious neutrality on the ground that it was the right and duty of the State to interfere for the protection of any class of subjects where a proved necessity existed.

The difficulty of enforcing a piece of legislation of this nature is obvious. In most cases of sexual intercourse with wives below the age of twelve, there was neither death nor permanent disablement, and even if there was, neither the victim, if alive, nor her relatives went to law against the offender, for reasons all too plain. There was, however, a sensational case in Madras of a child-wife killed on her nuptial bed, and another instance of a girl done to death by her sadistic husband was reported from Bengal. In the Madras case, the police recorded the dying deposition of the girl before she expired; her declaration was that her husband had set fire to her clothes, but the evidence available to the Coroner, who held the inquest, showed that it was a case of self-immolation which made him return a verdict of suicide. The incident, however, led to much publicity and press comment, and Gandhiji who had by now come to be looked upon as a modern interpreter of ancient Hindu law and something of an unofficial law-giver in his own right, wrote, in his paper *Young India*, a scathing criticism of child-marriage and the texts ordaining it. The orthodox view was ably presented by a correspondent, which was published in full in *Young India* of the 9th September 1926, along with Gandhiji's reply; both the letter and the reply are given below so that the reader may have a sound idea of the two different view-points on child-marriage prevalent at the time when legislation prohibiting it was contemplated.

The correspondent wrote:

> I am very much pained to read the following sentence in your article on *The Curse of Child-Marriage* published in *Young India* of the 26th August 1926: 'Only a man innocent of self-restraint and steeped in vice could call it a sin not to marry a girl before she reached the age of monthly periods'.

I fail to understand why you could not take a charitable view of those whose opinion differs from you. One can certainly say, that the Hindu law-giver was entirely wrong in prescribing child marriage. But I think it improper to say that those who insist on child marriage are steeped in vice. It seems to go beyond the limits of politeness in controversy. In fact, this is the first time that I heard such an argument against child marriage. Neither the Hindu social reformers nor the Christian missionaries ever said so, so far as I am aware. Imagine, therefore, the shock which I received when I found this argument in a writing of Mahatma Gandhi whom I believed to be perfection itself, so far at least as charity towards opponents was concerned.

You have condemned not one or two but probably every one of the Hindu law-givers. For so far as I know, every *Smritikara* enjoins early marriage of girls. It is impossible to hold, as you have suggested, that passages enjoining early marriage are interpolations. The practice of early marriage is not confined to nay province or class of society, but is practically a universal custom in India. It is also a very old practice dating from the time of the *Ramayana*.

I shall try to give briefly what I consider might have been the reasons why the Hindu law-givers insisted upon early marriage of girls. They considered it very desirable that every girl should have husband as a rule. If every girl has to be provided with a husband, the choice of husband should be made by the parents of he girl and not by the girls themselves. If the choice is left to the girls themselves, it will result in many girls not being married at all, not because they do not like marriage, but because it is very difficult for all girls to find out suitable husbands for themselves. It is also dangerous, for it might lead to flirtation and might cause looseness of morals. Youths who appear to be good might ruin the virtue of simple girls. Again, if the choice is to be made by parents, the girls must be married young. When they are grown up, they may fail in love and may not like to marry the bridegroom selected by the parents. When a girl is married young, she becomes one with her husband and his family. The union is more natural and more perfect. It is sometimes difficult for grown-up girls with fixed ideas and habits to adapt themselves in a new home.

The chief objection to early marriage is that it weakens the health of the girl and her children. But this objection is not very convincing for the following reasons: The age of marriage is now rising among the Hindus, but the race is becoming weaker. Fifty or a hundred years ago, the men and women were generally stronger, healthier and more long-lived than now. But early marriage was then more in vogue. The physique of educated girls who are marred late is not generally better than that of the girls who receive less education and are married early. From these facts, it would appear that early marriage does not cause as much physical deterioration as some people believe.

You have good knowledge of both European society and Indian society. You will be able to say whether, on the whole, Indian wives are more devoted to their husbands' than European wives; whether, among the poor the Indian husbands treat their wives more kindly than European husbands; whether there are fewer cases of unhappy marriages among Indians then among Europeans; whether sexual morality is higher in Indian society than in European society. If, in these respects, the Indian marriages are more successful than European marriages, then early marriage, which is an essential feature of Indian marriage, should not be condemned.

I cannot believe that the Hindu law-givers were actuated by any consideration except the true welfare of society in general (including both the men and women) in laying down the injunction of early marriage of girls. I believe that early marriage of girls is one of the features of Hindu society which have maintained its purity and prevented its disruption in spite of very hostile environments. You may not believe all this. But may we not expect that you should discard your idea that all the great Hindu law-givers who insisted on early marriage of girls were innocent of self-restraint and were 'steeped in vice'?

The Madras case reported by you seems to be very peculiar. The jury held that the girl committed suicide. But the girl said that her husband set fire to her clothes.

> In these conflicting circumstance it is very difficult to hold that the facts which you consider to be indisputable are really so. There have been millions of cases of girl wives below 13. Not one case of suicide due to cruel advances of the husband has been heard before. Probably there were peculiar features in the Madras case and early marriage was not the principal cause of death.

This is a beautiful specimen of the arguments of the orthodox who worked against the emancipation of Indian women. If he were alive at the time of William Bentinck, the writer would have held up Sati as a sign of the superior morals of the Hindus over the barbarians, and fought against its abolition.

But the fine logic of the correspondent was lost upon Gandhiji. As a rule, Gandhiji followed the middle path in criticism and seldom used strong language against his opponents. But in this particular case, his indignation was thoroughly roused, especially as the letter came from a highly placed man who had the benefits of a liberal education, and he replied as under:

> Well does the poet say: 'It costs very little to fashion a suitable philosophy in order to mitigate the rudeness of facts that secretly hurts one's conscience.' This reader of *Young India* has gone a step further. He has not only fashioned a suitable philosophy but ignored facts and erected his argument on unsupported statements.
>
> The charge of want of charity I must pass by, if only because I have not accused the law-givers but I have ventured to impute vice to those who could insist on marriage at an age too tender for bearing the burden of motherhood. Want of charity comes into being only when you accuse a live person, not an imaginary being, and that too without cause of impure motives. But is there any warrant for the writer saying that the original authors of the several Smritis who preached self-restraint wrote the verses enjoining marriage of little girls? Is it not more charitable to assume that the Rishis could not be guilty of impurity or gross ignorance of cardinal facts concerning the growth of the human body?
>
> But even if the texts ordering child, as opposed to early (for early marriage means marriage well before 25) marriage, be found to be authoritative, we must reject them in the light of positive experience and scientific knowledge.
>
> Nor does it follow that, if the parents are to continue to

make the choice of husbands for their daughters, the marriage must be contracted and consummated early. It is still less true to maintain that, if girls have to make their choice there must be courtship and flirtation. After all, courtship is not universal in Europe and thousands of Hindu girls are married after fifteen and yet have their husbands selected by their parents. Mussalman parents invariably select husbands for their grown-up daughter. Whether the choice is to be made by girls or their parents is a separate question and is regulated by custom.

The correspondent has tendered no proof to support the statement that children of grown-up wives are weaker than those of child wives. In spite of my experience of both Indian and European society, I must refuse to enter into a comparison of their morals. Granting, however, for the sake of argument, that the moral of European is lower than that of Hindu society, will it naturally follow that the lowness is due to the marriages taking place after full maturity?

Lastly, the Madras case does not help the correspondent but his use of it betrays his hasty judgment, based upon a total disregard of facts. If he will refer to the article again, he will discover that I have drawn my conclusion from proved facts. My conclusion is unaffected by the cause of death. It was proved : (1) that the girl was of tender age, (2) that she had no sexual desire, (3) that the husband made cruel advances, and (4) that she is no more. It was bad enough if the girl committed suicide; it was worse if the husband murdered her because she could not yield to his inhuman lust. The girl was fit only to learn and play, not to play the wife and carry, on her tiny shoulders, the weight of household cares or the yoke of lord and master.

My correspondent is a man occupying high position in society. The nation expects better things from those of her sons and daughters who have received a liberal education and who are expected to think and act on her behalf. We have many

> abuses in our midst, moral, social, economic and political. They require patient study, diligent research, delicate handling, accuracy of statement and clear thinking on them, and sober, impartial judgment. We may then differ, if necessary, as poles asunder. But we shall surely harm the country, our respective religions, and the national cause, if we do not toil to discover the truth and adhere to it, cost what it may.

Well, arguments convince nobody, but the Government, in spite of considerable opposition, appointed a Committee in the year 1928 to collect evidence on the question of the age of consent in and outside the martial state. The report submitted by the Committee showed that public opinion was sufficiently strong to warrant legislation. Accordingly, the Child-Marriage Restraint Act, sponsored by Harbilas Sarda, was introduced in the Central Legislative Assembly and after a heated debate, was passed in 1929. Brought into force on the 1st April 1930, the Act penalises the marriage of girls below fourteen and boys below eighteen years of age. "The husband, if of age, the parents or the guardians of the couple, the priest who celebrates the marriage, are all liable to imprisonment or fine or both".

Child-Marriage did not stop in India immediately the Act was passed. While the Bill was being debated in the Assembly, there was a rush of marriages of children, throughout the country (see page 301) and even after the passing of the Act, the orthodox were in a mood defiant enough to break the law and bear the consequences rather than face the prospects of hell predicted by sages like Parasara. Further, when prosecutions were actually launched and guilt proved, punishments were found to be so light that the offenders were inclined to treat the law as a big joke. In a case tried in 1934, for instance, the punishment awarded to an offender who had his two daughters aged seven and nine married, was a fine of Rs. 5 (Rupees five only). The Act, besides, did not operate in the Indian States, and few here cared to respect the law of British India. Again, the ceremony once performed was valid, though punishable, and this provided an incentive to the orthodox to take a chance with the law. The villages, moreover, were little affected by legislation in Delhi but were ruled by all-powerful custom in spite of the Sarda Act.

Yet a sound beginning had been made. The educated higher classes generally deferred the marriage of girls till about the age of twenty, and a convention against child-marriage rose all over the country. Breaches of the Sarda Act were vigorously hunted out by certain women's organisations that specialised in this work, and prosecutions launched, which had a deterrent effect on those who thought that the Sarda Act could be broken with impunity. In due course, the example of British India was followed by the Indian States, and by the end of the British period, child-marriage had become a thing of the past.

The Problem of Prostitution

The patronage prostitution had generally enjoyed from rulers and the astristocracy in ancient and medieval India ceased during the later British period. The odium attached to professional prostitution in the West, the austere attitude of later British highbrows against public levity in any form, the unpopularity of the 'Nautch' among English-educated Indians, all had a salutary effect on Indian public opinion about prostitution. Courtesans were no more considered necessary for the adornment of courts, for the splendour of state functions or for public entertainment.

But prostitution does not live by state patronage alone. As a matter of fact, the withdrawal of state patronage in no way adversely affected the trade; if anything, prostitution seems to have thrived in India under British disapproval.

While Gandhiji was travelling in Bengal in the year 1925, a gentleman handed him a letter in which he drew the leader's attention to the wide prevalence of prostitution in the region. Relevant portions of the latter are reproduced below, as it will give the reader a fair idea of the evil as then prevalent in Bengal:

I believe your attention has been drawn to the amazing

number of abduction cases now happening everyday in Bengal. These moral eruptions are an unmistakable indication that there is something wrong in the inner working of our social life.

Prevalence of prostitution and corruption in some of the Bengal districts is simply amazing. In most of the districts of western Bengal and in many of jute areas of northern and eastern Bengal, brothels are considered to be a necessary part of even a village bazar. One can easily guess the condition that obtains in big marts or, as they are called, 'bundars'. During the busy season most of the important jute markets have their prostitute quarters augmented by floating brothels. Numerous prostitutes infest these places and ply on their infernal trade in boats which remain moored alongside the market. In many parts of western Bengal, almost all fairs are infested with these unhappy women. They erect temporary sheds, on the Mela grounds, and cater for the people who visit the Mela. In some of the districts quite a number of prostitutes are found settled round a Zamindar's house or his *Kutchery*. For they are generally patronised by the Zamindar and his officers. Districts of Mymensingh, Pubna and Rajshahi are particularly notorious in this respect. As is naturally to be expected, cases of abduction and molestation of women occur in the largest number in these districts. Bengal has nearly 4 lakhs of Bairagi population (exact number 174,497 male and 203,610 female). Most of these people live by singing and begging. In short, the Bengali people spend more than 3 crores of rupees a year for the maintenance of these parasites. What is most unfortunate, this community is regarded as a waste paper basket of Hindu society. The majority of the abduction cases is in connection with women of this community. Under the garb of religion these unfortunate people lead a most sordid and corrupt life...

Conditions prevailing in and around Calcutta are as bad as can be imagined. The crushing poverty of many of the

> western Bengal districts induces hundreds of women to forsake their village homes and flock to Calcutta and its suburbs. Here they lead a dubious life by working as maid-servants, betel-leaf sellers, etc. A very low standard of morality among the masses is another cause of widespread prevalence of venereal diseases and leprosy in these districts.
>
> The theatres of Çalcutta are chiefly run by fallen women. These are resorted to by large number of students and even by noted public men. Important public meetings are held in these theatre halls. Lengthy appreciations of actresses and dancing girls find a place in the columns of daily papers (unfortunately some of the most influential nationalist papers). Besides, there are Bengali illustrated magazines specially devoted to the subject of drama and dancing. Outturn of debasing-literature in the Bengali language is perhaps greater now than it was ten years ago.

Making every allowance for the obvious Puritanic predilection of the writer, it cannot be denied that prostitution was on the increase during the later British period in India. Nor was Bengal an isolated instance; the position of other provinces was no better.

This increase in prostitution and the consequent moral degradation of the period may be attributed to the following main causes:

(1) A fertile breeding ground for prostitution was the growing industrial areas. During the later British period, a large number of industrial cities and ports of international importance had risen in India; unlike the ancient Indian cities which had a growth of centuries, these new cities grew rapidly and few of them had any local population of importance, as most of the citizens were immigrants from villages and towns who were attracted to the new cities by the opportunities offered by them for employment or money-making. Few of these immigrants could bring their wives with them because of low wages and poor

housing conditions, and in every one of these new cities there was a preponderance of male population over female. According to the Census of 1931, for instance, in Calcutta there were but 475 women to 1,000 men, and in Bombay, 553. The position of many other cities was almost as bad. This was naturally an ideal atmosphere for prostitution to flourish.

(2) The Government had, no doubt, withdrawn the ancient state patronage of prostitution in India, and the higher classes of Indians generally toed the line, but this, instead of eliminating the evil led to its spread. In ancient and medieval India prostitution, as we have seen, had a definite recognised place in society, and there were regular castes whose traditional occupation was singing, dancing and acting; in fact, in every social function, a singing or dancing party was an indispensable form of entertainment, and the total number of men and women who earned their livelihood by this occupation was quite considerable for the whole country. Social entertainments of this nature coming into disrepute during the later British period, large number of men and women of these castes became unemployed, and finding no alternate employment, the women migrated to the new cities where they were found in great demand.

(3) Under the British economic system with its centre of gravity on the industrial and commercial prosperity of Great Britain, the ancient village economy of India collapsed and the impoverishment of the village population enabled the trafficker in women and children to drive a flourishing trade.

(4) While prostitution was looked upon with disapproval, and there was a good deal of preaching against it, no positive efforts were made either by the Government or by public organisations to reclaim and rehabilitate fallen women.

In the more objectionable forms of prostitution, as every student of the institution knows only too well, economic factors play a greater role than ethical or emotional forces, and the general poverty of the population was in no small measure responsible for the alarming spread of the evil during the British period. The periodical wars that had effectively checked the overgrowth of population in medieval and ancient India had ended by 1857, and from then on there was a steady increase in population with no corresponding increase in the wealth of the country. Further, the doctrine of *laissez-faire,* which was then the economic fashion, tended to make the rich richer and the poor poorer, and poverty and riches, in extremes, always promote vice.

While the more objectionable forms of the trade, such as the keeping of establishments of abducted and unwilling women, can be stopped by law, the difficulty of combating voluntary prostitution by legislation is quite obvious. More effective methods would be to provide alternative employment for the men and women engaged in the profession, raise moral standards by sound education, give suitable work for destitute women to prevent their falling into the hands of the trafficker and to remove the disparity in sex ratio of the population of the big cities. The magnitude of the problem can very well be imagined when we consider the fact that the population of India at the end of the British period was something like 400 million, no work could be found for even a small percentage of her able-bodied, well-educated young men, let alone women, and the *per capita* income stood at about Rs. 245 and female literacy at 7 per cent. As such little was done during the British period to tackle the problem of prostitution except passing certain ineffective laws against the more aggressive forms of traffic in women and children.

The Institution of Devadasis was, however, abolished during the British period. Muthulakshmi Reddi's Bill for prohibiting the keeping of paid Devadasis in temples (the Inam-holding Devadasis as they were called) was passed into law by the Madras Legislative Council in 1927, and ten years later, a Bill against the dedication of children to temples. In other provinces the problem was not so serious as in Madras, and by the time the British left, there were no temples in India where Devadasis were overtly retained.

The Purdah

We have already noticed the salutary effect of the political struggle in India for bringing Indian women out of their ageold seclusion. Education and the prohibition of child-marriage were other powerful factors that worked against the veil. Among South Indian Hindus, who had never been very partial to the Purdah, women of all classes could be seen in the cities, towns and villages, taking active part in the social and public life of the community without much embarrassment, during the later British period. In fact, no positive action against the Purdah as such was needed to make South Indian Hindu women come out of the veil; the example of the women of the ruling class, the political struggle, and the general rise in education were enough to let Purdah die a natural death in the south, especially as seclusion of women was foreign to Dravidian genius and was an imposition on the upper classes to some extent by the Aryans and to a greater extent by the Muslims.

In the north, however, things were different. During the pre-Muslim period, Rajput nobles considered seclusion of women as a mark of aristocracy, and during the prolonged Muslim rule, the middle classes too, both Hindu and Muslim, adopted the veil practically all over North India. Hence here, a tough war had to be waged against the veil.

In the earlier stages of the battle of the veil, there were not sufficient women to come forward to lead the struggle and men were in the vanguard; and among these, Gandhiji was one of the foremost. He found that, in many places in northern India, when he addressed public meetings attended by women, he could not see his fair audience, all of whom were carefully screened off from profane male view, but could only hear discordant notes behind the veil. Gandhiji has left us the following interesting description of a Purdah meeting he addressed:

> Whenever I have gone to Bengal, Bihar or the United Provinces, I have observed the Purdah system more strictly followed than in the other provinces. But when I addressed a meeting at Darbhanga late at night, and among calm

> surroundings, free from noise and bustle and unmanageable crowds, I found men in front of me but behind the screen were women, of whose presence I knew nothing till my attention was drawn to it. The function was in connection with laying of the foundation stone of an orphanage, and I was called upon to address the ladies behind the Purdah. The sight of the screen behind which my audience, whose numbers I did not know, was seated made me sad. It pained and humiliated me deeply; I thought of the wrong being done by men to the women of India by clinging to a barbarous custom which, whatever use it might have had when it was first introduced, had now become totally useless and was doing incalculable harm to the country. All the education that we have been receiving for the past 100 years seems to have produced little impression upon us, for I note that the Purdah is being retained even in educated households, not because the educated men believe in it, themselves, but because they will not manfully resist the brutal custom and sweep it away at a stroke. I have had the privilege of addressing hundreds of meetings of women attended by thousands. The din and noise created at these meetings make it impossible to speak with any effect to the women who attended them. Nothing better is to be expected so long as they are caged and confined in their houses and little courtyards. When, therefore, they find themselves congregated in a big room and are expected, all of a sudden, to listen to some one, they do not know what to do with themselves or with the speaker. And when silence is restored, it becomes difficult to interest them in many everyday topics for they know nothing of them, having been never allowed to breathe the fresh air of freedom.

When Gandhiji, who had the greatest regard for the intelligence and ability of women, could speak so harshly, things must have been pretty bad in the twenties. But it must be mentioned that a good deal of progress had already been made during the hundred years of education of which he spoke; for if, before this period, a woman of a respectable household had expressed a desire to attend a public meeting presided over by a man, she would have been considered queer, if not actually mad.

Anyway, Gandhiji appeal, and the work of devoted men and women began to bear fruit in many places in India. In Patna, for instance, an organised demonstration against the Purdah took place on the 8th July 1928, and on that date the death of Purdah in Bihar was officially announced. The resolution, unanimously passed on the occasion which was graced by the presence of men too, declared as under:

> We, the men and women of Patna, hereby declare that we have today abolished the pernicious practice of the Purdah, which has done and is doing incalculable harm to the country, and particularly to women, and we appeal to the other women of the province, who are still wavering, to banish the system as early as they can, and thereby advance their education and health.

In the appeal that was issued on the occasion, it was specifically stated:

> We want that the women of our province should be as free to move about and take their legitimate part in the life of the community in all particulars as their sisters in Karnatak, Maharashtra and Madras, and in an essentially Indian way, avoiding all attempts at Europeanisation, for while we hold that a change from enforced seclusion to a complete anglicisation would be like dropping from the frying pan into the fire, we feel that the Purdah must go if we want our women to develop along Indian ideals. If we want them to add grace and beauty to our social life and raise its moral tone, if we want them to be excellent managers at home, helpful companions of their husbands and useful members of the community, then the Purdah as it now exists, must go. In fact no serious step to their welfare can be taken unless the veil is torn down, and it is our conviction that if once the

energy of half of our population, that has been imprisoned artificially, is released, it will create a force which, if properly guided, will be of immeasurable good to our province.

The funeral of the Purdah in Patna was given wide publicity in the country and Babu Brijkishore Prasad and Babu Rajendra Prasad, who had actively worked for the abolition of the Purdah in Bihar but were, at the time in London, sent their blessings to the movement.

Not only in Bihar but in all regions where the Purdah was prevalent, reformers and women's organisations declared war on the veil. In the Punjab, the Arya Samaj, especially the progressive College Section, intensified its campaigns for the education and emancipation of women, under the leadership of Lala Hans Raj and Lajpat Rai. The Sikhs who had all along believed in martial virtues for women, as opposed to seclusion, and had adopted the veil as a concession to the prejudices of the time, promptly discarded the Purdah.

All these efforts, together with the intensive Civil Disobedience campaigns of the thirties, liberated, towards the close of the fourth decade of the twentieth century, non-Muslim women of India from the oppressive rule of the Purdah. The Muslims, however, were slow to move with the times. Though some progress towards the emancipation of Muslim women from the Purdah was made by the example and efforts of individual Muslim ladies like Begum Hazrat Mohini, Begum Hamid Ali, Sakinatul Fatima Wazir Hasan, Shareefa Hamid Ali, Begum Shah Nawaz, Attiah Habibullah and Fatima Jinnah, and though a good number of young Muslim ladies went for college education and even for professions, the war on the Purdah did not produce as good a result on Muslim women as it did on their Hindu sisters.

It must also be stated that the general breakdown of the Purdah in regions that had been strongholds of the custom led to certain undesirable consequences. The trouble was mainly confined to North India. Young girls who went alone shopping, to public functions or to places of entertainment often attracted a good deal of unnecessary attention, and were even molested. Few of these cases of molestation were actually reported to the police because of the false sense of modesty of the victims, but protests were at times lodged with Gandhiji who had, by now, come to be reckoned a complaint-box, for all public grievances. Gandhiji gave publicity to the more glaring cases of molestation of women, and the following exerpts from *Young India* would show the predicament of emancipated women in some of the cities of North India. In the *Harijan* (altered name of *Young India)* of the 26th December 1938, Gandhiji wrote:

> There is a most pathetic letter from a college girl in the Punjab lying on my file for nearly two months. Her letter is written in chaste Hindustani, and here is my rendering of a portion of the letter:
>
> 'To girls and grown-up women there come times in spite of their wish to the contrary, when they have to venture out alone whether they are going from one place to another in the same city or from one town to another. And when they are thus found alone, evil-minded men pester them. They use improper or even indecent language, whilst they are passing by; and if fear does not break them, they do not hesitate to take further liberty....I want to give you my own experience of last night (26th October 1938). I was going with a girl companion of mine on a very special errand at about 7-30 p.m. It was impossible to secure a male companion at the time, and the errand could not be put off. On the way, a Sikh young man passed by on his cycle and continued to murmur something till we were within hearing distance. We knew that it was aimed at us. We felt hurt and uneasy. There was no crowd on the road. Before we had gone a few paces, the cyclist returned. We recognized him at once, while he was still at a respectable distance. He wheeled towards us, heaven knows whether he had intended to get down or only pass by us. We felt we were in danger. We had no faith in our physical prowess. I myself am weaker

than the average girl. But in my hands, I had a big book. Somehow or other courage came to me all of a sudden. I hurled the heavy book on the cyclist, and roared out: "Dare you repeat your pranks?" He could with difficulty, keep his balance, put on speed and fled from us. Now, if I had not flung the book at his cycle, he might have harassed us by his filthy language till the end of our journey. This was an ordinary, perhaps, insignificant occurrence; but I wish you could come to Lahore and listen to the difficulties of us, unfortunate girls....You will be painfully surprised to know that during Diwali and such other holidays, newspapers come out with warning women from venturing outdoors even to see the illuminations. This one fact should enable you to know to what straits we are reduced in this part of the world'.

This was not, however, an isolated instance. "Another Punjabi girl", commented Gandhiji, "to whom I gave the letter to read, supports the narrative from her own experiences of her college days, and tells me that what my correspondent has related is the common experience of most of the girls." Further, "a letter from an experienced woman, relates the experiences of her girl friends in Lucknow. They are molested in cinema theatres by boys sitting behind them using all kinds of language which I can only call indecent. They are stated to resort even to practical jokes which have been described by my correspondent but which I must not reproduce here."

To this evidence, I may add my own observations. The presence of young women in public places, in most parts of India where Purdah had been strictly enforced during pre-British days, attracted crowd, and one could invariably see hanging around ladies' compartments on railway platforms respectable looking young men, apparently gossiping but enjoying the pleasure of watching unveiled women. Good-looking, welldressed young women in bus-stops, railway stations, theatres or on public roads were often treated as exhibits in show-cases, when not actually molested, during the decades that saw the breakdown of the Purdah.

Well, now it is over fifteen years since India got independence, and large strides have been made in the matter of women's emancipation all over the country, but this undesirable feature has not completely vanished from the public and social life of some places in North India. In marked contrast is the case in the south where women have enjoyed comparative freedom from the Purdah down the centuries, and can move about freely without being the focus of male attention.

An Overall Estimate of the British Period

As stated elsewhere, the British period marks the most important phase in the history of the emancipation of Indian women. We may now give a resume of the gains of this period.

When the British rule started, illiteracy was the common lot of all respectable Indian women with negligible exceptions. According to the census of 1951, the percentage of feminine literacy in India, as already stated, had risen to 7.87. Co-education in many schools and colleges was introduced, and has continued to the present day.

Sati was stopped by law and widow-marriage was made legal for the Hindus. Polygyny and Purdah came to be looked upon as old-fashioned, though princes, Jagirdars and Zamindars, in many places, practised both; but they were considered survivals from the middle ages by the educated new middle class.

One of the most important changes of the British period was the slow disintegration of the joint family system of domestic life. The many disadvantages of the joint family have already been mentioned (page 227); the new English-educated classes preferred smaller families of the English type, consisting mainly of father, mother and children, and the possibilities industry and commerce opened up in the urban centres gave them opportunities for setting up their own families away from their ancestral joint families. These new families were, obviously, more suitable for the changing economy of the country and for building up sounder domestic relations, and the demand for the partition of the ancestral property and for breaking up the joint family into smaller units was made not only in cities and towns but even in remote villages where such innovations reach last. The general breakdown of caste, which enabled young men to take to occupations other than the ancestral, also hastened the disintegration of the joint family, as younger members of a village household, who did not have enough work at home, often moved to the new industrial cities and ports, where they found employment and earned wages sufficient to maintain families.

A sound convention had risen against the Purdah during the later British period, and feminine education had so far advanced that large Government service as well as in private concerns, as clerks, typists, stenographers, teachers, receptionists, nurses, etc. In fact while, during the earlier stages of British rule, the difficulty was to coax girls to take to public service, towards its end the problem was to find jobs for girl applicants. There were also serious complaints from male candidates that girls were depriving them of employment, especially as the army of unemployed young men began to gain in numbers year after year.

By far the most important feature of the later British period was the passing of the leadership of the feminist movement from men to women. Right down to the beginning of the twentieth century, men were generally fighting the battle of women and there were not a dozen women in the whole country who could effectively represent the cause of the sex. The Indian Social Conference, itself an organisation mainly of men, was, as we have seen, nestling under the wings of the Indian National Congress, and men were still the spokesmen of women. But towards the end of the second decade of the twentieth century the need for knights to take up arms in defence of Indian women had ceased; the feminist movement in India had come of age, and there was a large number of educated, able, energetic women who were competent to organise themselves and fight their own battles. Women's organisations sprang up in several parts of the country for promoting education, for espousing the cause of widows and destitute women, for providing homes for the homeless and for numerous other activities, and it was considered desirable to organise these independent activities on an all-India basis. Accordingly, the Women's Indian Association was formed in Madras in 1917, and this may be considered the first organisation that could speak with authority for the women of the country as a whole. Its official organ, *Stri Dharma*, gave effective expression to the feminine point of view on Indian problems. Originally the Association limited its activities to education of women, but in the seething socio-political atmosphere of the decades that followed, the Women's Indian Association could not confine itself to the avowed objective of the founders. Three other important feminist organisations rose later: The National Council of Women, which was affiliated to the International Council in 1925, the All-India Women's Conference, and the Federation of University Women, the last, mainly concerned with women's academic and professional interests.

A salutary feature of these women's organisations is their complete freedom from communalism or sectarianism; Hindus, Muslims, Christians, Sikhs, Parsis and Jews have all worked together in them with complete identity of interests. In this respect women have proved themselves an example to their dull-witted husbands, brothers and sons who have brought upon the land untold misery and suffering by their parochial and factional allegiances.

The spirit that animated the new women of India can best be appreciated from the writings they have left; for while actions pass into the mysterious realms of unseen forces, the written word remains. An interesting book embodying the trends in the feminist movement in India in the fourth decade of the twentieth century, written solely by women, was published in 1935 under the title *Our Cause,* and a perusal of it will show the reader the spirit of reform that inspired the women of the time. Two exerpts are given below by way of illustration.

Attiah Habibullah, a Muslim lady, wrote as under on the seclusion of women:

Purdah, having deprived women of any significance in political and economic spheres left them with a form of independence in the home only. Even here, however, woman's economic dependence on man, and the oriental ideology which makes man superior to woman, make it impossible for women to realise themselves as individuals. Brought up from childhood, to believe that they are important only in relation to men as daughters, wives and mothers, they have to fashion themselves on a pattern most likely to please men, and give them the greatest value in the marriage market. And marriage cannot be a matter of choice but a necessary evil. Believers in Purdah must necessarily believe that sex is evil and relationships arising out of it are sinful. Therefore no respectable man or woman may voluntarily express a wish to marry, nor, after marriage, talk of it and of the children born of its sin.

Illogically enough, this shameful, sinful alliance is praised in platitudes about one's mate and family.

Forcible repression of women has meant mental and physical disease, lack of discipline and rational care in the upbringing of children, lack of harmony and beauty in the home which has become the stronghold of convention and orthodoxy.

Men with their economic power found a means of escape. They divided women into two categories. Their wives, mothers and daughters, they forced to be guardians of morality at the expense of another class of women who exist only for men's pleasures. It is a strange comment on Purdah society that the cultural standards of its men should be gauged by the culture of its prostitutes.

To Justify this denial of all ethics, morality and justice, a dual code of morality has been evolved which regards as something 'honourable or at worst a slight blemish to be easily tolerated' in a man what in a woman is a deadly

> crime involving legal punishment and social ostracism. After all, men have no 'consequences' to fear, and the world considers a sin only when it is found out.
>
> It is in this false system of morality, conveniently upheld by men, that Purdah finds its greatest support and herein lies its weakness. Morality cannot exist by falsehoods and through negative beliefs. It must be borne of positive convictions. The only external safeguards should be material so that the existence may be made possible of a 'generation of men who never in their life chanced to buy a woman's surrender for money or any other instrument of power; and a generation of women who never happened to give themselves to a man for any consideration other than love'.
>
> Whatever the reasons for the existence of Purdah, however, strengthened by religion and custom it may be, the question arises whether it can continue to exist in any form whatsoever. It has not justified its existence by solving moral problems; and it has retarded all material progress... The civilised world has condemned Purdah, and the tendencies in the country are against it.

Another lady, the well-known Kamaladevi Chattopadhyay, wrote on the need for birth control to establish sex equality:

> Indivisibly linked up with her economic independence is woman's sexual independence. One without the other would be innocuous, and it alone will make sex equality a true reality for ever. Man's fight against woman's struggle to free herself from the penalty of undesired motherhood, is one of the bitterest wars waged by him, for he knows that her victory will deal a death blow to his vested interests and devastate for ever that atrocious structure of a 'female character'. In savage life, as well as civilised, woman's irrepressible urge to freedom and desire for a larger life has ever led her to seek escape from the sentence nature decreed upon her, and man has ever sought by law, religious canons,

public opinion and penalties to thwart her. The highest form of blessing upon a married woman in India is that she may be blest with eight sons, a usage which no doubt has its origin in imperialism, for the more the ambition for imperial glory the keener the encouragement given to breeding, and greater the consequent enslavement of women. No women can herself be free who cannot own and control her body, and who can be subdued and enslaved through that very quality of fertility which once raised her to the altar as a deity in the dawn of early civilisation.

The first argument against birth control is that it will lead to abuse and immorality. But let us look at morality as it prevails today.... Few have stressed the immorality of property rights of man over the body of woman, though religious and social codes and legal laws have been loud over the preservation of the chastity and purity of the unmarried. The crusaders in the cause of freedom must destroy that dead hand of the past which seeks to reach out to the present in its attempt to extinguish the flame of the new idealism, and crush the fingers that would carve out the new woman, new society and a new world.

Motherhood is one of the most sacred and unique functions of womanhood, and should not be left to the mercy of exigencies of accidental circumstances or allowed to be determined by ignorance. It must be a conscious task undertaken with joy and a full sense of its responsibilities, controlled and regulated according to the emotional urge and physical capacity of the woman. For this reason sound knowledge on sex, birth control and the use of contraceptives will have to be made easily accessible to every woman. From the point of view of national benefit, birth control is necessary for reasons of health, eugenics, social and economic considerations. To put forth the plea that a useful and necessary weapon should not be brought into public use simply because it may be abused, is utterly absurd and meaningless. One

> may as well advocate the stopping of the manufacture of matches simply because we can set anything on fire with a match-stick.

These forceful expressions would have shocked the most zealous social reformer in the beginning of the twentieth century. But by 1935 such revolutionary writings and speeches, demanding complete sex equality, had become a legitimate part of the feminist movement in India, and this should give the reader a fair idea of the advance made by the feminist movement in the country in three decades.